173654141

Video and DVD Industries

Video and DVD Industries

Paul McDonald

First published in 2007 by the
BRITISH FILM INSTITUTE
21 Stephen Street, London W1T 1LN

The British Film Institute purpose is to champion moving image culture in all its
richness and diversity across the UK, for the benefit of as wide an audience as possible,
and to create and encourage debate.

Set by Fakenham Photosetting Limited, Fakenham, Norfolk
Printed in the UK by St Edmundsbury Press, Bury St Edmunds, Suffolk

Cover design: ketchup/SE14
Cover photo: Paul McDonald

British Library Cataloguing-in-Publication
A catalogue record for this book is available from the British Library

ISBN 978–1–84457–168–0 (pbk)
ISBN 978–1–84457–167–3 (hbk)

Contents

Acknowledgments

There are a series of people to thank for their hand in bringing this book to completion. At BFI Publishing, Andrew Lockett was instrumental in getting the whole International Screen Industries series going in the first place, including this book. My thanks to Rebecca Barden for taking up the reins and steering the series onwards, and thanks to Sarah Watt and Tom Cabot for seeing the book through its final stages. During the course of research I have relied on the extensive knowledge and expertise of the staff at the BFI National Library, but I would particularly like to thank Sean Delaney and David Sharp for alerting me to sources I would not have known of otherwise. It would have been impossible to complete my research without a period of leave supported by the School of Arts at Roehampton University and a Research Leave Grant from the Arts and Humanities Research Council (AHRC). My thanks to Eddy Leviten at the Federation Against Copyright Theft for providing photographs used in Chapter 6. The book benefits greatly from the incisive and astute comments I received from Michael Curtin, my fellow editor for this series, and Peter Krämer, who both cast their eyes over an earlier draft of the work. Additional thanks also to Martin Barker and Gillian Doyle. Finally, my thanks to Tamar, Jessica and Chloe for joining me in the extensive and invaluable sofa-based research which had to be completed for this book as together we immersed ourselves in what Derek Zoolander describes as 'the wonderful world of dee vuh duh'. This book is dedicated to the memory of my father.

Introduction: The Video Business

Video serves many purposes. As Sean Cubitt (1993: xv) has noted, '[t]here is no essential form of video, nothing to which one can point as the primal source or goal of video activity'. When the videotape recorder (VTR) first appeared in the mid-1950s it was used by television broadcasters to transmit and archive programming. Two decades later the videocassette recorder (VCR) extended recording capabilities to consumers. VCRs were used not only to record programmes off air from television but also play pre-recorded audiovisual content in the form of pornography, feature films, music promotions, exercise tapes and instructional programmes. With video cameras, video consumers could also be video producers. Videocassettes replaced narrow-gauge film stock for amateur film-making, and video became a popular means of compiling records of family occasions, particularly weddings (Rollins, 1991; Talty, 1991). Video activists also used camcorders to document demonstrations and events organised by campaign and community groups. Activists valued video for the opportunities available for creating alternative or oppositional forms of information outside the official channels controlled by the press and broadcasting industries (Harding, 1997). When linked to a closed-circuit television (CCTV) system, video was also frequently used as a channel for surveillance.

Digital Versatile Disc or Digital Video Disc (DVD) was introduced on the consumer market in 1996. Coinciding with the introduction of systems for the digital delivery of satellite and cable services, interactive television, experimentation with digital cinema exhibition and mass adoption of broadband internet connectivity, DVD was a part of the digital revolution which traversed audiovisual media in the late 1990s. DVD not only replaced the VCRs and videocassettes but also introduced a new media object. Videocassettes had always remained a linear medium, working along the single plane of record, play, rewind and fast-forward. DVD, however, provided access to many different sources of content via menus. DVDs increased the storage capacity of video software units, providing space for the inclusion of other types of content beyond the main programme. By multiplying textual content, DVD has raised questions over whether there is a core or essence to the video commodity.

During the 1980s and 90s a huge global market developed around the VCR and sales of pre-recorded videocassettes, but by the mid-1990s growth in the sector slowed down and the video market appeared to have peaked. DVD, however, re-energised the market, creating a boom as players and discs rapidly sold in high volumes. Historically, then, the VCR and DVD have divided the consumer video market into two distinct waves of innovation and growth.

This is a book about the commerce of video. As already noted, not all uses of video (e.g. family records, video activism) are commercial. This is then a book about a certain version of video, concentrating on the industries which supply markets for video or DVD hardware and software. It is worth noting immediately that there is no single video or DVD industry. Instead, the video business involves participants from many industries. At one level, this is an effect of the structure on which the video market is built. Roy Armes has observed that consumer video follows the 'three-fold pattern of profits' found with other recording media, combining 'the sale of a consumer durable, pre-recorded products, and recording materials': 'the triple market created at the turn of the century for cameras, postcards, and photographic materials is echoed in the 1980s by the combination of domestic video recorders, taped movies, and blank cassettes' (1988: 113). The video industries therefore bring together involvement from the consumer electronics and media industries. At another level, the multiplicity of the video industries is a result of the multiple ways in which video-cassettes and DVDs are used. Cassettes and discs are used as carrier or storage media for many different kinds of content, including feature films, television programmes, pornography, music promotions, exercise and instructional workshops, corporate promotions and teaching materials. As these forms of content come from various categories of content provider, so, to follow Cubitt's terms, there is no 'essence' to the video industries. Instead, videocassettes and discs belong to the film, broadcasting, adult entertainment and music industries.

In the video industries, a broad distinction can be drawn between those businesses involved with the development, manufacture and marketing of electronic hardware, against those who make, distribute and sell items of video software. Broadly speaking, this is a distinction between the consumer electronics industry and the copyright and retailing industries. In the video software business, a further distinction can also be drawn between the legitimate market, based on the circulation and exchange of legally produced recordings, and the illicit business of industrialised video piracy.

As a market sector, consumer electronics covers a variety of home media goods:

- television sets
- VCRs
- DVD players/recorders

- audio systems – combined units including tuners, amplifiers, CD or Mini-Disc (MD) players, cassette decks and speakers
- audio separates – separate high fidelity (hi-fi) components, combined to create a system (e.g. record decks, cassette decks, speakers, amplifiers, tuners, pre-amplifiers and home cinema amplifiers)
- personal audio equipment – personal CD, MD, cassette or MP3 players
- portable audio equipment – cassette/CD players, radios
- PCs – where used for domestic leisure
- games consoles – cartridge or disk players, possibly with DVD-compatibility and/or internet enabled. (Taylor, 2002: 3–4)

Video therefore only represents a part of the consumer electronics business. In the consumer electronics industry, the major companies such as Hitachi, JVC, Matsushita, Philips, Sanyo, Sony, Thomson and Toshiba are involved in innovating new products through research and development programmes, together with the physical manufacture of hardware units. By licensing their patents, these companies can open up their technology for manufacture by other producers. Under Original Equipment Manufacturer or OEM arrangements, an electronics manufacturer can also make finished products for a secondary company, which buys in bulk and then resells under its own labels, placing its logo on the product. Both routes expand production and marketing, and are important to launching a new consumer product such as home video, for they expand the routes through which the product can be quickly and widely placed in the marketplace.

Transferring films and television programmes to tape or disc has provided the cinema and broadcasting industries with new sources of income. For Barbara Klinger (2006: 8), video has contributed to extending the 'textual afterlife' of film following initial theatrical exhibition. With video, film received 'its repurposed materialisation in the home' (p. 11). However, although feature films or television programmes may be repurposed for video releasing, the business model which supports this revenue stream is quite unlike theatrical film exhibition or systems of television delivery. As Paul Sweeting (2006b: 428–9) comments with regard to Hollywood cinema:

> Although the home video business is an integral part of the Hollywood movie system, it operates like no other part of show business. At the nuts-and-bolts level, it works more like the consumer packaged good business ... Unlike any other revenue stream, movies on home video involve manufacturing, warehousing and distributing physical product.

Rather than film or broadcasting, it may be more appropriate to think of video as a business which is closer to clothing or, to choose a media comparison, book publishing. As the following two chapters show, early recorded music formats and later audio CDs represented models of home entertainment media which prefigured the VCR/videocassette combination and subsequently DVD. Indeed, the structure of the video business is far closer to that of the recorded music industry than that of the film industry. Underpinning the video software business is a basic structure formed by producers, distributors, duplicators, wholesalers and retailers. Source material comes from producers of audiovisual works or the owners of rights to such works. As feature films, television programmes, pornography, music videos or instructional films represent just a few of the types of works which have appeared on videocassette or DVD, the variety of producers/rights holders range from large film companies and television broadcasters or networks to a vast array of independent production companies. Depending on the scale of the company, producers may either self-distribute video releases or sell rights to an external independent distributor. Video distributors acquire the rights for releasing titles in specific territories over a limited period of time. Either through their own offices or by outsourcing functions to external service providers, distributors create or commission the necessary packaging artwork and organise campaigns to market releases. A distributor may also organise preparation of a master tape, involving the telecine conversion of an original source such as film, and then pay for the mass reproduction of cassettes or discs at a factory run by a duplication or replication company. In some cases, video distributors may sell videocassettes or DVD units directly to retailers, although most distributors sell units through a wholesaler.

After receiving the cassettes and discs from the duplicator, the wholesaler divides the stock into smaller quantities for shipping to retail and rental outlets or 'rentailers'. Cassettes and discs are made available for rental through various types of outlet, from small individual video rental shops to large national chains. Video retail is also organised through diverse outlets, including department stores, supermarkets, garages and music or book stores. Retailers can arrange the buying of their video stock directly but in the case of department stores or supermarkets, where videos are sold as only a part of a large diverse range of products, the services of so-called rack-jobbers are hired to supply and manage the stock. As Sweeting (2006b) explains:

> *Rack-jobbers* are middlemen used by general merchandise retailers to manage and buy for a specific category of product, such as music or video, where the number of new product releases is high, requiring a degree of expertise to operate and stock a

department effectively. In return, the rack-jobber, which typically owns the inventory, splits the revenue with the retailer in an arrangement analogous to the manufacturer-operated cosmetics counters in large department stores. (emphasis in original, p. 434)

Alongside bricks-and-mortar retail outlets, additional sales channels are available through mail order and, more recently, online retailers.

While it is common in the video business to describe the owners of rights as distributors, as these companies usually do not handle the physical transportation of units to retailers and rentailers, it is a potentially misleading term. Harold Vogel's (2001: 467) suggestion that these companies are in effect 'publishers' offers what is probably a more appropriate description for this role. Similarly referring to creators of audiovisual works as 'producers' is deceptive, for they do not produce the actual videocassette or DVD units which circulate in the market. As in other cultural industries, such as film or recorded music, the producer only makes the original source from which copies are subsequently reproduced. It is the duplicators who actually produce the finished units and so their role is effectively that of a manufacturer.

Structure is only one way of understanding the video business. Historically, three major lines of tension have repeatedly emerged in the commerce of video. In one form or another, these continually appear and occur throughout the course of the book. It is these tensions which in many ways operate as the dynamics driving the business. One of the greatest areas of conflict has concerned competition over incompatible formats. In the 1970s, Sony's Betamax became the first commercially successful VCR format but ultimately lost out in the market to the rival Video Home System (VHS) from JVC and Matsushita. While Betamax and VHS were battling it out in the VCR wars, in the early 1980s a number of incompatible videodisc systems appeared on the market. Although a broad industry consensus supported the introduction of DVD, at the time of the launch, attempts were still made to introduce Digital Video Express or Divx as a rival digital disc system. Less than a decade after DVD came onto the market, a further format war emerged as Blu-ray and HD-DVD went head-to-head in their attempts to become the dominant format for high-definition DVD. Over successive decades, format wars have therefore divided hardware and software markets for video.

Control of video software has proved a second area of tension. Videocassettes and DVDs have presented the media industries with a double-edged sword. For producers and distributors of audiovisual content, videocassettes and DVDs offered the benefits of creating new markets and revenues, yet at the same time by packaging content in this way the reproduction and use of those works slipped beyond the control of rights holders. By making their properties available to the public, the media copyright industries have been confronted by the need to construct business models to maximise their remuneration from retail or rental transactions. Furthermore, alongside the legitimate market, the growth of the illegal market in video recordings has resulted in continuing struggles by the owners of copyrighted works to combat the impact of industrialised piracy. Videocassettes made recording easy for consumers but also for pirates, while DVDs provided both the legitimate and illegal industries with the means to produce high-quality copies. Videocassettes and DVDs may be hard, exchangeable objects, but as both these issues indicate, like all other media industries the video business is not based on things but on mechanisms for controlling and exploiting the intellectual property rights which pertain to images and ideas.

A final area of tension concerns the relationship of consumer video to other media. VCRs, videocassettes and DVD have introduced new platforms for home entertainment. Videocassettes and DVDs sit alongside other storage media such as CDs and videogames but also the delivery media of radio, television and the internet. Given the number of available substitutes and the limited quotas of leisure time which can be dedicated by anyone to media consumption, video media must continually justify their place among the range of media options. The video business is therefore always placed in competition against the broadcasting, computing and online industries, as video and DVD try to secure their place in the economy of consumer attention.

The effects of these tensions can be felt in the conduct of the video business at local, national, regional and global levels. Since its formation, the video business has been a global business. This book does not mount a global survey of the video industries or markets in all international territories but explores how transnational and globally extended industrial dynamics are central to understanding how the video business is organised and operates. As Annabelle Sreberny (2000) suggests, the global extensity of mass media industries can be mapped through the dynamics of global media firms, flows and forms. In the video business, companies in the consumer electronics and copyright industries organise their operations nationally and transnationally. For both the legitimate and illicit sides of the video business, networks for the distribution and sale of videocassettes and DVDs are employed to create global markets for video software. These markets circulate cassettes and discs as the carriers for various categories of content.

This book therefore examines the globality of the video and DVD business through the operations of transnational firms, the formation of national and international markets, and the circulation of audiovisual works. Although Japanese engineering produced the VCR, competing research and development programmes were conducted simultaneously by consumer electronics manufacturers in Europe and the US. To extend the supply of VCR hardware around the world, Sony, Matsushita and other Japanese companies established overseas production plants or formed licensing agreements with foreign manufacturers. In the case of the DVD, it was a partnership between the Japanese electronics manufacturer Toshiba and the US media and communications conglomerate Time Warner which initiated development of the disc format. Trade and the internationalisation of production formed a global market for VCR and DVD hardware, while globally extended distribution networks have provided the channels for flows of films and other content on cassette and disc. These networks are not confined to the legitimate media industries, for the global business of industrialised piracy thrives on inconsistencies in political and legal mechanisms to operate key centres of illegal manufacture in national territories, and to link these by underground cross-border distribution networks.

As a product of Japanese engineering, supported by content from large transnational media corporations, video and DVD are further symbols of the industrialised world's consumer modernity. Yet economic, social and cultural variations at the level of national and local contexts have resulted in substantial and significant differences in the adoption, use and reception of video media. Economic factors have undoubtedly influenced access to video hardware, and VCR or DVD ownership is unevenly distributed around the world, yet these technologies have still filtered into markets across the developing and industrialised worlds. While sales of VCRs and DVDs have spread around the world, the contexts in which these media are used have become many and various. For example, as VCR sales led to a boom in the operation of 'video parlours' as collective public viewing spaces attached to restaurants and bars in India or the former Soviet Union, so the idea of consumer video as 'home video' can be judged to be a culturally limited notion, largely confined to the industrialised world. Videocassettes and DVDs are not simply technological or commercial objects but also cultural forms, continually shaped at local, national and transnational levels by their integration into differing patterns of life and multi-layered formations of interpretation and taste.

At one level, the globality of video is therefore evident in the worldwide extension of markets for video hardware and software. Yet, although video products are sold across the world, small clusters of companies have remained at the core of the hardware and software sectors of the business. From the 1960s, various international projects were undertaken towards developing a consumer video recorder, but since the Betamax/VHS battle that started in the late 1970s, Japanese companies have dominated technological leadership in the video business. Although the content of recordings on cassette or disc has come from suppliers across international territories, Hollywood feature films have become the most visible type of content in the legal video market. From the early years of the videocassette market to the boom in DVD sales, the major companies in the Hollywood film industry have maintained their influence beyond the domestic US market. By distributing films to international territories on cassette or disc, the Hollywood majors have secured dominant shares in most of the world's richest video markets. Consequently, the majors have been able to exert wider influence over the video business. As witnessed with the development of the videodisc system DiscoVision and later with DVD and high-definition DVD, the majors have played an integral role in the launch of new video formats. Reflecting the status of Hollywood film in the legitimate market, Hollywood features have also become the leading source of illegal recordings in the pirate market. Consequently, through lobbying by the trade organisation the Motion Picture Association of America (MPAA) and its international arm the Motion Picture Association (MPA), the Hollywood majors have been at the forefront of international drives to curb industrialised piracy. To a large extent, the global video business is therefore structured across a core axis of Japanese hardware and Hollywood software.

This book explores aspects of the history and operations of video as a global business. Chapters 1 and 2 concentrate on matters of hardware, charting the historical developments in the consumer electronics industries which led to the commercial launch of the VCR, videodisc, video compact disc (VCD) and DVD. Chapter 3 examines the global market for consumer video, with the internationalisation of VCR production, the formation of the global VCR market, the popularisation of VCD in East Asian territories and the re-energising of the world video market by DVD. A range of case studies also explore how specific national circumstances affected the introduction and adoption of video technologies. Since the early years of the video business, Hollywood has remained the dominant content provider and distributor for video software both in the US and many overseas territories. Chapter 4 considers the contradictory responses which Hollywood presented to the introduction of home video as the major companies at first tried to resist video before embracing the medium for its new and lucrative revenue opportunities. Chapter 5 then looks at how the major Hollywood film companies are reshaping the US video market in the digital age. Finally, Chapter 6 examines the global economy of industrialised piracy and the legislative, enforcement and technological measures taken by governments and the copyright industries to combat piracy.

The historical parameters of this study are mainly concentrated on the market for home video which emerged following the launch of the VCR in the mid-1970s and which was subsequently re-energised with the arrival of DVD in the late 90s. However, the opening chapter sees home video as the product of technological innovations which not only emerged with the introduction of the VTR in the 1950s but which, from a longer-term perspective, came about with the introduction of new media technologies for home entertainment from the late nineteenth century onwards. This study could only trace developments in the video and DVD industries up until the end of 2006. At that time the video business was in the midst of a fresh wave of innovation following the recent launch of the high-definition DVD formats Blu-ray and HD-DVD. As these formats appeared on the market at more or less the same time, the video business faced new uncertainties as the prospect of a new format war loomed large, ending the nearly two decades of stability which had prevailed since VHS eventually triumphed over Betamax in the VCR wars. It was necessary for this study to stop at that point, but video is a continually evolving medium or range of media and the story of video is by no means complete.

A note on terms. As already outlined, the video market has experienced two waves of growth. With the first of these, VCRs and videocassettes established the idea of video as a consumer medium, so that 'video' came to stand for Betamax and VHS. 'Video' is applied here in this way to refer specifically to just these systems and the developments which occurred around them. Equally, however, DVD and other technologies such as videodisc and VCD are also video media. Moreover, although DVD created a new media object, the structure and organisation of the video industries continued along much the same lines as the business established in the VCR era. Consequently, 'video' is also used here as a generic term for a range of consumer media but also to identify the continuity of the video business or video market. Throughout this book, video is therefore used in both particular and general ways, and hopefully the context in which the term is used will clarify the differences between these applications.

I

Bringing Entertainment Home: The Consumer Electronics Industry and the VCR

The videocassette recorder or VCR was the product of two histories, one technological the other social. Technologically the VCR has a very specific history tied to the research and development programmes undertaken in Japan, the US and Europe from the early 1960s onwards aimed at creating a consumer-level video recorder. That history itself belongs to the broader history of video recording, which had commenced from the start of the 1950s with projects aimed at inventing a recording apparatus for use by the nascent television industry, resulting in the videotape recorder (VTR). Yet as the VCR and VTR both used magnetic tape, then video belongs to a longer history which stretches back to early attempts in the 1890s by the Danish electrician Valdemar Poulsen to use magnetic material for recording.

Before magnetic tape, from the late 1870s cylinders and then wax discs were used as recording media for sound. On 30 April 1877, the French poet and amateur scientist Charles Cros deposited with the Secretary of the Academy of Sciences in Paris a paper titled *Procédé d'enregistrement et de reproduction des phénomènes perçus par l'ouïe* (*Procedure for the Recording and Reproduction of Phenomena of Acoustic Perception*), outlining a system for recording and reproducing sound using a disc and lamp-blackened glass (Gelatt, 1977: 23–4; Kittler, 1999: 21). Cros lacked the financial backing to create a working version of his process but later in 1877 the American inventor Thomas Alva Edison produced his 'talking machine', the phonograph. Cros had nevertheless clearly grasped the fundamental idea of recording. To introduce the first book of his collected poetry, *Le Collier de griffes* (*The Neckless of Claws*), Cros wrote the poem *Inscription*, the final line of which summarised his scientific endeavours in recorded sound: 'Le temps veut fuir, je le soumets' ('Time would flee, I subdue it') (translated by and cited in Kittler, 1999: 22). Cros identified the technological effect of recording: to capture the moment and thereby arrest or subdue the passage of time.

Nearly a century later, when the Japanese electronics manufacturer Sony launched its Betamax VCR onto the consumer market, the company's co-founder, Akio Morita, took credit for neatly labelling the main benefit of the machine's recording functionality as 'time-shifting'. In speeches promoting Betamax, Morita eulogised the benefits of the VCR, claiming 'Now you can grab a TV programme in your hand' and 'With the VCR, television is like a magazine – you can control your own schedule' (Morita, Reingold and Shimomura, 1987: 208). Time-shifting was certainly innovative, because for the first time television viewers could record programming at one time for viewing at another. However, beyond the specific development of video recording for domestic viewing, the VCR was the product of the deeper modernist preoccupation – displayed by Cros, Edison and other media innovators of the nineteenth century – which was concerned with the wish to create technologies capable of subduing time.

As suggested in the Introduction, video has no essence. There is no essential purpose or use for which video can be employed and the VCR became a flexible medium with multiple uses. Yet despite its various possible applications, the VCR was always conceptualised by the developers who invented it, and the majority of consumers who bought it, as a domestic media technology. Once the VCR was integrated into the home, it joined a range of technologies already available for domestic media consumption, including the newspaper, magazine, book, record player, radio and television. VCRs joined what Hermann Bausinger has referred to as the domestic 'media ensemble' (1984: 349). Each of these media had the effect of creating a bridge between the private sanctuary of the home and the outside public world. As David Morley (2000: 87) notes, communication technologies have a disembedding effect in relation to the home, simultaneously

> articulat[ing] together that which is separate (to bring the outside world into the home, via television, or to connect family members, via the phone, to friends or relatives elsewhere) but, by the same token, to transgress the ... boundary which protects the privacy and solidarity of the home from the flux and threat of the outside world.

The VCR brought the outside world of cinema or television into the home but it further connected the home with forms of culture produced beyond its physical domain. As media technologies and forms traverse the boundary between the inside and the outside of the home, so that the outside is always present on the inside, then VCRs and other domestic media like recorded music, home cinema, radio and television contribute to the formation of what Morley terms 'mediated domesticity' (p. 86). The VCR is therefore not just the product of technological innovation but of a history of social change which has seen the home become the centre of media consumption while simultaneously linking the private domestic context into the wider currency of publicly circulated culture.

This chapter explores the historical emergence of the VCR, which it sees as the product of several factors. Initially, it considers how, from the late nineteenth century, a range of new media technologies were targeted at domestic use to make the home a key site of media consumption. The chapter then explores the development of magnetic recording and how this led to the introduction in the 1950s of the VTR as a video recording technology for the television broadcasting industries. As argued in the Introduction, video is not an industry but a collection of industries. One of these is the consumer electronics business, which is responsible for the manufacture and marketing of video hardware. The chapter traces the broad change which occurred during the twentieth century as Japan became the leading global force in consumer electronics. It also looks at pioneering attempts to launch video recording technology on the consumer market and how the Japanese companies Sony, JVC and Matsushita developed the first commercially successful VCRs, resulting in the format war between Betamax and VHS. Finally, the chapter concludes by reflecting on how the VCR transformed the dynamics of television viewing.

EARLY HOME MEDIA AND THE BUSINESS OF ENTERTAINMENT

According to Witold Rybczynski (2001), it was not until the seventeenth century that Western European societies began to regard the home as a place of private refuge. Whereas previously the home accommodated work and living, the separation of these two spheres resulted in the 'privatization of the home', giving rise to 'a growing sense of intimacy, of identifying the house exclusively with family life' (p. 39). Home became not simply a physical place but a concept associated with ideas of privacy, domesticity and comfort. From the start of the nineteenth century, the introduction of gaslight and ventilation systems contributed to what Rybczynski describes as 'the mechanization of the home': 'Domestic technology such as the gasolier and the ventilation duct represented an invasion of the home, not only by new devices, but by a different sensibility – that of the engineer and of the businessman' (p. 145). As the electrification of the home commenced by the end of the century, then technologies designed and sold to assist the comfort of domestic living became a feature of bourgeois living in the Victorian household.

Separated from work, the home became a place of leisure. From the late nineteenth century, mechanisation and electrification extended to the creation of technologies intended to amuse and entertain. New technologies for home entertainment were invented targeting a market broadly conceptualised as the bourgeois family gathered together in the privacy of the home during their leisure time. The trend which Rybczynski describes as 'the mechanization of the home' therefore led to the creation of what Barbara Klinger (2006: 5) describes as 'the technologized home', and as various mechanical and electrical media technologies were assimilated into domestic living, so the mediatised home took shape.

Recorded Sound

In the second half of the nineteenth century a number of inventions were devised to record and replay sound. It would not be until the last two decades of that century, however, that sound recording technology became commercially available. This early market for recorded sound was divided between competing systems based either on cylinder or disc formats. Patented on 24 December 1877 by Edison, the phonograph employed a cylinder wrapped in tin foil for recording. Working in Washington DC, Chichester Bell and Charles Sumner Tainter devised a similar system, the graphophone, patented in June 1885, using wax-coated cardboard cylinders to produce more durable recordings (Koenigsberg, 1990: xxiii). On 26 September 1887, Emile Berliner, a German émigré working in the US, patented the gramophone. Departing from the cylinder systems, Berliner's gramophone recorded and replayed sound on photoengraved discs.

Initially, the competing formats divided the market, impeding growth. At the start of the twentieth century, Eldridge Johnson was manufacturing and selling gramophones in the US. Johnson introduced innovations by adding a motorised drive, improving the sound box and developing an efficient process for recording which used wax discs (Gelatt, 1977: 133). After Berliner and Johnson agreed to pool their patents, on 3 October 1901 the Victor Talking Machine Company was incorporated. Use of the generic term gramophone was dropped as the company marketed its branded machine simply as the Victor (p. 134). By controlling all the key patents relating to disc systems, Victor was able to beat off competition from the Columbia Phonograph Company, its nearest rival, and as disc-based systems emerged as the dominant format, the industry achieved the standardisation needed for market growth.

When recorded sound technology first appeared, questions surrounded its potential uses. Edison believed the phonograph would serve many purposes, including dictation, elocution, education, articulate clocks, the preservation of languages and as a 'Family Record' (p. 29). Of these possible applications, Edison preferred to see the phonograph as a 'talking machine' for use in offices to record business correspondence. Marketing the machine therefore concentrated on its use in commerce, and the phonograph was priced too high for a mass consumer market. In contrast, when Berliner first presented the gramophone on 16 May 1878 to members of the Franklin Institute in Philadelphia, he promoted the machine for its entertainment value. He envisaged the gramophone would see 'prominent singers, speakers, or performers derive an income from royalties on the sale of their phonautograms' (p. 63). In the copy for an advertisement from Christmas 1900, the gramophone was sold as a popular and accessible entertainment technology, welcome 'everywhere and by everybody'.

> No matter how remote your habitation, it brings within the family circle the actual voices of orators, singers, comedians, and story-tellers, who perhaps at that very moment are delighting Metropolitan audiences with the same eloquence, melody, humour, and dialect that is coming from the Gramophone in the quiet of a country home hundreds of miles away. (illustration in Moore, 1976: 40–1)

Technology was therefore only one factor distinguishing the gramophone from the phonograph. Berliner's machine was conceived principally as a medium for commercial entertainment, to be used and consumed in the home, and supported by sales of recordings of popular performances.

By the end of the 1890s, the recording industry was well established in the US, and the domestic market was providing the foundation for US companies to expand into international territories. From 1888, the Edison-Bell company established a secure base in Europe, exporting phonograph and graphophone merchandise to the region through its London office (Gelatt, 1977: 100). France responded well to the new technology and in 1897 Columbia opened its first overseas office in Paris. It was Berliner, however, who most actively pursued the global extension of his business. William Barry Owen was entrusted with exclusive rights to sell gramophones and recordings in Europe from his London office, and in May 1898 he founded the Gramophone Company (p. 105). According to their trading agreement, Victor handled sales in East Asia together with North and South America, while Gramophone looked after Europe, Africa, Australia and the rest of Asia (Gronow and Saunio, 1998: 11).

Home Cinema

Before the arrival of cinema at the end of the nineteenth century, shadowplays, magic lanterns, peepshows, panoramas and dioramas all entertained through displays of visual spectacle in public spaces, including theatres and fairgrounds. Optical toys, such as the Thaumatrope, Phenakisticope, Zoetrope, Viviscope and Praxinoscope, also provided visual entertainment in the home. Between 1894 and 1895, Edison's Kinetoscope, along with the Bioscope of Max and Emil Skladanowsky, and the Cinématographe of Louis and Auguste Lumière, emerged as early examples of film technology. As Edison and the Lumières commercially exploited their technologies, the consumption of moving pictures was located outside the home in the public spaces of Kinetoscope parlours and theatre, vaudeville or fairground presentations. However, as Peter Krämer (1996: 15) has shown, Edison originally conceived of his motion picture apparatus as not only a technology for use in the home but also as a device which he hoped would receive audiovisual signals transmitted to the home by the telegraph and telephone. For Krämer therefore, this vision of 'the "cinema" arose, then, out of what . . . could be called Edison's "televisual imagination"' (p. 16). As similar ideas were articulated by contemporaries of Edison,

> the big screen literally putting the home in contact with the world outside, blurring and dissolving the boundaries between the most private spaces and the public sphere, was the perceived end point and centre piece of late nineteenth century developments in media technologies. (p. 17)

Some of these intentions were pursued when, between 1896 and 1912, a series of projectors aimed at the home market appeared in Europe and the US (Mebold and Tepperman, 2003; Singer, 1988). Possibly the first of these was W. Watson's Motorgraph, which came onto the market in Britain at the end of 1896. Many other examples followed. In 1897, the American Parlor Kinetoscope Company released a domestic version of Edison's machine and between 1904 and 1906 the Ikonograph appeared. However, due to the dangers of highly flammable nitrate stock, growth of the home cinema market remained limited.

When several European and US companies launched new projectors in 1912, there was a resurgence of interest in home cinema. Of the systems to appear at this time, the most notable were the Edison Home Projecting Kinetoscope, or 'Home P.K.', and the Pathéscope, manufactured by the French studio Pathé Frères (Singer, 1988: 44). Instead of the 35mm prints used in cinema exhibition, both projectors ran narrower, substandard gauges on safety film. While the Home P.K. catered for home entertainment, Edison also marketed the system to schools, businesses and churches. Through a system of mail order exchange for sale and return, a range of comedies and drama titles were made available. Despite the Edison name, however, pricing, technological imperfections and poor marketing all prevented the Home P.K. from establishing a strong consumer market, and in 1914 the system was withdrawn.

From 1902, Pathé had risen to prominence in the French film industry due to cheap production costs, an extensive international distribution network and the company's dominance of the fairground or *fêtes forianes* market (Abel, 1998: 22–5). Pathé became the first vertically integrated film company in the world when in 1906 it began to add a circuit of permanent cinemas to its existing production and distribution holdings. Introduction in France of the K-O-K home projector during 1912 was therefore part of the company's programme of diversification. After the K-O-K was renamed the Pathéscope, from 1913 the projector was marketed in the US and other parts of Europe. Alongside manufacturing projectors, Pathé also made available many of the titles from its film catalogue for the home system as films were reduced from 35mm to play on the idiosyncratic 28mm gauge of the Pathéscope.

Although the Pathéscope was more successful that the Edison machine, it did not stimulate a large-scale market for home cinema: Pathé intentionally marketed the K-O-K or Pathéscope as the 'cinématographe de salon', targeting only the more affluent class of consumer (Mebold and Tepperman, 2003: 140). After the introduction in 1921 of Bell and Howell's Filmo 70 camera with projector, followed two years later by Eastman Kodak's introduction of its Ciné-Kodak camera and Kodascope projector, an amateur market was formed around the 16mm gauge (Winston, 1996: 60–3; Zimmermann, 1995: 27–31). Kodak subsequently fed the amateur market with the introduction in 1932 of the 8mm gauge, followed in 1965 by the Super-8 format. Even so, home cinema remained a minority pastime, largely confined to the middle and upper classes, and to the realm of the hobbyist or enthusiast rather than the mass consumer market. Substandard film gauges opened up the idea and possibility of film consumption in the home but without generating the consumer base to form a viable market for home viewing as a secondary or alternative exhibition window for professionally produced film.

Broadcasting

With the arrival of radio and television broadcasting, the home was further opened up to new mass media options. Recorded sound and home cinema both brought entertainment into the home through storage or carrier media formats. On wax discs or 28mm film, songs and dramas circulated in tangible forms. These storage media artefacts could be reproduced in mass volumes for export and sales across international markets. Broadcasting, however, entered the home not in the form of hard artefacts but by signals, introducing channels for electronic delivery media into the home.

From its beginnings in 1919, radio broadcasting flourished in the US and later in parts of Europe. Although experimental television services began during the mid-1930s in Germany, Britain, France, the USSR and the US, the Second World War halted their development. After the war, television broadcasting resumed in Britain, the US, Germany and France, and during the 1950s, Japan, Australia, Holland, Belgium, Scandinavia, China and most of Latin America introduced full television services (see contributions to Smith, ed., 1998). As radio and television became internationally popular, national broadcasting systems emerged.

Television made an obvious contribution to the future development of the VCR, for the television receiver became the box through which video recordings were played. But arguably it was radio rather than television which played the more significant role in establishing the context in which the VCR would later emerge, for more than any previous domestic media, radio routinised the consumption of entertainment in the home. While public leisure spaces, theatres and cinemas attracted audiences to amusements outside the home, radio broadcasting drew large and regular audiences in the privacy of their homes. With the popularisation of radio and later television, the home became the primary locus for the consumption of professionally produced entertainments.

Home Entertainment as an Industry

In its earliest years, the recorded sound business illustrated one of the most common trends in the commercial launch of new media technologies: format incompatibility. Phonograph recordings could not play on gramophones and vice versa. Likewise, the prints which ran on the Home P.K. and Pathéscope were not interchangeable. Similar tensions arose in the late 1970s as Betamax and the Video Home System (VHS) divided the home video market, establishing a pattern which was replayed over subsequent decades with incompatible videodisc systems and high-definition DVD formats.

Despite the different technical formats, the phonograph and gramophone industries shared a common business model for home entertainment media. For both media, a market was formed around a range of companies which supplied the hardware of cylinder and disc players, or an array of interchangeable software recordings. Likewise, Edison and Pathé's home cinema systems relied on the combination of hardware and software to supply the consumer market. As infrastructures for the production, distribution, duplication and retailing of mass reproduced content were established, so recorded music and home cinema formed new markets for media software. In the case of Pathé, the company's strength in production and distribution was capable of supporting the home cinema system and making the Pathéscope a commercial success. With its unique 28mm gauge, the Pathéscope was entirely incompatible with other competing systems, for example the 22mm gauge of the Home P.K., and so consumers were locked into using Pathé as the only supplier of films for the projector. Imitating the distribution networks which supported their 35mm business, Pathé created a rental scheme allowing consumers to hire a number of films through mail order each week. With its home projector, Pathé therefore prefigured the type of business practices found later with home video, introducing not only a technology for consuming films in the home but also establishing networks of film exchange serving consumers which pre-dated the rental of video recordings through high street stores or over the internet. As Pathé films were simply reformatted prints of films produced and shown on 35mm, the French studio also demonstrated the possibilities of securing additional value from copyrighted assets by creating a secondary or ancillary market for the studio's back catalogue of film titles.

Recorded sound and home cinema offered new opportunities for consuming entertainment. The phonograph and gramophone allowed for the consumption of the spoken word or musical entertainment outside the theatre or concert hall. Film also separated the recorded from the live performance, with home cinema providing an alternative and domestic window for film exhibition. In each case, recording formats operated as storage or carrier media which had various cultural, commercial and legal implications. Recording disembedded the place of consumption from the place of production, making the recording available as a tangible artefact for commercial exploitation. As they were circulated and exchanged in markets for cultural works, carrier media were subject to intellectual property laws determining their rightful use. Whether the gramophone disc or 28mm film print, storage media were therefore not only technological products but also commercial and legal objects.

Broadcasting brought mediated performances into the home but in most other respects the radio or television industries were quite different from the recorded sound or home cinema business. Radio or television required the consumer to own items of media hardware but did not involve any complementary software industry as such. By delivering content which was either identical or similar to that obtained by the carrier media of recorded music or home cinema, radio or television offered a rival substitute in the economy of consumer attention. Early radio broadcasting, therefore, became the first step towards forming the competitive division between carrier and delivery media in the home entertainment ensemble. As video matured as a consumer market during the 1980s, its popularity grew alongside the introduction in many international markets of cable and satellite as new delivery systems for multi-channel television. Similarly, as DVD was launched in the mid-1990s, its introduction was set against the arrival of digital cable and satellite, together with broadband internet, which all provided additional routes for channelling audiovisual content and services into the home. Whether on cassette or disc, home video media have therefore had to constantly negotiate their place in the market vis-à-vis various alternative delivery media options.

MAGNETIC RECORDING AND THE DEVELOPMENT OF THE VIDEOTAPE RECORDER

For two decades before the VCR arrived on the consumer market, the VTR became widely used in television broadcasting as a professional producer technology. Processes for recording television pictures began in 1927 with John Logie Baird's Phonosvision, a mechanical system using a stylus for transferring images to the vibrations stored on wax discs (Abramson, 1955). Film recording processes were also pioneered in Germany, England and the US during the 1930s. But it was through a concentrated period of research and development from the late 1940s until the mid-50s that video recording was advanced and finally realised.

Magnetic Sound Recording

Essential to the development of video recording was the range of tests and trials conducted in the use of magnetic tape as a recording material. Early patents for magnetic recording technology emerged in the last years of the nineteenth century. Poulsen, an employee of the Copenhagen Telegraph Company, demonstrated a device using wire to record magnetic impulses back in 1893, and in 1898 he patented the Telegraphone, the first magnetic recording machine. Working in Germany, Dr Fritz Pfleumer improved on wire recording with a system for applying magnetic powder to paper or plastic-backed strips, an early form of magnetic recording tape, which he patented in 1928. Building on Pfleumer's patent, the German companies Allgemeine Elektricitäts-Gesellschaft (AEG) and Badische Anilin- und Soda-Fabrik AG (BASF) formed a partnership, with AEG working on the recording machinery while BASF developed the magnetic stock. BASF started manufacturing plastic-based tape in 1934 and the following year AEG publicly demonstrated the Magnetophon, the first magnetic tape recorder.

German radio stations worked with the Magnetophon and its use by the Wermacht during the Second World War brought the system to the attention of John T. Mullin of the US Army Signals Corps after the war. Mullin brought the Magnetophon to the US, where he demonstrated an improved version of the technology. It was at one of these demonstrations that the singer and radio star Bing Crosby first became interested in the possibilities of magnetic recording. Crosby had built a successful radio career on the National Broadcasting Company (NBC) network but left after they refused his request to use recordings to ease the strains of live broadcasting. After joining the new American Broadcasting Company (ABC) network, Crosby encouraged the use of acetate recordings over the air and hired Mullin to magnetically record his 1947–8 season. With a view to promoting advances in magnetic recording for audio, Bing Crosby Enterprises invested in the Ampex Corporation, a wartime manufacturer of aircraft motors. At the time, Ampex regarded sound recording as a new business opportunity and after adapting the Magnetophon, from 1948 the company began to produce the Model 200 recorder. Impressed with the Ampex machine,

Crosby bought twenty recorders, which he then sold to ABC for radio broadcasting (Rosenbloom and Freeze, 1985: 116).

Television Recording

In the early 1950s, television continued to be admired for its 'liveness'. Recording was necessary, however, not only to produce original programming but also
to store live output for retransmission. This latter need was particularly pressing in the US, where the national networks faced the problem of trying to deliver
a uniform programme schedule across four time zones, creating a three-hour
time difference between the east and west coasts. Initially, radio broadcasters
used acetate discs to record programmes broadcast in the east for delayed
retransmission in the west, and after 1948 began employing magnetic tape
(Abramson, 2003: 26–7). Television broadcasters found a similar solution in
kinescope recording: by pointing a film camera at a television monitor, a programme broadcast live in the east was recorded in the west and the film rapidly
processed for retransmission. However, kinescoping was costly and produced
poor results. Although kinescoping used 16mm film which was a third of the
price of 35mm, the costs of film stock and processing quickly became apparent,
as by 1951 the television industry was using an estimated 550 million feet of film
each year (p. 48). Furthermore, the results could only poorly register grades in
the grey scale between black and white (Ginsberg, 1981: 11).

Noting the advantages gained by the radio industry, television executives
acknowledged that magnetic tape could provide technical and financial benefits
compared to film recording. Optical losses associated with the use of the lens
in the kinescope process would be eliminated along with the costs of processing. A tape recording could also be played back immediately and the tape reused
(Abramson, 1955). Early attempts to record television signals on magnetic
material had started in 1927 when Boris Rtcheouloff filed a patent in Britain for
a proposal to use Poulsen's Telegraphone, but this did not produce an effective
solution. Speaking on 27 September 1951 at celebrations for his forty-fifth year
of working in radio broadcasting, David Sarnoff, General Manager of the Radio
Corporation of America (RCA), addressed engineers at the RCA laboratories in
Princeton, New Jersey. In his speech, Sarnoff told the assembled that on this
anniversary he wanted to ask the RCA engineers for three 'presents' to be delivered within the next five years: 'a true amplifier of light', 'an electronic air
conditioner for the home' and a 'videograph' for recording black-and-white and
colour television pictures on magnetic tape (Lyons, 1966: 302). This last item
was of particular importance to RCA, as the company's NBC subsidiary ran one
of the three television networks in the US and so was familiar with the problems and limitations of kinescoping. Responding to Sarnoff's request, RCA

engineers immediately embarked on a project to develop video recording using magnetic tape. Also in 1951, Ampex began its own video recording project, while elsewhere in the US similar projects were under way, with General Electric (GE) in Syracuse and the Allen Shoup Laboratory in Chicago. Ampex and RCA, however, emerged as the leading rivals in efforts to create a working magnetic recorder for television.

At Ampex, the five-man team of Charles P. Ginsberg, Charles E. Anderson, Fred Pfost, Alex Maxey and Ray Dolby developed an experimental VTR model, the Mark IV, which received its first public demonstration on 14 April 1956, the eve of the thirty-fourth annual convention of the National Association of Radio and Television Broadcasters (NARTB) in Chicago (Abramson, 2003: 70). In front of 200 CBS affiliates, the Mark IV was used to record a speech by CBS chief engineer Bill Lodge, and then played back only a few seconds later. Simultaneous with the Chicago event, Ampex also held a press conference at the company's factory at Redwood City, California, using a Mark III model to demonstrate the technology (Ginsberg, 1981: 14; Rosenbloom and Freeze, 1985: 122).

Ampex's model had clear advantages over the RCA project, combining ease of operation with reduced tape use, and following the Chicago demonstration, RCA capitulated and all three US television networks placed orders for Ampex machines. On Friday 30 November 1956, the Columbia Broadcasting System (CBS) used video recording for the first time with a delayed broadcast of the 15-minute news show *Douglas Edwards and the News* from Television City in Hollywood (Abramson, 2003: 75). NBC began using the Ampex machine from January 1957 and ABC followed in April. Initially, Ampex could only satisfy demand by providing broadcasters with custom-manufactured prototypes but by the end of 1957 a production model, the VR-1000, was available, priced at US$45,000. A large console machine, weighing approximately 900 pounds, the VR-1000 could record black-and-white video for up to 64 minutes at a speed of 15 inches per second on a 12-inch reel of 2-inch-wide Mylar magnetic tape. An audio track could be laid down along one edge of the tape (Ginsberg, 1956: 302).

Colour television had started in the US during 1954 and Ampex looked towards developing colour capability. After trying to develop its own system, at the end of 1957 Ampex made a three-month cross-licensing agreement with RCA to grant the free exchange of technical information between the companies: Ampex made available patents related to the VR-1000 in return for licences to components in RCA's colour television system. RCA began manufacturing its own VTRs in 1959 but Ampex took the lead in the market. By 1961, Ampex had sold nearly 900 machines, of which around 300 were bought by foreign broadcasters. RCA's share of the VTR market remained at 25–35 per cent (Rosenbloom and Freeze, 1985: 123).

Ampex's design team for the VR-1000: left to right, Charles E. Anderson, Shelby Henderson, Alex Maxey, Ray Dolby, Fred Pfost and Charles P. Ginsburg

In the UK, the public service broadcaster, the British Broadcasting Corporation (BBC), had started to develop its Vision Electronic Recording Apparatus (VERA) from 1952 and publicly demonstrated the equipment on air during April 1958 (Briggs, 1995: 835). However, the commercial broadcaster Associated-Rediffusion, part of the Independent Television (ITV) network, implemented video recording for the first time when it used an Ampex machine on 26 June 1958 to broadcast the current affairs show *This Week* (p. 837). When VERA's fuzzy images were greeted by an unfavourable public reaction, the BBC disbanded the project and adopted the Ampex technology.

VERA was the only significant television recording project outside the US at this time. International sales of Ampex technology were aided by the introduction in April 1959 of the 'Inter-Switch', a modification enabling recording and playback for 525 lines/60 fields (the NTSC standard in the US), 405 lines/50 fields (UK), 819 lines/50 fields (the French standard) or 625 lines/50 fields for the rest of the world (Abramson, 2003: 85). By the end of the decade, during which television had become popularised around the world as a medium of mass entertainment, Ampex was therefore marketing a video recording technology adaptable for use by broadcasters across international territories.

Quadruplex and Helical-Scan Recording

Tape speed, image quality, safety and cost implications were all issues facing the first wave of VTRs. Early VTRs were all based on the same principle: tape was mounted on spinning reels and ran longitudinally across a fixed head to record a signal along the length of the tape. This required running huge lengths of tape at very high speed in order to achieve a recording of even a few minutes. When RCA demonstrated a prototype recorder in 1953, the tape speed ran at 30 feet per second (Lardner, 1987: 56).

Ampex's VR-1000 found a solution to these problems by constructing a revolving drum carrying four heads spinning laterally across the width of the tape to provide transverse scanning. With this quadruplex arrangement, the drum revolved quickly while the tape speed decreased, thereby reducing the length of tape required for longer recording times. However, as the change from one head to the next could cause breaks in the signal, a 'venetian blinds' effect frequently resulted.

A significant advance on these early systems came with the development of helical-scan recording. Instead of the tape passing over multiple video heads, it was wrapped in a helical loop around a drum holding a recording head, which was mounted at a slight angle to the line of the tape, transverse scanning a signal diagonally across the tape (Nmungwun, 1989: 145). Helical-scan removed the signal problems of the quadruplex arrangement and offered the additional benefits of slow motion and still-framing. Japanese electronics manufacturer Toshiba publicly demonstrated their VTR-1 helical-scan recorder in September 1959, using 2-inch-wide tape operating at a speed of 15 inches per second. Nippon Hōsō Kyōkai (NHK), the Japanese state broadcaster, began trials with the VTR-1 in December 1961. Other helical-scan recorders appeared that year, with Ampex introducing the VR-8000 and Victor Corporation of America, a division of JVC, marketing the Telechrome JVC Model 770 in the US. Three years later, Sony put their PV100 helical VTR on the market and American Airlines adopted the later PV-120AL model for in-flight entertainment.

VTRs were developed as a professional television production technology aimed at servicing the broadcast industry. But various technological innovations resulting from the research and development of the VTR later contributed to the making of the VCR. In particular, reductions in the speed and use of tape by helical-scanning, together with slow motion and still-frame functionality, aided the construction of compact and versatile units vital to the development of a video recorder suitable for the consumer market.

JAPANESE LEADERSHIP IN THE CONSUMER ELECTRONICS INDUSTRY

Although the US company Ampex took credit for developing the first workable videotape recorder, it was Japanese companies which would eventually introduce commercially marketable video machines for the home consumer. This change encapsulated broader developments in the consumer electronics industry. Initially driven in the first half of the twentieth century by the success of European and American companies through the manufacturing and selling of radios and later television receivers, the consumer electronics business was transformed from the 1960s onwards as Japanese and later South Korean and Taiwanese companies came to the forefront of the industry. By the time the VCR came onto the market in the 1970s, American industry had ceded technological leadership in the consumer electronics business to Japanese engineering.

The Decline of the US Consumer Electronics Industry

At the end of the nineteenth century, the electronics industry in Europe was led by the German companies Siemens & Halske AG and AEG, together with the Dutch company Philips, which established businesses in telegraphy, telephony, electric lighting or electrical components ('Siemens AG', 1990: 97; 'AEG', 1988: 409–10; Cohen, 1996). The foundations of the consumer electronics industry arose from the commercialisation of radio. In 1904, Siemens and AEG formed the joint venture Telefunken to market radio technology. Philips departed from its background in the components industry to undertake manufacturing of completed electrical products, starting in 1927 with its first radio set. Meanwhile in the US, GE, American Telephone and Telegraph (AT&T) and Westinghouse also began producing early radio transmitters and receivers (Chandler, 2001: 15).

After acquiring the US subsidiary of Marconi Wireless in 1919, GE formed the Radio Corporation of America retaining a majority stake in the new company. RCA was established at the request of the US government, which wanted to see the creation of a major US interest in the nascent radio industry to combat foreign competition. Headed by Marconi's former commercial manager, David Sarnoff, RCA marketed radio equipment produced by GE and the manufacturer Westinghouse. GE assigned all its radio patents to RCA, which, in a move to unite the radio business, acquired the patents of its main competitors. After negotiating patent agreements with Marconi, Telefunken and Philips, RCA secured a dominant hold on the radio business in the US; only the Philadelphia Electric Storage Company (Philco) and Zenith Radio Corporation remained as significant challengers (p. 23). As RCA diversified, it established a presence in other areas of home entertainment. In 1926, the formation of the NBC network saw RCA move into radio broadcasting, while the purchase of the Victor Talking Machine Company in 1929 established the company in the recorded music business as RCA Victor. RCA produced its first television receiver in 1939 and in the early 1950s beat its main broadcasting rival, CBS, to successfully market colour television.

For nearly four decades RCA stood pre-eminent in the US electronics industry, but from the late 1950s its position weakened. With the aim of opening up the US electronics industry to competition, in 1958 the Justice Department instructed RCA, AT&T and the computer manufacturer IBM to make their patents available to other companies. From 1965, RCA also began to invest heavily in research on electronic data-processing in a failed attempt to challenge IBM's dominance of the computer business. A programme of acquisitions – which saw RCA diversify into publishing, sports apparel, car hire, frozen foods, real estate and carpets – also resulted in mounting debts and undermined the company's consumer electronics business. Difficulties also beset Philco: after it was sold to the Ford Motor Company in 1961, Philco was broken up and in 1973 the consumer electronics division was sold to GTE Sylvania, which after RCA was the second largest producer of consumer electronic components in the US.

RCA, including NBC, was taken over by GE in 1986, and the following year was split up with the consumer electronics division sold to Thomson SA, the electronics manufacturer owned by the French government. This was not an isolated case. From 1974 to 1981, most of the leading names in the US consumer electronics industry were sold off to overseas companies. Philips purchased Magnavox in 1974 and in 1981 acquired Philco and Sylvania. Japanese companies also entered the acquisition spree: in 1974, Matsushita bought the Quasar production and distribution facilities of the communication equipment manufacturer Motorola, while in 1976 Sanyo acquired both Warwick and Fisher Radio. Two years later, Admiral was split up and sold off to Mexican, Taiwanese and Canadian companies. The sale of RCA to Thomson therefore came at the end of a wave of acquisitions which marked what Alfred J. Chandler describes as 'the death of the US consumer electronics industry' (2001: 46).

The Rise of Japanese Electronics

By the mid-1950s, the Japanese consumer electronics industry had established a strong production base in its home territory. As Japanese manufacturers developed commercial applications for transistors, from the late 1950s the industry entered a new phase with the internationalisation of production and marketing.

In the same era as European and US companies were entering the consumer electronics business, in 1918 Konosuke Matsushita established his company, the Matsushita Electric Devices Manufacturing Works, in Osaka. Initially making bicycle lamps, the company expanded into electric irons and heaters, dry-cell batteries and, in 1931, began radio and tube manufacturing (Chandler, 2001: 51; 'Matsushita Electric Industrial Co., Ltd', 1990: 55). Following incorporation of the company in 1935 as Matsushita Denki Sangyo (Electrical Industrial), Konosuke Matsushita was among leading industrialists who backed the right-wing militarist administration, profiting from the government's armament programme. After the Second World War, the occupying authorities brought an anti-trust action, splitting up the company. Matsushita Electric Industrial (MEI) remained as a manufacturer of consumer goods, while Matsushita Electric Works (MEW) was split off as an industrial counterpart and a new company, Sanyo Electric Industrial, was established by Konosuke Matsushita's brother-in-law, Toshio Iue (Bowman and Martin, 1993: 302; Salamie, 2001: 399). Under the leadership of the company's founder, Matsushita Electrical was formed in 1952 as a joint venture 35 per cent owned by Philips (Chandler, 2001: 52). New consumer product lines appeared in 1953, including televisions, washing machines and refrigerators.

With the relaxation of anti-monopoly laws after the Korean War, Matsushita was able to undertake its first significant acquisition, buying a 50 per cent stake in the Victor Company of Japan (JVC). Founded in 1927 as the Japanese subsidiary of the Victor Talking Machine Company, the US gramophone and records manufacturer, JVC was sold in 1929 to RCA, which in turn sold minority interests to the Mitsubishi and Sumitomo financial groups (Salamie, 1999: 511). Ownership gradually transferred solely to Japanese hands during the late 1930s as RCA sold off its interests in JVC to several Japanese concerns, the majority going to Nihon Sangyo (later Nissan Motor Company). When Matsushita bought into JVC, the two companies competed over very few product lines and JVC was granted operational autonomy. Later, however, this relationship would evolve into a state of what David E. Salamie describes as 'competitive cooperation' (p. 512).

While war damaged the infrastructure of Japanese industry, post-war stability encouraged investment in civilian technology (Nakayama, Boulton and Pecht, 1999: 28–9). In the context of reconstruction, radio provided a valuable channel of public education for the occupying forces, together with communication and entertainment among the Japanese populace. As existing receivers in Japan were of poor standards, the US military placed an order for four million sets, energising an expansion in component manufacture and set assembly among established firms and small new entrepreneurs (p. 29). It was in this context that

Masaru Ibuka opened an engineering workshop in October 1945 to mend broken radios and make shortwave adapters. The following year, Ibuka, together with Akio Morita, founded Tokyo Tsushin Kogyo K. K. (the Tokyo Telecommunications Engineering Corporation) and the company began to develop its own products, including the introduction in 1958 of Japan's first transistor radio, the TR-55 (Nathan, 2001). Development of audio recording began in 1950 with the Model G Tapecorder, the first tape recording machine made in Japan, and in 1958 the company adopted the name Sony.

Matsushita, JVC and Sony provided the domestic foundations for the Japanese consumer electronics industry and would be at the forefront of moves in the 1950s to internationalise the industry. Key to this manoeuvre was the US market. Initially, Japanese companies established arrangements during the 1950s and 60s with US partners for sales of products, including radios and television sets, before turning in the 1970s to opening their own production facilities in the US. On a trip to the US in 1951, Konosuke Matsushita was reportedly seduced by 'rich America', hoping to make it his company's main market in the future ('Matsushita Electric Industrial Co., Ltd', 1990: 55). From 1959, the company began to expand its overseas marketing, starting with sales and distribution in the US under the Panasonic brand (Chandler, 2001: 54). After gaining significant market shares in foreign territories, particularly the US, in 1968 JVC formed the subsidiary JVC America (Salamie, 1999: 512). Looking to the US, in 1955 Sony signed an agreement with Superscope and Agrod to act as their marketing agents in the country, together with a distribution agreement with the electronics wholesaler Delmonico International. Once the Delmonico agreement was dissolved in 1960, the Sony Corporation of America was established to oversee marketing activities in the US.

These moves gave Japanese industry a foothold in the US consumer electronics market. Similar moves followed with the internationalisation of production. Starting in the 1960s, Matsushita opened plants in Taiwan, the Philippines, Spain and the UK (Chandler, 2001: 54). From the early 1970s, Japanese manufacturers invested in US-based production facilities. Sony led the way, building a colour television plant in California during 1972, and two years later, as part of the Quasar deal, Matsushita acquired a similar facility in Illinois.

Fears of the market becoming flooded by Japanese hardware brought a reaction by the US industry, which led to the signing in 1977 of the Orderly Marketing Arrangements, limiting Japanese exports of colour television sets until 1980 to 1.56m units per annum (Gregory, 1981: 8). As Japanese exports declined, Taiwan became the main exporter of televisions to the US, with South Korea a close competitor. To bypass export restrictions while still maintaining the level of overall output, in 1978–9 Japanese manufacturers Mitsubishi,

Toshiba, Sharp and Hitachi built new plants in California and Tennessee, and by 1979 these were producing over 2.3m colour television sets for the US market (p. 9). Japanese exports also diminished the share of the global market held by European manufacturers such as Philips, Thomson and the German company Grundig. Although Thomson had a strong presence in the US through its own-ership since 1987 of the RCA brand name, Chandler (2001: 78) argues that the company lacked the necessary technical and functional capabilities to commer-cialise new products or improve existing ones. With Japanese manufacturers producing television sets to meet the boom in demand from the Chinese market, Japan ended the 1970s once again at the forefront of the global consumer elec-tronics business.

The development of the VCR was therefore conducted against a background of industrial change which saw the balance of power in the consumer electron-ics industry tipping from American to Japanese interests. As Sony, JVC and Matsushita eventually introduced the first commercially successful consumer video recorders in the mid-1970s, the VCR was marked as a product of Japan-ese engineering. Consequently, although the VCR cannot be held responsible for effecting the changing balance of power in the consumer electronics industry, it did become emblematic of Japan's new technological leadership in the global electronics business.

EARLY HOME VIDEO

At the same time as the professional VTR was introduced to the broadcasting industry, RCA, Ampex and Sony were just some of the companies engaged in exploring the possibilities of launching video as a consumer medium. Several factors prevented the professional standard VTR becoming a consumer tech-nology: machines were too costly and too large for the home, while open-reel threading of the tape required a certain amount of technical virtuosity. Pricing and operational simplicity were therefore two of the main hurdles confronting the development of a home video system.

First Generation Home Video – Telcan, CV-2000 and EVR

From the early 1960s, several companies were working towards expanding the video recording business into the educational and consumer markets. In the UK, the earliest attempt to produce a domestic video recorder came with Telcan, the system developed by the small company Nottingham Electric Valve. Telcan ran standard ¼-inch audio tape on a reel-to-reel system built into the top of a tele-vision set. While demonstrated on British television in 1962, the system was never marketed. A few years later, again in the UK, Wesgrove Electrics began to sell their own home system, which was available to consumers in kit form for a little under £100 (Hain and Browne, 2003d). Ampex had formed a new division in 1963 for consumer and educational products, and that year launched the Signature V, an elaborate home entertainment unit combining their VR-1500 video recorder with a black-and-white camera, television receiver and music centre (Nmungwun, 1989: 146). Retailing at US$30,000, the unit was unrealistically priced for the consumer market.

By the late 1960s and early 70s, home video was on the verge of becoming a commercial reality. Appearing on the market in 1964, Sony's CV-2000 ('CV' being short for consumer video) was marketed at a fraction of the cost of professional models. While recording good black-and-white images, the reel-to-reel system was difficult to operate and the CV-2000 failed to open a consumer video market but was adopted for medical and industrial purposes instead (Rosenbloom and Freeze, 1985: 146; Sony, 2005b).

In the US, CBS worked in collaboration with Motorola and the chemical companies ICI and CIBA to develop the Electronic Video Recorder (EVR). A monochrome EVR was demonstrated in December 1968 and two years later CBS gave a public demonstration of the Colour EVR. Despite its name, the EVR had playback capability only. Pre-recorded content was stored on 7-inch (18cm) spools running 8.75mm film. Although CBS developed an international consortium – the EVR Partnership – to sell players and spools around the world, the EVR failed to launch onto the consumer market. With sales only reaching the corporate and education sectors, the cost implications of short production runs for spools sank the project and, in 1972, CBS halted the venture.

After losing out to Ampex in the making of a marketable VTR, RCA was keen to establish an early mark in home video. From 1964, RCA sank millions into developing its own consumer system, SelectaVision. The project used holography to record images on transparent PVC tape read by a laser. With a view to the consumer market, RCA placed a focus on cheapness and functional simplicity. SelectaVision was given a public demonstration in 1969 but was eventually overtaken by EVR and consequently never went to market.

Cassette Loading – Sony's U-matic

Telcan and CV-2000 operated on the same principle as audio recording and the VTR, as they used open reels to carry tape which had to be threaded through the recording mechanism. Despite its commercial problems, EVR found a compact and consumer-friendly solution for feeding recording material. Cartridge and cassette carriers provided easy operation and proved decisive for the launch of commercially successful home video. With their enclosed and compact design, cartridges and cassettes provided convenience together with protection and durability, key requirements for the popular diffusion of video technology

Pioneering home video: the
Electronic Video Recorder

to the consumer market. Sound recording had led this innovation. In the late 1950s, US radio stations in Bloomington and Washington, DC, had started using cartridges as a means for playing short spot commercials. Philips introduced the first audiocassette player in 1962 and 8-track audio players went on the market in 1965. By 1964, RCA had also developed a videotape cartridge for the broadcast industry.

After the CV-2000, Sony had worked on producing a cassette format for video recording and in October 1969 demonstrated their Color Videoplayer. Using ¾-inch videotape, cassettes could record up to 90 minutes. Promotions hailed 'A New Era for Community and Family Lifestyles' and the Japanese daily newspaper *Yomiuri Shimbun* announced 'The Era of Packaged Movies and Film Entertainment is Around the Corner' (Sony, 2005a). With other electronics manufacturers announcing their plans to launch videocassette machines, Sony called on the industry to arrive at a shared standard. In March 1970, Matsushita, JVC and five non-Japanese companies joined Sony to agree a unified standard. Agreement was reached on a U loading format, which wrapped the tape behind a rotating recording head, and in September 1971 Sony revealed its U-matic colour videocassette system at the Keidanren (Japanese Federation of Economic Organisations) in Tokyo.

Early models, the VP-1100 and VO-1700, went on sale and although both were aimed at home use, size and expense hampered sales of U-matic hardware. Colour television was still a recent development and ownership of colour sets still relatively low – less than 40 per cent of Japanese households – and so U-matic was launched at a time when consumers had no pressing need for a colour video system. U-matic made little impact in the consumer market but found a place in the media industries, where it was widely adopted as a professional format.

Home Recording – Cartrivision and VCR

In the same year as CBS closed the EVR project, the first consumer video recorder went on the market. Cartrivision, developed in the US by Playtape Inc. with manufacturing and financial help from Avco Corporation, was designed to play pre-recorded cassettes and record from television. From June 1972, Cartrivision machines went on sale through Sears stores in the Chicago area. Avco manufactured an ordinary cassette for recording and the system was supported by pre-recorded material. A catalogue of 111 specially produced recordings was made for sale-only and identified by their black cases (Lardner, 1987: 83). A separate catalogue of 200 rental-only titles was also available, with special red cases. These were available through the Cartridge Rental Network, established specifically to distribute the Cartrivision cassettes. As a partner in the network, the Hollywood film company Columbia Pictures released for rental a catalogue of classic titles from the company's film library, including *Casablanca* (Michael Curtiz, 1942, US), *It Happened One Night* (Frank Capra, 1934, US), *Red River* (Howard Hawks, 1948, US) and *Dr Strangelove or: How I Learned to Stop Worrying and Love the Bomb* (Stanley Kubrick, 1964, UK). Rentals were regulated through the inclusion of a locking device in the red cassettes: only rental outlets had the machine necessary for rewinding the cassettes, preventing consumers from watching a film for a second time.

While the system made it onto the consumer market, a series of problems

Like to tape TV programs off the air for a video library? Or rent a feature movie recorded on a video cartridge? That highboy cabinet at the left, above, houses a 25-inch, solid-state color TV receiver and a Cartrivision video-tape system. The combination receiver/recorder/playback unit is Montgomery Ward's Airline system. Other Cartrivision and 25-inch console styles are available from Montgomery Ward; Sears, Roebuck; and various department stores throughout the country.

The price of the set shown, about $1600, includes an optional black-and-white $250

TV camera for making home video-tape movies. Blank tapes are about $12 for 15 minutes, $24 for one hour, and $37 for 116 minutes. You can rent feature movies for a one-time showing at $3-$7. Prerecorded cartridges (sports, hobbies, etc.) sell for $13 to $40.

At the right, above, is a Cartrivision video-tape player ($700) that plays back prerecorded cartridges through your color TV. It's expected to be in stores by May, 1973. To operate the player, you simply connect a wire to your television set's antenna terminals, and run the cartridge.

The Cartrivision concept

befell the enterprise. Cartrivision was a difficult concept for sales staff and consumers to understand. Moreover, as the Cartrivision cabinet combined a television receiver with the recorder, consumers were not convinced of the reasons for disposing of their existing television sets. Furthermore, the non-rewindable cassettes did not fit well with the distractions of home viewing. As sales struggled to reach projections, it became impossible for Avco to sustain the high levels of investment necessary for starting up the venture and within a year of going to market Cartrivision was bankrupt.

Philips also pitched a new system at the consumer market. In 1974, the N1500 went on sale to consumers, combining a tuner (for receiving TV signals from an aerial) with a modulator (necessary for playing recordings through a TV set) and an analogue clock timer (to pre-set timing for single television recordings) (Hain and Browne, 2003a). Plastic cassettes housed two spools mounted on top of one another with the tape running diagonally between them. Initially, the recording capacity was for 45 minutes only, but one-hour cassettes quickly became available, selling for the relatively high price of £14.50. Although directed at the consumer market, the N1500 was mainly adopted by industry and educational institutions. Philips labelled their format VCR, coining the term later applied as the generic label for all home videocassette systems. From 1976, the N1502 went on sale to the consumer market and in 1978 the launch of the N1700 introduced the revised format, VCR-LP. 'LP' stood for long play, as two hours could be recorded on a standard one-hour VCR cassette (Hain and Browne, 2003b and 2003c). By this time, however, the future development of the home video market had become firmly focused on the competition between two formats: Sony's Betamax and JVC's VHS.

BETAMAX, VHS AND THE VCR WARS

Betamax and VHS did not pioneer home video but they were the first systems to prove commercially successful by establishing a mass market for video on a global scale. Developed, manufactured and marketed by Sony, JVC and Matsushita, these VCR formats affirmed the ascendancy of Japanese consumer electronics in the global market.

Sony's Betamax

With the Model G tape recorder, TR-55 transistor radio and Trinitron colour TV system (1968), Sony had established a distinguished record of product innovation (Nathan, 2001). This continued with video recording. With the PV100, Sony had been actively involved with advancing the helical-scan VTR, while the CV-2000 represented an early gesture towards creating a consumer-friendly unit. U-matic became an industry standard by the first half of the 1970s and Sony continued to look towards breaking into the home video market.

Morita regarded home video as a vital area for development and on 16 April 1975 Sony announced it would be launching Betamax as a cassette-based system. For its ½-inch cassettes, Betamax adapted the ¼-inch U-matic format with the same pattern of tape feed. When Betamax went on sale in Japan on 10 May 1975, the original SL-6300 deck cost ¥229,800, approximately the price of a large colour television set and 60 per cent of the price of a U-matic machine (Sony, 2005c). At the same time, another model, the LV-1801, went on sale priced at ¥449,800, combining the SL-6300 with an 18-inch Trinitron colour television. With a built-in tuner and plug-in clock unit, Betamax machines could be used to time-shift television recordings. This was not an altogether new concept, for the Philips VCR provided the same function. Cassettes were 60 minutes in length and sold for ¥4,500. In the following year, Betamax units went on sale in the US priced at US$2,295, and from February 1976, cheaper decks became available from US$1,295. Meanwhile, sales in the UK began during 1978 with the SL-8000, priced at £600.

The Issue of Incompatibility

Betamax was an attractive product and a base of home video consumers began to form in territories where the Sony hardware was introduced. Very quickly, however, the commercial existence of Betamax was threatened as the rival VHS came onto the market. Betamax appeared first, but through a mixture of technological and commercial factors, it lost ground to VHS and Sony eventually withdrew the format.

Central to the conflict which ensued was the issue of format incompatibility. Sony had witnessed the business benefits of opening up a system to competitors back in the 1950s with audio tape recording: after releasing its patents, Sony's share of the Japanese market diminished from 90 to 30 per cent, but with the open standard allowing the market to grow tenfold, Sony gained overall (Lardner, 1987: 72). Creating an industry consensus around a uniform standard for

Made in Japan: Sony's
SL-6300

video recording also motivated Sony's decision to invite the backing of other manufacturers before U-matic was launched. That consensus was possible because all participants recognised that compatibility and collaboration were essential to creating a viable market for video. Sony even integrated modifications recommended by its competitors into the eventual design of U-matic.

Building on these lessons from the past, as Betamax was nearing production, late in 1974 Sony invited Matsushita and JVC to adopt Betamax as an industry standard. This time, however, the other manufacturers did not reach agreement. When Matsushita and JVC had first seen U-matic demonstrated it was still at the point where they could actively offer input towards developing the system. Yet, since the agreement over U-matic, Sony had gone on to become by far the largest beneficiary of the format. When Betamax was demonstrated to Matsushita and JVC in December 1974, the system was already developed to a stage where it was ready to go to market. It was clear therefore that Sony intended to launch Betamax irrespective of the collaboration or advice of its competitors.

Due to these tensions, the main movers in home video development failed to resolve a unified standard. While Sony was developing Betamax, Matsushita worked on its own VX format and JVC developed VHS. Matsushita went ahead, launching the VX-100 in Japan during September 1975, four months after Betamax. In October the following year, JVC put VHS on the market. Recognising the superiority of JVC's format over its own system, on 10 January 1977 Matsushita publicly announced that it would be backing VHS in the future, thereby creating a clear bifurcation of the market.

Betamax and VHS shared certain similarities. Both were cassette-loaded, using ½-inch tape, with helical-scanning and employing azimuth recording (an arrangement ensuring tape heads did not receive interference between different tracks). These similarities were strong enough that when Sony first saw a demonstration of VHS, the company's executives claimed that it was a copy of Betamax. There were, however, several major differences which rendered the systems incompatible. Betamax employed a tape-handling mechanism similar to that of U-matic, pulling the tape out of the cassette and threading it behind the drum bearing the recording heads. JVC adopted an M-loading pattern for VHS which kept the tape at the forward side of the drum. This was not the only difference. Misguidedly, Morita had adamantly held on to the idea that tapes with a 60-minute recording capability would be enough to satisfy consumer needs. By using thinner tape, VHS was able to offer two hours recording time, which proved a more attractive option among consumers.

A further format joined the VCR wars in 1980 when Philips and Grundig began to market their Video 2000 format. Uniting Dutch and German electronics, V2000 represented a European challenge to the dominance of

Japanese technology. Incompatible with either Betamax or VHS, a key advantage of V2000 was its long-play facility. By slowing the tape speed, cassettes were able to complete four hours of recording on one side and could be flipped over to record the same on the other side, imitating the compact audiocassette which Philips had introduced. However, V2000 proved complex and costly in its production and entered the market too late to pose any serious challenge to Betamax and VHS.

JVC's OEM Strategy and the Triumph of VHS

Technical differences alone were not enough to diminish Betamax's share of the market. Incompatible formats rapidly divided the main players, but the deciding factor in the format wars was the strategic alignment of other electronics companies with the formats under licensing or Original Equipment Manufacturers (OEM) arrangements (Cusumano, Mylonadis and Rosenbloom, 1992).

Due to its distinguished record of product innovations, Sony had a general policy of avoiding OEM arrangements to preserve the distinction of its own brand name. When Betamax first came on the market, Sony did not therefore immediately look towards establishing licensing and OEM arrangements. Only when the launch of VHS was immediately pending did Sony agree to license Betamax to Toshiba and Sanyo. In contrast, JVC had a relatively small manufacturing capability and on its own was unable to supply a mass market. Consequently, JVC immediately aimed to attract backers for the launch of VHS. By the end of 1976, Hitachi, Mitsubishi and Sharp were all aligned with VHS. Matsushita was not only the major shareholder in JVC but also owned a huge manufacturing capability with an extensive international marketing network. The company's decision to halt the VX system and follow the JVC format therefore gave enormous backing to VHS.

After establishing these arrangements in Japan, JVC commenced negotiations for European alliances, recruiting Nordmende, Telefunken, Thomson and Thorn, among others. Through its previous track record of sales, Sony had a stronger presence in the US market than JVC. In a departure from company policy, Sony struck an OEM deal with the US television manufacturer Zenith. Sony had shown Betamax to RCA in September 1974 and the demonstration was impressive enough for the American company to halt its own home video development. However, Betamax's short recording capability dissuaded RCA from following the format. Instead, it was Matsushita who reached an OEM deal with the American company in March 1977 after agreeing to RCA's request for VCRs capable of recording at least three hours, enough to 'record a football game' (Lardner, 1987: 161). Reviving the SelectaVision name from its earlier home-grown video project, RCA put its own branded VHS machines on the US market, priced at US$1,000, US$300 cheaper than Betamax machines. Following the Matsushita–RCA alliance, other major US companies joined the VHS family during 1977, including GE, Sylvania, Magnavox and Curtis Mathes. Betamax was therefore left with few partners in the US. Sony responded with longer recording times and lower prices but Betamax was unable to beat off the challenge of VHS. Betamax units remained relatively complex to make compared to VHS, while Matsushita aimed for low-cost production, reducing component parts, automating manufacturing and scheduling large production runs (Cusumano, Mylonadis and Rosenbloom, 1992: 80).

VHS sales were already surpassing Betamax by the late 1970s. Philips and Grundig withdrew V2000 in 1984, aligning themselves with VHS, and when Zenith left the Betamax group for VHS in the same year, Sony effectively lost its main foothold in the US. Betamax continued to be used as a professional format for many years, but with regard to the consumer market, from 1988 the format war was over after Sony began to produce its own VHS machines. As Michael A. Cusumano, Yiorgos Mylonadis and Richard S. Rosenbloom (1992) have shown, VHS won the format war because JVC's OEM strategy drew the support of nearly all the major names in consumer electronics (table 1.1).

Frequently, video folklore has held on to the belief that Betamax was the better-quality format, producing sharper, crisper images than VHS. According to this view, technical superiority fell victim to market forces. However, this view is debatable. In the early years of the video market, in the US successive reviews compared the competing formats and found no actual difference between the two or otherwise arrived at contrary evidence suggesting VHS offered superior picture quality (Klopfenstein, 1989: 28). But above all else, VHS won the format war because it was better placed to meet the demands of high-volume manufacturing and mass marketing.

SHIFTING TIME AND SPACE

Subduing or arresting time describes the basic technological effect of video recording. Capturing time was the core aim of the VTR projects undertaken by RCA and Ampex and the VCR systems launched by Sony and JVC/Matsushita. For the television industry, the VTR provided an efficient and cost-effective solution for the storage and retransmission of programming, while the user-friendly recording capability of the VCR changed the technological, industrial and social dynamics of television viewing. With the VCR, the delivery medium of television signals, produced by the public institution of the broadcasting industry, was transformed into a storage medium, the videocassette, in an act of production undertaken by the private viewer. VCRs gave private viewers the means to subject the temporality of television scheduling to the technological effect of recording by capturing slices of time for consumption later.

Japan	US	Europe

VHS (39)

Japan	US	Europe
JVC	Magnavox (Ma)	Blaupunkt
Matsushita	Sylvania (Ma)	Zaba (J)
Hitachi	Curtis Mathes (Ma)	Nordmende (J)
Mitsubishi	J.C. Penny (Ma)	Telefunken (J)
Sharp	GE (Ma)	SEL (J)
Tokyo Sanyo	RCA (H)	Thorn-EMI (J)
Brother (Mi)	Sears (H)	Thomson-Brandt (J)
Ricoh (H)	Zenith (J)*	Granada (H)
Tokyo Juki (H)		Hangard (H)
Canon (Ma)		Sarolla (H)
Asahi Optical (H)		Fisher (T)
Olympus (Ma)		Luxer (Mi)
Nikon (Ma)		
Akai Trio (J)		
Sansui (J)		
Clarion (J)		
Teac (J)		
Japan Columbia (H)		
Funai		

Betamax (12)

Japan	US	Europe
Sony	Zenith (S)*	Kneckerman (Sa)
Sanyo	Sears (Sa)	Fisher (Sa)
Toshiba		Rank (To)
NEC		
General (To)		
Aiwa		
Pioneer (S)		

V-2000 (7)

Japan	US	Europe
		Philips
		Grundig
		Siemens (G)
		ITT (G)
		Loewe Opta (G)
		Korting (P)
		B&O (P)

Source: Cusumano, Mylonadis and Rosenbloom (1992: 73)

Note: * During 1984, Zenith moved from the Betamax group to VHS.
Suppliers are identified by initials: G = Grundig, H = Hitachi, J = JVC,
Ma = Matsushita, Mi = Mitsubishi, P = Philips, S = Sony, Sa = Sanyo,
T = Tokyo Sanyo and To = Toshiba.

Table 1.1 Group Alignment with VCR Formats (1983–84)

For John B. Thompson (1995) one of the key characteristics of modern mass communication – as seen with the development of telegraphy in the mid-nineteenth century – was the introduction of technologies for uncoupling time and space, relaying messages across great distances without delay. One effect of this decoupling was to create the experience of 'despatialized simultaneity':

> Simultaneity presupposed locality; 'the same time' presupposed 'the same place'. But with the uncoupling of space and time brought about by telecommunications, the experience of simultaneity was detached from the spatial condition of common locality. ... In contrast to the concreteness of the here and now, there emerged a sense of 'now' which was no longer bound to a particular locale. (p. 32)

For Thompson, a further characteristic of mass communication involves the instituting of a structured break created between the contexts in which symbolic forms are produced and those in which they are received, so that the time and space of reception is not the same as the time and space of production. For example, in the case of television broadcasting, the production of pre-recorded programming is temporally and spatially removed from the viewer sitting at home. Even when broadcasting is live, production remains at a distance from the viewer. Yet the temporal organisation of the television schedules nevertheless means that television broadcasting retains an ordered sense of time, so that viewers receive the same content at the same time. Unlike the cinema, where the audience is bound together in the auditorium, television scheduling creates the sense of despatialised simultaneity by making the same audiovisual programming available at the same time to viewers scattered across space.

VCRs stretched these spatial and temporal dynamics even further. Broadcasting spreads the availability of audiovisual entertainment into many spaces but is always contingent on an aerial, satellite dish or cable to receive signals. To record programming off air, the VCR also needs to be linked to a receiving instrument but once the recording is made it can be transported to multiple other locations independent of such links. Alongside the production of programming, broadcasters also produce the ubertext of the television schedules. With the VCR, time-shifting fractured the temporal organisation of the schedules by allowing ordinary television viewers the freedom to uncouple the time of viewing from the time of scheduling. Using the pause, fast-forward and rewind functions of the VCR also disrupted the linear flow and duration of audiovisual content. With the VCR, the viewing of audiovisual content through the television did not only become spatially flexible but also temporally flexible, freed from the constrictions of institutionally organised time, as television programming and other forms of audiovisual content could be watched not only anywhere but at anytime.

While time-shifting was crucial to the commercial success of the videocassette recorder, the VCR was equally a playback or exhibition technology. Video recorders extended the channels through which to consume pre-recorded audio-visual content. Following the launch of the VCR, a vast market in pre-recorded software developed as cassettes were used as carriers for pornography, television programming, music promotions, exercise instruction, how-to guides and lan-guage courses. Potentially, the VCR could be used to watch any type of audio-visual content transferred to videocassette; however, feature films became the most prevalent category of content circulated on pre-recorded videocassette. As discussed earlier, the idea of creating devices for showing moving pictures in the home had been a preoccupation for the pioneers of film technology (Krämer, 1996). That same preoccupation was still evident over fifty years later in the famous essay 'The Birth of a New Avant-garde: La Caméra-stylo' by the French film-maker Alexandre Astruc (1948). In this work, usually cited as a defining statement of cine-auteurism, Astruc not only mounted a polemic arguing for the expressive capabilities of film but also saw new opportunities for the circulation of films:.

> It must be understood that up to now the cinema has been nothing more than a show. This is due to the basic fact that all films are projected in an auditorium. But with the development of 16mm and television, the day is not far off when everyone will possess a projector, will go to the local bookstore and hire films written on any subject, of any form, from literary criticism and novels to mathematics, history, and general science. From that moment on, it will no longer be possible to speak of *the* cinema. There will be *several* cinemas ... (emphasis in original, p. 19)

Writing shortly before the major popularisation of television ownership in the 1950s, and nearly three decades before the arrival of the VCR, Astruc was predicting a future in which the home would become a new and possibly equal space with the auditorium for the consumption of films. He foresaw not only the mass consumption of film in the home but also a whole distri-bution infrastructure created to service this form of exchange. To a certain extent, the home cinema systems of the 1910s had already realised Astruc's vision, but it would only be with the emergence of the video software busi-ness in the late 1970s that the consumption of film in the home became a large-scale enterprise.

The VCR/videocassette coupling offered not only temporal but also spatial

IF YOU MISSED IT ON B.B.C. OR I.T.V.– SEE IT ON JVC.

THE FIRST THREE-HOUR HOME TV RECORDER

Promoting time-shift early British advertisement for VHS

flexibility. Classrooms, bars, galleries, shop displays, aircraft and buses all became spaces for the consumption of video. However, the main location of the VCR was domestic, as consumer video came to mean home video. VCRs domesticated cinema, taking a previously public entertainment, the theatrically exhibited feature film, and creating an additional channel for its exhibition in the privacy of the home. As such, the VCR came to represent one of Astruc's 'several cinemas'. With its temporal and spatial flexibility, the VCR not only liberated the time and space of viewing – the questions of *when* and *where* to watch – but with the plethora of content available to view, it also extended the options for *what* to watch.

CONCLUSION

For Thompson (1995) mass communication extends the availability of symbolic forms across time and space, circulating those forms to a broad public (p. 30). 'The fact that media products are available in principle to a plurality of recipients means that they have an intrinsically *public* character' (emphasis in original, p. 31). As an exhibition technology, the VCR provided a new window for the public circulation of films and other forms of audiovisual content. At the same time, the VCR fragmented that public. Unlike the theatre or cinema audience assembled together in the public space of the auditorium, recorded music, radio, television and video addressed an audience separated by their location in the confines of the home who may watch the same television programmes or films but not necessarily at the same time.

Intentionally or not, Cros identified one of the key social implications of recording when he said 'Time would flee, *I* subdue it' (my emphasis). By sub-duing time, recording gave freedom to the private individual, for once it was captured, recorded time could be adjusted to personal use. The VTR served institutional purposes but the VCR was conceived as a technology for individ-ual use. As a product of industrialised manufacturing, sold to a broad public through the market, and used for recording or viewing widely distributed con-tent, the VCR was undoubtedly a mass medium. But with its use predominantly located in the closed privacy of the home, allowing personal control over the recording and exhibition of content, the VCR became a mass medium based on popularising the individualisation and privatisation of media consumption.

2

Disc to Digital: From Videodisc to DVD

In the 1960s and 70s, contemporaneous with developments in the use of magnetic tape for video recording, many projects were undertaken to produce disc-based video systems for the consumer market (*Screen Digest*, 1978a and 1978b). By November 1960, Philips had developed an early disc player and in March 1966 Sony announced two disc players: the monochrome Videomat and the Video Colour Demonstrator. Californian company Magnetic Video Recording (MVR) launched similar machines with the Model VDR-210F Videodisc in 1965, followed in 1967 by the Videodisc Slow Motion VDR 250 Recorder. Other disc players in development during the 1960s included Vision-disc from Radiovision (Westminster) Ltd and Westinghouse's Phonovid.

By the early 1970s, a range of disc systems vied to become the first consumer system (Abramson, 1973). OROS (Optical Read-only Storage) from the US company Teletron, Optidisc from SEPO in France and Polygramovision from Rudolph Stepanek in Australia were among the international array of projects working in this area. These innovations failed to progress beyond the development stage, but by the late 1970s and early 80s the first consumer videodisc systems were appearing on the market.

Videodisc ultimately failed to steal the home video market from the VCR but after the compact disc (CD) transformed the recorded music business, the consumer electronics industry turned once again to considering the prospects of using disc-based media for video. A new age of digital home video emerged as the CD became the foundation for Philips's CD-i format and Video CD (VCD). But it was only after Digital Versatile Disc or Digital Video Disc (DVD) came onto the market from the mid-1990s that the home video business was revived and entered its second wave of innovation and growth.

This chapter reviews the range of videodisc initiatives together with the emergence of the CD and VCD. It then looks at the interactions between consumer electronics, the Hollywood film companies and the computing industry which led to the development of DVD. Consumers have turned to DVD for the benefits which the format offers in the way of enhanced audiovisual presentation and inclusion of 'extras' materials to accompany the core programme. DVD has created a new media object and the chapter therefore examines the character-istics of this object in an effort to understand the form of commodity which is at the foundation of the contemporary video market.

VIDEODISC
While the VCR market remained divided by the battle between Betamax and VHS, rival videodisc systems fought to secure a place in the consumer market. Significant differences emerged between the methods used by these systems depending on whether they read discs by mechanical, magnetic, optical or capacitance methods.

Mechanical Videodisc – TeD and VISC
Mechanical recording for videodisc involved similar methods to audio discs. A stylus cut a master disc, which was then used for stamping duplicates. John Logie Baird's Phonovision had used mechanical methods of recording and play-back from 1927 and pre-recorded discs went on sale in London during 1935 under the brand name Radiovision. However, with signal coverage in the UK still restricted, television ownership did not reach the level of density required to make Radiovision a realistic consumer product.

   Mechanical recording for video returned during the early 1970s with TelDec or TeD (Schubin, 1980: 15–17). Demonstrated in Berlin during June 1970, TeD resembled an audio disc, with a stylus reading the 'hills and dales' of grooves stamped into a 210mm plastic flexible disc. When spun at 1,500rpm, these discs became rigid, storing 5 minutes of black-and-white video recordings. Developed in Europe by a joint venture between the German company AEG Telefunken and the English recorded music company Decca, TeD was released onto the German market on 17 March 1975 and became the first consumer videodisc system. To extend the playing duration, attempts were made to launch a twelve-disc changer for the system, providing up to 2 hours' viewing (including 4-second intervals between disc changes), but the limitations of playing time eventually contributed to the collapse of the TeD venture (Howe, 2005a and 2005b). Discs could easily be damaged through handling and the addition of protective paper sleeves slowed delivery times (Schubin, 1980: 17). By 1980, the system was withdrawn.

   Matsushita also showed interest in developing a mechanical videodisc in 1979 with their VISC system. VISC (short for video disc) was originally designed to use conventional audio discs but Matsushita quickly abandoned these plans in 1980 to back the alternative VHD system from the company's JVC subsidiary (p. 12). Like audio discs, both TeD and VISC offered a crude form of random access, for the stylus could be placed at any point across the playing surface of the disc (p. 18).

Magnetic Videodisc

Ampex had led the way in using tape for magnetic video recording and would experiment with using similar methods for recording on disc. The Ampex HS-100B was developed for use by the broadcasting industry to make high-quality television recordings, and other magnetic discs were developed for industry by Quantel, Precision Echo and Bosch. Limited storage capacity and the high cost of equipment, however, prevented magnetic disc recording from becoming widely adopted by broadcasters. Storage limitations also hampered attempts to construct a magnetic disc system for the consumer market. In 1974, MDR (Magnetic Disc Recording) Holdings demonstrated a machine intended for the consumer market at Vidcom in Cannes. Difficulties with playback quality and a storage limitation of 20 minutes on each side of the double-side disc, however, prevented the product from going to market (p. 13).

Optical Videodisc – DiscoVision/Magnavision

After the failed attempts to launch mechanical and magnetic disc systems, it was optical and capacitance systems which eventually formed the first short-lived consumer market for videodiscs. Both worked on totally incompatible principles. Mechanical, magnetic and capacitance disc systems all involved some form of contact between the disc and a stylus, while optical discs relied on a laser to read signals.

During the 1970s, MCA was a leading media company in the US. A major producer of television programming, it owned the Hollywood company Universal. After the introduction of Betamax and VHS to the US market, in the late 1970s MCA mounted a high profile lawsuit against Sony, claiming the off-air recording possibilities of Betamax infringed copyright (see Chapter 4). At the same time, MCA also recognised that video could provide a valuable new revenue stream and commenced a research and development programme to produce a videodisc system. MCA developed videodisc as a read-only medium to protect against copyright infringement, which, they argued, was possible with Betamax.

David Paul Gregg had undertaken foundational work on videodisc from the late 1950s and, after MCA acquired Gregg's patents and a controlling interest in his company, Gauss Electrophysics, from February 1968 MCA's videodisc programme began. In 1969, MCA's President, Lew Wasserman, persuaded the board to invest in the project, and a new research division, MCA Laboratories, was formed (Cellitti, 1998). On 12 December 1972, MCA demonstrated Disco-Vision (as the system was originally named) to the press and industry. Along with the entertainment value of playing pre-recorded films and other programming, MCA envisaged their system would also be employed in a range of other contexts. Libraries could use videodiscs for cataloguing and storing books, while teachers might employ discs in the classroom for question and answer assessments. Other possibilities existed for the weekly publishing of credit card verification data, while television programmes could be distributed on disc rather than by film prints or magnetic tape, with the benefit of easy cueing (*American Cinematographer*, 1973: 216–17).

Simultaneous with MCA's project, Philips was working on its own optical disc system, VLP (video long play). This shared many similarities with Disco-Vision, for prior to the acquisition of its patents by MCA, Gauss Electrophysics had made a full technical disclosure to Philips in the hope of establishing a partnership. To avoid competition, in September 1974 Philips and MCA agreed to collaborate by forming a hardware–software alliance, integrating Philips's expertise in electronics development and manufacturing with MCA's ownership of rights to television and film properties. During January 1976, this partnership and others experimenting with optical disc systems introduced the first optical videodisc standard (Schubin, 1980: 27).

It would be 1978 before the Philips/MCA format was ready for marketing. MCA amended the name of the system to DiscoVision, and Magnavox, a subsidiary of North American Philips, began marketing the system in the US as Magnavision. On 15 December 1978, Magnavision went on sale in three shops in Atlanta, Georgia, priced at US$695 (Sigel, 1980: 54). Philips shipped ready-made Magnavision machines from its Eindhoven plant in the Netherlands, but the majority of machines available in the US were assembled from parts imported by Magnavox to its plant in Greeneville, Tennessee.

DiscoVision/Magnavision was aimed at the home entertainment market but MCA looked beyond its partnership with Philips towards targeting industrial and institutional customers. To realise this aim, in October 1977 MCA and the Japanese consumer electronics manufacturer Pioneer formed the joint company Universal Pioneer Corporation (UPC) for manufacturing industrial videodisc players. Pioneer was relatively small compared to the giants of Japanese electronics, Matsushita or Sony, which were battling it out in the VCR wars. However, the benefits of involvement in the home video market were already clear and Pioneer launched a consumer version of DiscoVision from June 1980 in the US (*Screen Digest*, 1980a). Pursuing the data storage potential of the format, MCA also formed a further partnership in 1979 with IBM, the world's largest computer manufacturer, creating the joint venture DiscoVision Associates (DVA). IBM became a 25 per cent owner of UPC and reportedly set out to commit US$5m a year with a view to the format becoming a computer peripheral, although this initiative never progressed beyond the development stage (Schubin, 1980: 31; *Screen Digest*, 1979b).

To feed consumer interest, MCA announced a catalogue of 200 titles accompanying the launch of DiscoVision/Magnavision. Predominantly film titles, the catalogue included recent hits (e.g. *National Lampoon's Animal House* [John Landis, 1978, US] and *Jaws* [Steven Spielberg, 1975, US]) and classic titles (e.g. *Psycho* [Alfred Hitchcock, 1960, US] and *Frankenstein* [James Whale, 1931, US]) from the Universal feature film library. Other Hollywood companies were also included in the catalogue, with titles from Paramount (e.g. *The Godfather* [Francis Ford Coppola, 1972, US] and *Love Story* [Arthur Hiller, 1970, US]), Warner Bros. (e.g. *Bonnie and Clyde* [Arthur Penn, 1967, US] and *The Wild Bunch* [Sam Peckinpah, 1969, US]), and Disney (e.g. *The Littlest Outlaw* [Roberto Gavaldón, 1954, US] and *Miracle of the White Stallions* [Arthur Hiller, 1962, US]) (*Screen Digest*, 1979c: 28–9). Recent releases were priced at $15.95, while classics cost $9.95. Some non-fiction titles were also available at $5.95. MCA later diversified the catalogue, releasing its first music videodisc in 1980 with a recording of the Swedish pop group ABBA.

Capacitance Videodisc – CED/SelectaVision and VHD

RCA had lost out to competitors in its attempts to develop videotape recording but the wave of videodisc innovation during the 1970s saw the company working on a capacitance disc system. Capacitance videodisc systems used devices able to store electrical charges up to a certain level or capacity. Such devices, or capacitors, comprise two plates, respectively storing positive and negative charges. In the case of the capacitance videodisc systems, a stylus and a disc made of a conductive material acted as the components of the capacitor (Schubin, 1980: 19). Like mechanical discs, hills and dales cut into the discs varied the space between the metal coating of the disc and the electrode of the stylus causing the capacity to change, and from these variations the video signal could be reconstructed.

Research and development towards RCA's capacitance disc system (CED) used a minute stylus to play grooved vinyl discs and was intended to be a cheaper and technically simpler format than the MCA/Philips system. As DiscoVision/Magnavision quickly hit marketing problems, even before CED went on sale many observers were forecasting that RCA was poised to steal the videodisc market. On 19 March 1975, RCA demonstrated its prototype Engineering Model 2 (EM2) to the press at the company's Rockefeller Center headquarters in New York. Reviving the SelectaVision name which RCA had previously used for its videotape project, on 22 March 1981 a basic consumer model, the SFT100, went on sale in the US. RCA sold its own models, while Hitachi, Sanyo and Toshiba manufactured under licence. After its launch on the US market,

MCA's videodisc system: The
DiscoVision release of *Jaws*

from October 1983 CED models went on sale in the UK, the only overseas
territory where the system became available. In both territories, a catalogue of
film, television, concert, music video, exercise and sports titles supported the
launch of the format.

By the start of the 1980s, JVC's VHS format was already winning the VCR
war. The company therefore occupied a confident position at the vanguard of
home video and developed its own disc system, VHD/AHD (Video High Den-
sity/Audio High Density), to play either video or hi-fi audio discs. Although
VHD was another capacitance system, it was entirely incompatible with CED.
VHD discs were smaller (10 inches) and did not have grooves. Instead, the stylus was guided by an electronic servo system across spiral tracks in the disc,
allowing the stylus to read variations in the length and depth of pits in the tracks
recorded as the programming signal on the disc (Hendley, 1985: 15; *Screen
Digest*, 1978a: 207). This arrangement provided several benefits over CED.
As the stylus only traversed the surface of the disc, contact between disc and
stylus was reduced, lessening the wear on discs. Other functional benefits were
also available, with reverse and freeze-frame facilities added as features, while
machines were capable of switching between NTSC and PAL standards for use
in either the US and Japan or Europe. JVC saw VHD as serving the needs of
industry and consumer entertainment, and Matsushita, GE and Thorn-EMI
backed the system. JVC launched VHD in Japan during April 1983 and from
early 1984 Thorn-EMI, acting as JVC's agent, introduced the system to a limited
market in the UK.

The Demise of Videodisc

DiscoVision/Magnavision was only available on the consumer market for a short time before the technical and commercial problems of the system became apparent. Manufacturing was unable to produce enough machines to meet the high demand from consumers and the supply of discs faced greater problems. Reports circulated that MCA's duplication plant at Costa Mesa, California, was experiencing a 50 per cent rejection rate from the faulty discs it was pressing. Disc masters were more difficult to produce than tape equivalents, with the result that it took months rather than weeks for finished discs to reach the market after the initial transfer of a film or programme (Sigel, 1980: 55). While MCA had promised a catalogue of 200 titles to entice consumer interest, extended delays in issuing many titles on disc became a source of frustration among consumers who bought the system. Although the range and volume of discs remained limited, Magnavox reported the costs of importing parts from Philips in Europe as the reason for announcing in August 1979 a 12 per cent price increase to US$775. MCA also raised the price of discs to US$24.95 for recent releases and US$19.95 for classic titles. Aside from these official increases, scarcity in the supply of machines saw some retailers massively over-pricing players and taking advantage of the unfulfilled demand by selling discs over the list price (*Screen Digest*, 1979a, 1979d and 1979f). At the end of 1980, two years after the system went on sale, industry analysts offered a highly speculative estimate of only 18,000 Magnavision players purchased in the US to date (*Screen Digest*, 1980b).

Philips's involvement in the venture soured after MCA formed its partnership with Pioneer, and the Dutch company became frustrated by MCA's inability to handle the disc production problems. These frictions eventually led to Philips parting ways with MCA and forming a partnership with Sony, with whom MCA was continuing to fight its legal battle over the VCR. Sony and Philips agreed to exchange patents, with Sony working on videodisc development using Philips's VLP format to produce a machine for the industrial market (*Screen Digest*, 1979e). Later, this partnership with Philips led to the development of the CD (see below). After Philips's departure, in 1980 MCA renamed its disc system Laservision and once disc players went on sale from October 1981 in Japan, and the UK during May 1982, hopes grew of selling the system to international markets. But MCA eventually pulled out of the venture altogether in 1982, turning over DiscoVision Associates to Pioneer, which continued to manufacture the system as LaserDisc, later becoming known just as laserdisc (*Screen Digest*, 1982a).

After all the anticipation which had built up around RCA's SelectaVision, from the very start sales were slow and remained that way. A significant weakness of CED was the friction and wear caused by the stylus and groove combination, for repeat plays of any CED disc diminished picture and audio quality. In July 1981, CED, models from RCA and Hitachi were competitively priced, selling at US$499.95–525.00 compared to prices ranging between US$699.00 and US$769.00 for Laservision machines (*Screen Digest*, 1981a). Yet it was estimated that at the end of 1981, only 55,000 units had been sold in the US, and by the end of 1983, a total of 370,000 units in the US and UK (*Screen Digest*, 1984a: 89).

Margaret B. W. Graham proposes several reasons for why CED failed to take off (1986: 214). During the first eighteen months it was on the market in the US, the number of dealers handling the system declined by about two-thirds. Dealers felt it was too soon after the arrival of the VCR to push another new home video technology. With a retail price substantially below that of Laservision, RCA was also marketing with low profit margins for dealers, offering little incentive to promote CED against the higher profits enjoyed from VCR sales. Dealers were also required to stock discs, which was not the case with videocassettes. RCA was surprised by the popularity of the cassette rental business, and having made agreements with rights holders for CED discs to be available for sales only, the company was unable to quickly change over to rental arrangements (p. 215). Amongst CED owners sales of discs had been greater than anticipated, and demand for new titles was high. However, with only a relatively small population of CED owners, there was no urgent justification for extending the catalogue (p. 216). RCA had made their system cheap and technically simple but its lack of sophistication led to criticism among the trade press. As the rise of VCR ownership resulted in hardware and software prices falling, RCA discounted the price of its disc players, but it quickly became apparent that CED was unlikely to become anything other than a specialist technology. With the whole of RCA carrying a US$2.9 billion debt burden at the start of the 1980s, and straining under the chaos of its widely diversified operations, there was the demand internally for the company to concentrate on its core businesses. Consequently, in April 1984 RCA announced its withdrawal from CED, and other manufacturers ceased production.

In the mid-1970s, with the Betamax/VHS battle still unfolding, there was the opportunity for a standardised videodisc format to have stolen the ground from the VCR. Yet, regardless of the specific problems of DiscoVision/Magnavision and CED, the first consumer videodisc systems suffered two major weaknesses. Instead of arriving at a standard format, research and development imitated the incompatibility dividing the VCR market. What these early videodisc systems did have in common, however, was that they only played pre-recorded, read-only storage media. Consequently, videodisc lacked the recording, time-shift

With SelectaVision RCA aimed to make its mark in the home video market

facility which was making the VCR such a compelling product for the consumer market.

RCA's withdrawal did not mark the end of videodisc. Systems continued to cater for a limited consumer market and VHD was used in Japan for karaoke. In December 1984, around eighteen companies were continuing to supply approximately fifty-seven different videodisc player models to markets in the US, Europe and Japan, using either the laserdisc or VHD systems (*Screen Digest*, 1984b). Stockpiled CED players also made a small contribution to hardware sales. This array of models did not result from any significant growth in the market, for it was estimated that only around 40,000 videodisc players across all formats were sold in any month worldwide. Due to enduring consumer allegiance, particularly in Japan, Pioneer continued production of laserdisc, but as the impact of DVD began to be felt from the late 1990s, the company stopped manufacturing laserdisc players and the last disc titles were released in 2000.

DIGITAL ENTERTAINMENT

Videocassettes and mechanical and capacitance videodisc systems were all forms of analogue media: they stored and displayed image and sound information in forms that used continuous values. From the early 1980s, home entertainment in general, including video, would be transformed as digital media formats were introduced onto the consumer market. Digital media take an analogue source, for example a photograph, and transfer it into numerical form. Initially, the source is sampled, breaking it into discrete units of data, such as the pixels which make up a digital image. That data is then quantified as each unit is allocated a numerical value (Manovich, 2001: 28). Through this process, source material is digitally encoded to produce a numerical representation, allowing data to be not only mathematically described or reproduced, but also programmed and manipulated (p. 27).

Compact Disc

Philips introduced the compact audio cassette in the early 1960s. Cassettes provided a new portable format for recording or listening to music, but as sales of vinyl recordings decreased during the following two decades, the recorded music industry raised major concerns about cassettes as a tool for home taping and industrialised piracy. Philips had continued to explore product innovations with the V2000 VCR and VLP videodisc systems, and after leaving the DiscoVision/Magnavision partnership, the Dutch company researched the potential for using optical discs as storage media. Through the partnership formed with Sony, Philips developed the CD as a new digital media format. After the CD was commercially launched in 1982 as a carrier for audio recordings, the format went on to re-energise the global market for recorded music.

In the late 1970s, a range of electronics companies were researching the possibilities of digital audio disc. As those projects neared fruition, in September 1977 twenty-nine manufacturers from around the world formed the Digital Audio Disc (DAD) Conference with the aim of establishing industry-wide agreement on a standardised format. Convening during June 1980 in Salzburg, DAD met to consider three systems: an electro-static system from JVC, a mechanical system developed by Telefunken and an optical system from Philips and Sony which read discs using a laser (Nathan, 2001: 141). DAD decided to approve both the electro-static and optical systems but after many major manufacturers began to license the Philips/Sony technology, the optical system emerged as the clear favourite.

Technical specifications for the system demonstrated by Philips and Sony at Salzburg were documented in the first of what became a series of colour-bound books. The 'Red Book' detailed standards for Compact Disc Digital Audio (CDDA), and commercial use of the standard was licensed through Philips. Compact Disc Digital Audio became a registered trademark and the logo is still seen on CD cases, covers and discs today. Compact disc became the platform on which a number of additional media formats were created and other standards for optical disc formats were published in further colour-coded books. For example, in 1985, the 'Yellow Book' was published as the specification for Compact Disc Read-Only Memory (CD-ROM).

Commercial exploitation of CD audio commenced on 1 October 1982 when Sony launched the first CD audio player, the CDP 101, onto the Japanese market (p. 144). Unlike the VCR, which allowed home recording, CD was a read-only medium. The availability of software was therefore essential to getting the format off the ground. Through Sony's existing partnership with CBS Records, CBS/Sony Records, a catalogue of fifty titles was immediately made available to the public. This was weighted towards classical recordings in the belief that consumers of such works would be foremost in their appreciation of CD's enhanced sound quality.

Although the CDP 101 was prohibitively priced at ¥168,000 (US$700), Sony's introduction in November 1984 of the D-50 player – retailing at half the price – expanded the market for compact disc, and sales of CD hardware and software rose dramatically during the 1980s. CD units overwhelmed sales of music in other formats. In 1991, 2,893.3m recorded music units were sold worldwide, of which vinyl LPs accounted for 291.6m, cassettes 1,492.8m and CDs 997.5m. By 2000, 2,511.2m CDs were sold against 800.9m cassettes and 13.5m LPs (IFPI, 2001: 17). Part of the reason for the popularity of CD can be explained by consumers not only buying new titles on CD but also duplicating titles they already owned on vinyl. CD audio was therefore at the forefront of demonstrating one of the key lessons of the new digital era: digital media provide lucrative platforms for new but also old media content, adding to the value of the music, film or television libraries kept by rights holders.

Just as the phonograph and gramophone had prefigured the formation of the home video market by popularising the idea of consuming mass-reproduced pre-recorded entertainment media in the home, so CD audio played an indirect but nevertheless important role as a precursor for the arrival of DVD in the late 1990s. Vinyl records and cassette tapes had created a mass market for recorded music but CD audio introduced consumers to the idea and benefits of digital media. CDs effectively pioneered digital home entertainment, selling consumers on the idea that digital meant quality. Although music could be listened to quite easily at home on LPs and cassettes, CDs differentiated the consuming experience by promoting digital quality as delivering better sound. CD functionality also enabled easier and more accurate options for randomly accessing the content of recordings.

Digital Video – CD-i and Video CD (VCD)

After the success of compact disc as a carrier for audio entertainment, developers looked towards using CD as a platform for digital video. In 1986, the 'Green Book' was published as the specification for CD-Interactive or CD-i, which Philips promoted as a multimedia platform for use by industry and consumers. The first CD-i players appeared on the market in 1991 and two years later Philips attempted to launch the format for video. In June 1993, the Hollywood company Paramount signed an agreement to provide fifty feature film titles for CD-i (Parisi, 1993: 1). From October that year, a plug-in peripheral, the Digital Video Cartridge, became available, allowing playback of VHS quality video (Landis, 1993a). Paramount also released its first titles for the platform in that month, with CD-i editions of recent hit films, including *Top Gun* (Tony Scott, 1986, US), *The Hunt for Red October* (John McTiernan, 1990, US), *Naked Gun 2½: The Smell of Fear* (David Zucker, 1991, US) and *Star Trek VI: The Undiscovered Country* (Nicholas Meyer, 1991, US). Philips saw great potential for the format to play not only video but also allow the users to interact with programming (*New Media Markets*, 1993). However, CD-i was an expensive alternative to the VCR: in 1993, a VCR might cost in the region of US$180, while CD-i models produced by Philips or Magnavox cost between US$399 and US$499, with an additional charge of US$249 for the Digital Video Cartridge (Landis, 1993a). CD-i failed to create a market for digital video, and after attempts to reinvent CD-i as a gaming console lost out to the arrival in late 1994 of the Sega Saturn and Sony PlayStation, Philips discontinued the format in 1996 (Philipscdi.com, 2006).

Although CD-i did not succeed as a platform for video, Philips was able to channel the insights gained from the venture into creating the video CD format. Fundamental to the development of digital video media was the work of the Motion Picture Experts Group (MPEG). MPEG was originally convened in 1988 as a working group of the joint technical committee for Information Technology of the International Organisation for Standardisation (ISO – not an acronym but short for the Greek 'isos' meaning 'equal') responsible for agreeing international technical standards. ISO was formed as a non-governmental network of accredited experts representing a collective of national standards agencies. Under the convenorship of Leonardo Chiariglione, MPEG (formally named ISO/IEC JTC 1/SC 29/WG 11) was entrusted with the '[d]evelopment of international standards for compression, decompression, processing, and coded representation of moving pictures, audio, and combination, in order to satisfy a wide variety of applications' (ISO, 2001). In November 1992, the group agreed the ISO/IEC 11172 or MPEG-1 standard, part of which provided the capability for encoding video information at 1.15Mbits/s, equivalent to VHS quality.

MPEG-1 became widely used for audio compression in the MP3 format but was also adopted for the encoding of video on CD. By early 1993, competing projects were under way aimed at employing MPEG-1 in the creation of a commercial video CD format. In February that year, British company Nimbus Technology and Engineering, a subsidiary of the CD producer Nimbus Records, announced it had developed a system for compressing full-motion video together with sound on a single CD (Dean, Pride and McClure, 1993). The year before, JVC, in partnership with Philips, demonstrated a separate video CD system aimed at the karaoke market in Japan, and in 1993 they published the video CD format as the 'White Book' standard. Sony and Matsushita placed their support behind the JVC/Philips project in June 1993 and two months later the four partners announced agreement on the basic specifications for their own video CD system. Although the Nimbus and the White Book formats both conformed to the MPEG-1 standard, they were incompatible. As the guardian of the CD standards, Philips was able to prevent the Nimbus project reaching the market and the White Book format emerged as video CD.

VCD went on sale in the US from November 1993. To introduce US consumers to the concept of VCD, from November 1993 a test promotion for the format was conducted in the San Francisco area with fifty-two outlets of the Blockbuster video rental chain accommodating kiosks displaying the hardware and software. Players from Panasonic and Magnavox, together with an attachment for the Sega Genesis games console, were available and could be rented for US$19.95 over three nights (Nichols, 1993). Among the initial run of software available were games, children's programmes and reference works.

VCD offered several benefits over VHS, with better sound reproduction and the inclusion of chapter stops for fast cueing. Discs could be played on various platforms, from dedicated VCD players, or standard audio CD players with VCD adapters. Yet a number of commonly held criticisms confronted the format. Its picture quality was only equal to VHS and noticeably inferior to laserdisc, while the system lacked the recordable facility of a VCR (e.g. Clark, 1993; Landis 1993b). With a maximum compression ratio of 200:1, the MPEG-1 standard could store up to 74 minutes of video on a standard 120mm compact disc. This capacity became a crucial limitation for the format. As the VCR had shown, development of an associated software market was necessary to drive consumer interest in new media hardware. With its limited storage capacity, VCD was unable to carry an entire feature film on a single disc, a problem which Nimbus believed they had solved. Furthermore, in many cases the VCD image proved inferior to good-quality VHS recordings. As Don Rosenberg, executive Vice-. President of the US-based Video Software Dealers Association, commented in November 1993, video CD 'is not knock-'em-dead in the quality department' (quoted in Landis, 1993b). With these widely recognised limitations, even before it was launched commercially commentators judged the format had limited marketability and forecast that its use would be confined to educational resources, music videos and reference materials (McClure, 1993).

DVD

VCD demonstrated that compact disc standards were unlikely to satisfy the purposes of digital video: the format simply did not have the storage capacity to deliver high-quality full-motion video. DVD developed from research conducted towards finding a digital disc medium capable of providing the necessary storage capacity for video presentation. Competing projects and incompatible formats again divided developments in this direction, but the major consumer electronics companies eventually agreed to support a single format. Wider industry backing was also achieved when the major Hollywood film companies became involved with the project as potential providers of software content, together with the computer industry as a future user of the format. Unlike the competition which plagued the launch of the VCR, this tripartite gathering of interests gave broad-based industry support to DVD as a uniform digital video disc format.

The Development of DVD

In an effort to reach an industry consensus on digital video, in September 1994 the major Hollywood companies – Columbia, Disney, MGM/UA, Paramount, Universal and Warner Bros. – came together to request a unified digital disc standard. This focused on seven key requirements. As Jim Taylor (1998: 40–1) summarises, they wanted a format with room for a full-length feature film on one side of a single disc, providing superior picture quality, strong copy protection and compatibility with high-quality audio systems. They also required discs which could store several languages, had the facility for multiple aspect ratios and could hold several versions of a programme on one disc.

Two consortia emerged at the forefront of digital disc development. After partnering on CD, Sony and Philips worked together again and on 16 December 1994 they announced their single-sided, 3.7 gigabyte format, MultiMedia CD (MMCD). Since March 1992, the Japanese electronics firm Toshiba had worked on its own disc format in partnership with US media and communications company Time Warner. This partnership therefore brought together two of the major names in media hardware and software. After the project attracted the support of other electronics manufacturers, including Matsushita, Hitachi, Mitsubishi, Pioneer and Thomson, on 24 January 1995 this alliance announced its own Super Density (SD) format. As JVC and Matsushita's strategy had shown in the VCR wars, the destiny of competing formats was largely decided

by the ability of format creators to expand manufacturing and marketing by gar-
nering the support of other producers. In the new digital disc war, both sides
built competing alliances. A number of electronics manufacturers, including
Acer, Aiwa, Alps, Bang and Olufsen, Grundig, Marantz, Mitsumi, Nokia, Ricoh,
TEAC and Wearnes, formed the MMCD family, while Nippon Columbia, Samsung and Zenith were among the companies backing the SD standard (p. 41).

Unlike the VCR wars, the battle for a universal digital disc standard was not
confined to the electronics industry alone. As leading providers of video software, the major Hollywood companies had a vested interest in any future digital
format. Furthermore, several of the Hollywood majors were directly connected
to the consumer electronics business: Sony had bought Columbia in 1989 and
Matsushita acquired Universal the following year, while Toshiba owned an
interest in the entertainment group of Time Warner (see Chapter 4). Although
collectively the Hollywood majors were interested in seeing agreement on a uniform format, through their corporate parentage these particular companies
aligned themselves with different sides: through Sony, Columbia was aligned
with MMCD, while Toshiba and Matsushita brought Warner Bros. and Universal into the SD family, which also had the support of MGM/UA. Meanwhile,
Disney and Paramount stayed out of the fray (Rawsthorn, 1995).

Alongside the consumer electronics industry and the Hollywood majors, the
computing industry represented a third party of companies interested in the
development of DVD. As CD drives were built into PCs, compact discs had
added to the range of media which could be played on computers or used for
data storage. The IT industry was therefore interested in the development of
any digital video format, for there was every chance it would be used on computer platforms in the future. Eventually, the involvement of information
technology businesses became the deciding factor in the format battle. In April
1995, the IT companies Apple, Compaq, Hewlett Packard, IBM and Microsoft,
later joined by Fujitsu and Sun, formed a technical working group to exert pressure on the opposing parties in digital video disc development towards
compromising and reaching a single standard. As Taylor outlines, these
companies stipulated necessary requirements of their own. These included calls
for a single format to cover computer and video entertainment, a common file
system, backwards compatibility with CD and high data capacity (1998: 42).

When the MMCD and SD-DVD alliances refused to compromise and reach
agreement, the IT consortium recommended adoption of the Universal Disc
Format (UDF) developed by the Optical Storage Technology Association
(OSTA) as the basis for a single standard. At this point, Sony and Philips lost
ground in the battle after IBM announced its support for the SD format, and
from August 1995 the two opposing camps agreed to enter negotiations towards

a single format. After the computing group outlined their preference for a standard combining elements of MMCD and SD, both sides made concessions and finally reached agreement in principle on 15 September 1995. They agreed the standard would incorporate most of Toshiba's innovations along with Sony's signal modulation system. Sony and Philips, together with the seven electronics companies behind SD and Time Warner, adopted the name DVD for the format and formed the DVD Consortium (later renamed the DVD Forum) to advance the development of a common standard for the launch.

However, further complications arose over the issue of copy protection. Fearing digital reproduction would encourage widespread copyright infringement, the Hollywood majors, collectively represented by the Motion Picture Association of America (MPAA), reached an agreement in March 1996 with the Consumer Electronics Manufacturers Association (CEMA) to propose legislation relating to digital recording and the protection of intellectual property. As this agreement was reached without the involvement of the computer industry, the following month the Information Technology Industry Council (ITIC) objected to what they saw as a mandatory standard imposed by other business sectors and rejected the MPAA/CEMA proposals (p. 47). To resolve the issue, the three sides formed the Copy Protection Technical Working Group and on 29 October 1996 a provisional agreement was reached on DVD encryption. Although a number of issues relating to copy protection remained outstanding, and these delayed the much anticipated launch of DVD in North America, from 1 November 1996 Japan became the first territory to introduce DVD players to the consumer market.

At the request of the computing industry, the DVD standard was backwards compatible with CD: audio CDs or VCDs could be played on DVD players but not vice versa. Any DVD player was therefore automatically also a CD player. While using 120mm discs which looked identical to CDs, DVD worked with smaller tracks and different modulation and error correction methods. These differences gave DVD seven times the storage capacity of CD. DVD was never intended to be a specific video disc format but was designed as a flexible storage medium which could be employed for many uses, not just video. Hence, there was a certain ambiguity concerning what DVD stood for when the format launched. 'Digital Versatile Disc' described the broad potential of the standard but as video presentation became the most common use of the format, so 'Digital Video Disc' became the equally appropriate and widespread designation.

A further turn in the development of DVD has come as manufacturers have introduced DVD recorders to the consumer market. When DVD was initially launched it was as a play-only technology. Time-shift recording had however contributed to the VCR becoming a compelling addition to the home media ensemble and encouraged expectations that the same functionality should be available for DVD. Electronics manufacturers have developed three different solutions in this area: DVD-RAM, DVD-R and DVD+R, each using 12cm optical discs. DVD-R or DVD+R can be used in the same way as CD-Recordable (CD-R) but provide greater storage capacity than the CD format: both are based on removable discs, offering 4.7Gb of storage, which can irreversibly be written to once. Although recordings using DVD-R or DVD+R are permanent, DVD-RW or DVD+RW offer re-writable variations on these formats which can be re-used approximately 1,000 times. DVD-RW or DVD+RW record data along a single spiral track but DVD-RAM stores data in concentric tracks and discs can be re-written in the region of 100,000 times (Bennett, 2004).

While the electronics industry reached consensus over use of DVD for pre-recorded video, recordable DVD introduced new conflicts through development and support for these incompatible formats. Pioneer developed DVD-R during 1997 and DVD-RW followed two years later. On 13 December 1999, Pioneer introduced the world's first consumer DVD-RW recorder, the DVD-1000, to the Japanese market (*Screen Digest*, 2000b). Retailing at ¥250,000 (US$2,400), the DVD-1000 was priced substantially above the average consumer price range. DVD-RAM attracted support from across the electronics business, with Hitachi, JVC, LG Electronics, Matsushita, Samsung, TEAC and Toshiba joining forces to form the RAM Promotion Group (RAM-PRG). Through its Panasonic brand, Matsushita launched its DVD-RAM model in the US during August 2000, priced at US$3,999 (*Screen Digest*, 2000a). Philips meanwhile embarked on an alternative format, working from 1997 on the development of DVD+R. DVD-R and DVD-RAM both benefited from the approval and backing of the DVD Forum but DVD+RW did not win similar endorsement. With the support of the Forum, Philips gathered a consortium of other companies to establish the DVD+RW Alliance. Members of the Alliance came from the fields of computing (Dell, Hewlett Packard), chemicals (Mitsubishi, a manufacturer in storage media including CD-Rs marketed through its Verbatim brand), office equipment (Rioch), electronics (Philips, Sony, and Thomson) and musical instruments and sound equipment (Yamaha). DVD+RW was launched in 2001 and the following year DVD+R came onto the market.

Potentially these differences could have created a format war preventing consumer adoption of DVD recorders. However the introduction of hybrid format recorders, with dual DVD±R or DVD+/-R (and DVD±RW or DVD+/-RW) capability, meant the market did not need to settle on a single format. After prices fell an explosion of models came onto the market, and by 2005 many consumers were confidently purchasing DVD recorders in volume as they upgraded their home media technology, replacing DVD players with hardware offering all the functionality associated with the VCR.

The DVD Commodity

With the VCR, consumers had been drawn to the technology by the facility for home recording, together with the new opportunities for watching pre-recorded programming in the home. Despite the fact that until the introduction of DVD recorders, DVD offered consumers only the latter option, sales exploded across international territories. In Western Europe, for example, DVD reached over 50 per cent penetration of television households by the end of 2004, six years after the official European launch. VCRs had taken nearly twelve years to reach the same level of penetration (*Screen Digest*, 2005b).

What made DVD such an attractive product for consumers'? If DVD was just another storage medium, a substitute for the videocassette, why did the format capture a popular market so quickly? Both questions invite a consideration of the DVD as a certain form of commodity. The appeal of DVD came down to two key features which differentiated the medium from the VCR and videocassette. DVD created an innovative home media commodity which promised consumers improved sound and image quality, together with new flexible options for accessing media content. It is necessary to examine these attractions in greater depth in order to understand how and why DVD became marketable as a distinctive media commodity.

The Aura of DVD Quality

Foundational to the claims for DVD quality was the high resolution of the DVD image and clarity of sound reproduction. NTSC presentation by laserdisc, for example, offered 567 × 480 lines of resolution while DVD provided 720 × 480 (Solman, 2001: 54). Combined with CD quality sound, DVD promised an experience previously unseen or unheard with the VCR.

Screen resolution was only part of DVD's claim to quality. Production of cassettes for the VCR relied on analogue methods of reproduction. A telecine machine transferred a film or other source material from celluloid to a tape master, from which commercial tape copies could be reproduced. From celluloid-to-tape and from tape-to-tape, the analogue transfer process successively lost some of the data which made up the original source and consequently image and sound became degraded. With digital media, however, because numerical data can be exactly replicated, then hypothetically perfect and exact copies can be reproduced. As Lev Manovich (2001: 54) summarises: 'In contrast to analog media where each successive copy loses quality, digitally encoded media can be copied without degradation.'

Commenting just before the DVD boom on the reproductive quality of laserdisc , Charles Tashiro (1996/7: 16) noted

> faith in the potentially perfect copy persists, expressed in the exploitation of ever-newer technologies, striving always to get closer to the film original, but never quite arriving ... As a result, change is valued for itself, and with each new technical capability, both collectors and producers feel compelled to improve on what has come before.

This same logic sold DVD to the consumer market. Like other digital media such as CD, DVD appealed through this promise of providing something new to bring the consumer closer to the original. In his 1936 essay 'The Work of Art in the Age of Mechanical Reproduction', Walter Benjamin (1977: 387) had observed that with mechanical reproduction the copy eliminated the 'aura' of an original cultural work: 'making many reproductions ... substitutes a plurality of copies for a unique existence'. The appeal of DVD quality can be understood as an attempt to compensate for this loss. While the DVD copy is removed from the original source and obviously the product of mass reproduction, digital reproduction can make a strong commercial appeal by promising to unite the consumer's copy with the fullness of the original work. Compared to the degraded image and sound of the VHS copy, the digital copy can therefore claim to be closer to the original source or otherwise give the consumer more of the original, thereby regaining, or at least preserving, something of the original's aura.

This intimate connection between copy and original is, however, deceptive. For the transfer of a film, for example, in many cases the mastering process may use a print struck from the master negative. In such cases, the mastering process is not creating DVD copies from an original but rather drawing copies from a copy, as digital reproduction follows on the back of mechanical reproduction. With films, as with all audiovisual works, the fidelity of reproduction is always contingent upon the photographic or recording qualities of the source and the condition of the prints or sound recordings used for the mastering. In the case of a film print, data may therefore be lost at source due to scratches, colour deterioration or other damage. As a step towards preparing for release on DVD, a film distributor or other rights holder may choose to subject the original to a process of restoration to rectify faults in the image, or otherwise clean up the sound by digital remastering. Ironically, in such instances the DVD copy may therefore be providing the consumer with data now lost from the source.

While these scenarios problematise the belief that DVD copies fully reproduce the source, in these instances it is the actual original source which in some way or other is flawed or incomplete. However, further problems are inherent to the process of digital reproduction itself which prevent the digitally encoded copy from fully capturing the original. Criticising the view that digital reproduction delivers pure and exact copies without degradation, Manovich argues

> there is actually much more degradation and loss of information between copies of digital images than between copies of traditional photographs. A single digital image consists of millions of pixels. All this data requires considerable storage space in a computer ... Because of this, the software and hardware used to acquire, store, manipulate, and transmit digital images rely uniformly on *lossy compression* – the technique of making image files smaller by deleting some information. Examples of the technique include the JPEG format, which is used to store still images, and MPEG, which is used to store digital video on DVD. The technique involves a compromise between image quality and file size – the smaller the size of a compressed file, the more visible the visual artifacts introduced in deleting information become. (emphasis in original, 2001: 54)

For DVDs, compression is necessary because film prints hold a tremendous amount of data which exceeds the storage capacity of discs. Data or information from the source is compressed by the MPEG-2 standard for the 'generic coding of Moving Pictures and Associated Audio', initially approved at the November 1994 meeting of MPEG (ISO, 2001).

When the Los Angeles film laboratory Crest National was involved in production of a DVD edition of John Carpenter's *Halloween* (1978, US), it had to compress the film for video. At 93 minutes long, the film contained approximately 134,000 frames, each of which was scanned at a rate of 44 megabytes. As a DVD disc is unable to store that much information, the data was necessarily reduced:

> The theory is simple: because much of a film's image information is redundant from frame to frame, you only have to encode information that changes. The idea is that a computer chip on the DVD player will de-code the compressed images and put the redundant elements back into the picture. (Fisher, 2000: 100)

Getting the film to disc therefore necessarily involved losing some of the data contained in the source.

Besides compressing information from the source, the mastering process can introduce 'artefacts' which do not result from the original photography and sound recording of the film. These can arise from

film scratches, film-to-video conversion, analog-to-digital conversion, noise
reduction, digital encoding, digital decoding, digital-to-analog conversion, NTSC to
PAL video encoding, antitaping alterations, composite signal crosstalk, connector
problems, electrical interference, waveform aliasing, signal filters, television picture
controls, and much more. (Taylor, 1998: 60)

Gregory Solman (2001: 55) also notes how in DVD editions of film titles, the
quality of transfers can result in an image quality so clear that DVD copies may
reveal the artifice of special effects or contrasts between studio and location
shooting which are otherwise imperceptible in other contexts: 'Is it the nature
of the DVD beast to scare up problems that remain hidden in film projection
and inefficient lower-resolution consumer formats such as VHS?'. In such cases,
DVD does not lose the quality of the original but rather uncovers details which
were present but invisible with the source.

DVD quality is therefore based on a misleading but highly marketable myth.
Instead of digitisation transparently and perfectly transferring data from the
source to the copy, DVD mastering *mediates* the original, passing it through a
series of intervening phases which subtly transform sound and image. As
Manovich comments,

> rather than being an aberration, a flaw in the otherwise pure and perfect world of
> the digital, where not even a single bit of information is ever lost, lossy
> compression is the very foundation of computer culture, at least for now.
> Therefore, while in theory, computer technology entails the flawless replication of
> data, its actual use in contemporary society is characterized by loss of data,
> degradation, and noise. (2001: 44)

DVD quality does not deliver a complete, unblemished reproduction of the original. Instead, DVD quality is a comparative concept, measured less by the
relationship of the copy to the original than by the reproductive capabilities of
DVD when compared against other home entertainment media like the videocassette or VCD. As DVD can never completely and fully deliver the original,
and because the mastering process actually transforms data from the original,
then DVD quality is sold on the aura and not the actuality of perfect fidelity.

The Extra Value of DVD Extras
Choice and control were fundamental to the commercial appeal of the VCR.
Time-shifting liberated televised entertainment from the broadcast schedules
and as an associated market in pre-recorded videocassettes emerged, so consumers were provided with a rich variety of software from which to choose. By

using the pause, fast-forward and rewind functions, the VCR/videocassette combination gave the consumer control over the flow of sounds and images. Choice and control therefore granted video consumers options for when, what and how to watch entertainment in the home.

Initially marketed to consumers as a play-only medium, DVD repeated the functionality of the VCR by giving the viewer control over the flow of pre-recorded material. Where DVD crucially departed from the previous medium was in the additional optionality it gave to consumers. Videocassettes always worked across a single linear, horizontal axis of control: pre-recorded material could be played, fast-forwarded, or rewound. DVD expanded these possibilities by introducing multiple axes of control, with tiered menus for accessing different levels of content, together with subtitling options and sound selection for choosing between different musical or vocal tracks to accompany the image. DVD facilitated therefore a whole 'architecture' of choices.

The benefits of this extended optionality became most obviously demonstrated through the inclusion on discs of various DVD 'extras' to supplement the core programme. Not all DVDs include these: many titles are given what is known as a 'straight' release, where the disc includes only the film with maybe a scene access menu and/or trailer. Special edition releases, however, include an array of additional materials beyond the core programme.

Inclusion of these extra materials on video releases did not start with DVD. From the early 1980s, laserdisc had been used to explore the possibilities for including supplementary materials alongside feature films. Leading this innovation was the New-York based video distribution label the Criterion Collection, established in 1983 as part of the Voyager Company (Kendrick, 2001: 127). When Criterion was established, the label held a partnership with Janus Films. Since the 1950s, Janus had become a leading distributor of international art-film releases and was responsible for establishing the reputation in the US of European auteurs such as Ingmar Bergman, Michelangelo Antonioni and Federico Fellini. The partnership gave Criterion access to the Janus library of European and international titles which established the label's identity. Since piloting extras on laserdisc, from 1998 Criterion has moved exclusively to DVD and maintained its reputation for preparing special editions rich in supplementary materials. While preserving and building its core catalogue of film classics from international cinema, it also periodically releases a few recent popular titles. Criterion summarises its own identity with the slogan 'A continuing series of important classic and contemporary films', which appears on all the label's releases.

Criterion introduced director commentary tracks with its laserdisc editions of *King Kong* (Merian C. Cooper and Ernest B. Schoedsack, 1933, US) and *Black Narcissus* (Michael Powell and Emeric Pressburger, 1947, UK). With *Citizen*

Kane (Orson Welles, 1941, US), inclusion of still frames from the storyboard and comparisons of different scripts provided extras for the label's first special edition (Neopolitan, 2003; Schauer, 2005). Among video distributors, when preparing films for release on videocassette, it had become common practice to pan-and-scan films produced in widescreen aspect ratios. Panning-and-scanning selected only a portion of the whole widescreen image to fill the 1.33:1 ratio of the television screen. Ultimately, this did a fair degree of damage to the film, for it cut out large amounts of the image and forced attention on certain portions of the frame. As Steve Neale (1998: 131) notes, panning-and-scanning modified a film 'by reframing shots, by reediting sequences and shots, and by altering the patterns of still and moving shots used in the original film'. Criterion departed from this practice, working against the drift of the market, when they decided only to present films in their original aspect ratios. With widescreen ratios, this inevitably meant 'letterboxing' the image, for the full width of the image could only be presented by resigning parts of the screen to black empty areas above and below the image. Other Criterion policies involved dedication to using only the best possible film elements (i.e. prints and sound recordings) for their transfers, restoration work on damaged prints and consultation with living directors to produce 'Director Approved' editions (Crowdus, 1999; Schauer, 2005).

Through the inclusion of extras, adherence to original aspect ratios and the label's art-film repertoire, Criterion created the laserdisc as an object of distinction: supplementary materials deepened understanding of a film's production, while letterboxed presentation moved the home viewing experience closer to what was originally seen in theatres. As laserdisc only captured a limited and marginal market, however, these extras remained rare features. Laserdisc therefore catered for an exclusive category of collector which did not characterise the larger body of consumers who formed the popular video market. But as DVD rapidly became a popular medium, the format routinised the inclusion of extra materials and original aspect ratios as widespread and familiar components of the home video product. DVD therefore mainstreamed the features which previously had marked the distinction of laserdisc.

DVD had only been on the market for a couple of years before conventions were quickly established in the types of extras commonly included on discs. Feature films, for example, were supported by the inclusion of scene access menus, theatrical trailers, deleted scenes or outtakes, on-screen biographies of the performers and other creative personnel involved with making the film, short 'making-of' featurettes and other documentaries, music videos for songs from the soundtracks of films, galleries of production stills, options for subtitles and a choice of language tracks. Together these items 'present the DVD as an event, where the film is but one part of a package allowing the buyer to get immersed in the film's historical and cultural legacy' (Seguin, 2003a: 22).

Frequently, DVD packaging identifies these items as 'special', 'extra' or 'bonus' features, suggesting they have a supplemental status. While they are undoubtedly additional to the core programme, for after all they are 'extras', arguably these items are not supplemental but essential to the value of DVD. It is the amassing of extras which not only differentiates the DVD special edition from a VHS release, even a VHS special edition, but also distinguishes the DVD event or commodity from the film watched in a theatre or otherwise on broadcast television. As was seen with the CD market, consumers will purchase digital media to replace items they already own on analogue media. Consumers buy copies of films on DVD which they already own on pre-recorded videocassette or which they have recorded to cassette from off-air transmission. In these cases, the purchasing decision is motivated by the aura of digital quality. However, there is less of an incentive to buy a simple straight release of a film on DVD when compared against the many further offerings which become available with a special edition release. DVD extras may be supplemental to the core film but they nevertheless represent the essential extra value of DVD as a format.

Material for DVD extras is obtained from many sources. Classic titles may be supported by trailers, documentaries or newsreel footage sourced from film archives. For new releases, it is already common practice in film and television production to record interviews with directors or actors, or to shoot on-set behind-the-scenes footage as material for electronic press kits (EPKs). Since DVD became a popular medium in the late 1990s, this material is now produced and used for making-of documentaries or featurettes on DVD. These typically explore the processes of film production, integrating footage of the film being shot with interviews involving the director and leading members of the cast. In some cases, particularly when a film was produced several years before the DVD is released, these documentaries involve the archival work of piecing together sources to provide a historical account of a film's production. But in other cases, especially with films produced after the launch of DVD onto the market, and for which a DVD release is inevitable, the making-of documentary draws together material which previously would only have been included as part of the EPKs sent to journalists. As Craig Hight (2005: 7) observes, documentaries of this type 'serve as extended trailers'. Through their combination of production footage and interviews, this type of making-of featurette creates a particular form of address to the viewer.

> They offer the obligatory praise from core cast and crew for their colleagues, a celebration of the film, and enough teaser clips from the film itself to build anticipation for its release. In EPK versions of [making-of documentaries], there

are no doubts voiced about the creative or (potential) commercial success of the film, no evidence of tensions (creative or otherwise) in its production, little if any exploration of the wider political or economic contexts of its production – in fact nothing that would disrupt the corporate agenda of the studio that owns the film. (p.7)

Paul Arthur (2004: 40) notes, with the making-of documentary, '[a]mong the intrinsic principles . . . is the validation of directorial artistry, counterbalanced by airing of less ballyhooed collective contributions'. Making-of documentaries therefore invariably aim to go behind the scenes of film-making but only go so far, creating a particular vision of the processes and conditions of media pro-duction.

Another familiar feature of the DVD extras package is the commentary track. Commentary from directors, actors and other creative personnel provides pos-sibilities for opening up new insights on a film. As Thomas Doherty (2001: 78) observes, with the director's commentary, 'the conceit is both home-spun and starstruck: you and the *auteur* shoulder to shoulder, planted on your living-room couch . . . [an] imaginary friendship nurtured in the vicarious dialog between pantheon artist and mortal fan . . . a wholly new order of intimacy'.

Together these extras produced an interactive object which exceeds and maybe even displaces the core programme as the prime attraction. As Graeme Harper (2001: 24) observes, 'DVDs promote and develop the idea of film as "game"':

No longer do audiences simply enter a text expecting to follow its narrative from Point A through to Point Z and to respond to the film text *a posteriori* in ways which reflect personal, cultural, historical and/or aesthetic bias. The expectation that supplementary materials provides is not, in reality, supplementary at all. In the extreme case . . . the core film narrative disappears entirely, forming the basis of a new narrative whose story is connected with the core but constructed under far more 'personalised' methods.

While these possibilities exist, it is debatable whether the inclusion of extras on DVDs actually transforms the viewing experience or disrupts the linear pro-gression of watching the core programme. Many titles released on DVD are just 'straights', and even if extensive extras are included on a disc, this does not necessarily mean the consumer will choose to consult these but may simply watch the core programme in a linear manner. Rather than presuming DVD has any actual impact on the viewing experience, it is probably more appropri-ate to judge that the significance of DVD extras resides in how they offer the possibility of interactivity even if the viewer never chooses to access those options.

DVD Production

Where DVD extras have certainly had an impact is on the work of producing titles for video release. For feature film releases, decisions over the materials to be included as DVD extras are now considered at pre-production and shot during principal photography. Ken Graffeo, Senior Vice-President of marketing at Universal Studios Home Video, notes this trend when he comments

> When we do production now, we're actually talking, at a script stage, about what else we can do – whether it's a deleted scene or an outtake that won't be part of the movie – that we could produce just for the DVD. ... It is a studio-wide focus, and we're working very closely with our theatrical marketing [department] to see if there's certain content that, rather than using it in publicity, they can hold for the DVD to give it that exclusivity. (insert in the original, quoted in Reesman, 2001: 56)

In cases where a video distributor picks up the rights to a film, the company may put together a package of extras from already existing materials or create new interview and documentary materials produced either by the distributor or outsourced to an external production company. As film rights are sold on a territorial basis, unless a film is handled by the distribution division of one of the Hollywood majors who have a global reach through their extensive international distribution offices, then a film is likely to be handled by different distributors between countries. This influences the packaging of extras, as a distributor will only hold rights to extras material for a particular territory. Frequently, the extras content for DVD editions of the same film is not therefore globally uniform. For example, in the case of the feature film *La vita è bella* (Roberto Benigni, 1997, It), produced by the Italian company Melampo Cinematografica, Disney's speciality video distribution subsidiary Miramax Home Entertainment handled the DVD release in the UK and the US. The US edition came with a *Making Life Beautiful* featurette, English-language track, US theatrical trailer and collection of trailers from US television, while the UK edition received a simple 'straight' release without extras.

Finding material for extras, particularly if the film to be released is not a recent production, involves archival research and liaison with rights holders. At video distribution companies, the importance of DVD extras has resulted in the creation of a new category of audiovisual worker, the DVD producer. It is the role of the DVD producer to co-ordinate the package of extra materials, identifying sources for extras material and securing the rights to that material. One example of this role is Curtis Tsui, a DVD producer for Criterion. At Criterion, the decision to produce a special edition is based on consideration of the historical and cultural value of a film, together with the availability of material for extras (Seguin, 2003b). When Tsui decided to produce a special edition of *Fa yeung nin wa* (*In the Mood for Love*) (2000, HK/Fr), from the director Wong Kar-Wai, the choice was based on the director's international reputation and on how the film's setting of 1960s Hong Kong was rich in possibilities to explore through additional materials.

Tsui and co-producer Bona Flecchia researched the availability of extras material. As the video division of the French television network TF1 had already released a DVD special edition of the film with extras, including a director's commentary, Criterion reached an agreement to incorporate these on their edition. Tsui also licensed the director's earlier film, *Hua yang de nian hua* (2000, HK/China). This 2-minute short edits together a montage of moments lifted from a collection of old nitrate prints of Hong Kong films found in a Southern California warehouse, which previously had belonged to a defunct Chinatown cinema. Wong was commissioned to create the short film by the Hong Kong Film Archive and he cut together the footage against the soundtrack of the Chinese song 'Blossoming Flower'. For Criterion's edition, Tsui obtained the rights to the original footage and the song. Tsui also secured rights to the short story 'Intersection' by the Hong Kong writer Liu Yi-chang which the director claims inspired *In the Mood for Love*, and the story is reprinted in the booklet accompanying the DVD. Among the other extras is a recording of a press conference at the 2000 Toronto film festival, attended by the film's two stars, Maggie Cheung and Tony Leung, and rights for this were held by the Canadian company Rogers Cable. Once the extras material had been identified, Criterion licensed the DVD rights for the main feature from USA Films, which held rights for the whole of North America.

Collecting

Across the first wave of home video, the market remained heavily concentrated on consumers renting rather than buying cassettes. In 1996, the year before the global roll-out of DVD, worldwide consumer expenditure on video rental was estimated to total US$19,693m, compared to US$14,929m from retail, a proportional split of 57/43 per cent (*Screen Digest*, 1997c: 249). By 2004, combined VHS and DVD rentals accounted for 31.9 per cent of worldwide expenditure on video software, while DVD retail accounted for 61.9 per cent, with a further 4.8 per cent of spending on VHS retail (the remainder was spent on VCD rental and retail) (*Screen Digest*, 2005d: 334). As the price of players and discs dropped

A wealth of extras: Criterion's edition of *In the Mood for Love*

dramatically after only a few years on the market, DVD consumers have swayed the market heavily towards the ownership of video software. Instead of renting, consumers have become drawn to DVD as a collectable format (Rothman, 2004).

For Barbara Klinger (2006: 62), the currency of extras, special editions and limited special editions circulated through DVD fits 'the goal of media industries in relation to collectors [which] is to tap into a middle-class consciousness about the superiority of ownership'. Klinger suggests video has created two categories of collector. The 'high-end collector' pays for expensive hardware on which to present his or her extensive collection of pricey DVD editions. As Klinger suggests, the high-end collector is driven by a combination of technophilia and cinephilia: 'the desire for cinema is inextricably linked to the desire for the newest and best technology' (p. 63). The 'low-end fan', on the other hand, will buy cheaper technology and build a collection of obscure titles.

Klinger's categories certainly characterise recognisable types of DVD consumer; however, what these do not take into consideration is how DVD has spread the practice of privately amassing discs beyond the dedicated collector to a wider body of consumers. DVD collecting is divided by different degrees of acquisitiveness. The label 'collector' has connotations of high culture deriving from art or antique collecting and evokes the idea of someone who makes a long-term investment of time and money in searching for and hoarding a particular category of artefacts. Collectors are media consumers but a particular elite category of consumer. Individual collectors do acquire vast personal stocks of DVDs but even so, the global shift in the video market from rental to retail could not be explained by this small, elite constituency of collectors alone. The collector does not characterise the majority of DVD shoppers who purchase discs, sometimes by design, sometimes on impulse, but without the intention of seeing these fit into any larger library. Nonetheless, through repeated purchases the more ordinary category of DVD shopper does still build a collection, though probably of more modest proportions than that of the collector. With the introduction of DVD, video collecting has therefore become a more generalised practice which exceeds the realm of the elitist collector.

CONCLUSION

In technological terms, videodisc and CD-based systems provided viable alternatives to the VCR, but these new platforms were defeated by market conditions. DiscoVision, Magnavision and SelectaVision appeared too soon after the VCR first went on sale. If, by the early 1980s, the VCR market had settled on a single format, that alone would have presented a major obstacle to establishing a foothold for videodisc. Yet as MCA and RCA were trying to launch new and rival technologies into a market already divided between Betamax and VHS, the disc alternatives not only faced competition from the VCR systems but also considerable confusion and caution among consumers. Judged on their own merits, the videodisc systems provided perfectly good platforms for video exhibition, but without the recording function of the VCR, the videodisc systems delivered less to the consumer. Videodisc was a video player but the VCR was both player and recorder.

Videodisc did not altogether fail but only gained a limited market and became a kind of unforeseen prototype for DVD. When DVD first came onto the market, it was also a read-only medium but succeeded in attracting a popular consumer base by delivering a distinctive new media product. Improving the presentation of sound or picture could only ever provide DVD with qualitative differentiation over VCR. Quality is always a vague concept, open to many interpretations, and in the case of digital reproduction the improvements over analogue media are by no means certain or even detectable. Extras, however, provided the DVD commodity with more obvious, tangible and quantitative differences over the VCR: DVDs could do what pre-recorded videocassettes could do, only more. DVD not only introduced a new format for playing entertainment but also provided consumers with an interface which transformed what was possible with home video. Confined to a limited elite market, videodisc had been a technology of social and cultural distinction. DVD mainstreamed the qualities of videodisc by appropriating the features of original aspect ratios, commentary tracks and special editions. These technological innovations energised the second wave of the video business, expanding the work of video production and transforming buying trends in the video market.

3

Porous Media: Global Diffusion of Video and DVD

After rapid sales across international territories, in less than a decade the VCR had become a global media technology. Two decades later, the absence of any format war meant the international diffusion of DVD happened even quicker.

As suggested in the Introduction, spatial flexibility has seen VCRs and DVD used as exhibition technologies in multiple consumption contexts. The global video market accentuates that flexibility as VCRs, cassettes, DVD players and discs become mobile and adaptable media, travelling across borders and malleably fitting into diverse market conditions and patterns of life. As Tom O'Regan (1991) notes,

> Video product flow and viewing cannot be easily monitored. Light in weight and easily reproducible, the video cassette is able to cross customs checkpoints, bypass cumbersome censorship bottlenecks, and evade law enforcement agencies. Furthermore, being electronic, video can easily and efficiently be reproduced without expensive investment in equipment. Thus the monitoring and regulation of video relies more upon the good will of the population than upon the efficiency of the state regulatory apparatus. (p. 118)

For these reasons, he describes video as having a 'porous nature', due to the 'combination of its light weight, its reproducibility and the difficulties facing its detection ... facilitat[ing] transfrontier circulation and piracy' (p. 120). While O'Regan is thinking about instances where video sneaks past attempts to block imports, regarding it as 'porous' is a good way of generally conceptualising how cassettes and discs circulate in the global audiovisual economy, permeating boundaries, 'seeping' into and becoming 'soaked up' in the practices of everyday living.

This chapter looks at the formation of the global video market through the internationalisation of VCR production and growth of the world VCR population. Consumer video has achieved global ubiquity, but as is now widely recognised, the workings of global media markets do not rest on the homogenisation of national contexts. Like all globalised media, international markets for VCRs and DVD are built on the economic, political, social and cultural differences which characterise and define regional, national or local contexts. In the global video market, those differences are most readily evident in the divergences represented by unequal levels of sales for video hardware, variations in the uses of video, national regulatory schemes imposed to control video, divergences in intellectual property law and the formations of taste which influence software purchases. To grasp the shaping of the global video market, the chapter therefore provides a series of case studies looking at how video was adopted into selected national contexts. In particular, it considers contexts in which the porous nature of video resulted in attempts to halt its diffusion for the purposes of regulating and controlling culture, and how video nevertheless circumvented those controls. The chapter then looks at how DVD re-energised the global video market before concluding with analysis of the conditions which led to Video Compact Disc (VCD) becoming a popular medium in East Asian territories.

FORMATION OF THE GLOBAL VIDEO MARKET

Internationalisation of Japanese VCR Production

Through the research and development programmes of Sony and JVC, Japan became the international centre of video innovation and development. As VCR production was predominantly conducted by Japanese manufacturers, aligned with either the VHS or Betamax 'families', so Japan also became the world centre of VCR production. During the 1980s, as these companies expanded their operations internationally, Japanese technology and manufacturing fed the formation of a global VCR market.

By the end of the 1970s, Sony, JVC and Matsushita, together with Akai, Hitachi, Mitsubishi, Sanyo, Sharp and Toshiba, were all operating production plants in Japan. According to the Electronic Industries Association of Japan (EIAJ), in 1976 Japanese manufacturers produced 208,163 units, 139,224 of which were exported (*Screen Digest*, 1981c: 234). By 1983, annual production capacity from the Japanese manufacturers had reached 18,260,000 units, with exports of 15,237,483 units (*Screen Digest*, 1984c: 114). To supply the expanding global market, during the 1980s Japanese companies opened international plants to make VCRs, with Western European territories becoming the main overseas locations for Betamax and VHS production. During the first half of the 1980s, plants in West Germany, France, Spain, Italy and the UK all commenced VCR production. In other international regions, Brazil, China, India, South Korea, Taiwan and the US also became locations for VCR production. For an analysis of this global spread of VCR production see table 3.1.

Manufacturer	Start	Location	Monthly Output		
			VHS	Beta	8mm
Japan					
Aiwa	1983	Tokyo		5,000	
	1985	Tokyo			10,000
Akai Electric	1979	Tokyo	*40,000		
Canon	1984	Fukushima			30,000
Funai Electric	1986	Tokyo			100,000
General Corporation	1981	Kawasaki		*10,000	
Hitachi	1978	Tokai	**280,000		
	1984	Fukushima	**70,000		
	1984	Haramichi	**50,000		
JVC	1976	Isezaki	**400,000		
Matsushita	1976	Kadoma	**1,000,000		
Mitsubishi	1977	Kyoto	**180,000		
NEC	1981	Tokyo		**50,000	
	1984	Gotemba	**30,000		
Philips/Marantz	1986	Sagamihara	100,000		
Pioneer	1986	Tokyo			5,000
Sanyo	1977	Judo, Tokyo		*167,000	
	1982		**170,000		
Sharp	1979	Osaka	**220,000		
Sony	1977	Ichinomiya, Kisarazu, Tokyo		**250,000	
	1985				300,000
Toshiba	1977	Komukai, Fukuya		**120,000	
	1984		**180,000		
Europe					
Akai-France	1983	Honfleur	7,500		
Fisher Industrie Deutschland	1984	Nordlingen	**15,000		
Grundig	1984	Nüremberg, FDR	*15,000		
Hitachi	1983	Landsberg, FDR	**30,000		
	1985	Hirwaun, Wales, UK	10,000		
J2T	1982	West Berlin, FDR	35,000		
	1982	Newhaven, England, UK	25,000		
MB Video	1983	Osterode am Harz, FDR	**20,000		
Mitsubishi	1983	Livingston, Scotland, UK	**20,000		
Orion	1986	Kenfig, Wales, UK	10,000		
Philips	1984	Liesing, Austria/Krefeld, FDR	165,000		
Sanyo	1983	Lowestoft, England, UK		**15,000	
Sharp	1985	Wrexham, Wales, UK	**5,000		
Sony España	1986	Barcelona		5,000	
Sony France	1986	Ribeauville			5,000
Sony Wega	1982	Cologne, FDR		**5,000	
Thomson-Brandt	1983	Tonnerre, France	*85,000		
Toshiba	1984	Plymouth, England, UK	**10,000		
Vidital	1986	Rome, Italy	8,000		
Brazil					
Philco	1982	Saõ Paulo	*1,500		
Sharp	1982	Manaos	*5,000		
China					
Matsushita	1985	n/a	*2,500		
State/Sony	1984	Amoy		*1,750	
South Korea					
Daewoo	1984	Seoul		**17,000	
Goldstar	1985	Seoul	**85,000		
Philips/Dongwon	1986	Seoul	40,000		
Samsung	1985	Seoul	**80,000		
Taiwan					
Sanyo	1983	Taipei		3,000	
Tatung	1982	Taipei	12,500		
USA					
Hitachi	1986	Anaheim	8,000		
Matsushita	1986	Vancouver, Washington	20,000		

Source: adapted from *Screen Digest* (1986b)

Note:
All output figures are for 1986 unless otherwise indicated. * = 1984 figures   ** = 1985 figures.

Table 3.1 World VCR Manufacturing (1986)

Japanese companies internationalised VCR production by expanding manufacturing through overseas plants and agreeing licensing arrangements with other manufacturers, or negotiating partnerships with producers in international territories. Sony, for example, was producing Betamax VCRs through its three Japanese plants in Ichinomiya, Koda and Kisarazu, before internationalising production from 1982 through its German plant at Cologne. Four years later, Sony España began making units in Barcelona. Betamax production was also undertaken under licence by Daewoo in South Korea and Sanyo in Taiwan. Meanwhile, in China Sony agreed a six-year contract from 1984 to partner with the state in Betamax production.

The World VCR Population

Following the launch of Betamax in 1975, over the next three to four years VCRs spread rapidly to international territories. Although sold in large numbers, during the late 1970s VCRs only reached a small fraction of the world television population. High prices ensured that the VCR remained a luxury item or status symbol, acquired mainly by the enthusiastic 'early adopters' of consumer technologies in the industrialised nations, or by the wealthy elite in developing countries. It was not until the 1980s, as VCR prices fell and the pre-recorded cassette market evolved, that a worldwide boom in VCR sales created a substantial global market for consumer video.

With the excitement caused by this boom, various bodies attempted to measure and estimate the size of the VCR population at national, regional and international levels. Governments, industry bodies from broadcasting or the film industries, and media research agencies all tried to gauge the size of the world video population based on production volumes, export or import figures, sales to dealers and consumer expenditure. Representative of this trend was the work undertaken by the London-based research agency and industry periodical *Screen Digest*. From 1982, *Screen Digest* began collating and reporting data from agencies in various national territories to estimate the size of the global VCR population. Problems existed with the availability and reliability of this data, and *Screen Digest* initially relied on very few sources, including export records from Japan as the world's largest VCR manufacturer, together with figures from the International Federation of Phonogram and Video Producers and the Motion Picture Association of America (MPAA). Over the next few years, new information sources became available on additional territories and *Screen Digest* was able to revise and expand their picture of the world VCR population.

By the end of 1976, the first full year VCRs were available on the consumer market in many countries, shipment of units to retailers indicated the world

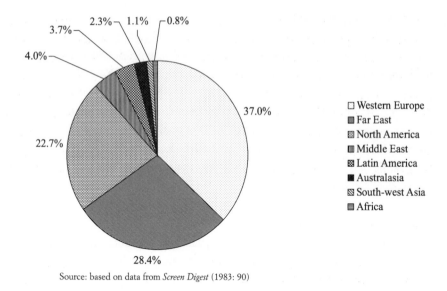

Source: based on data from *Screen Digest* (1983: 90)

Figure 3.1 Estimated Regional Distribution of the VCR Population (1982)

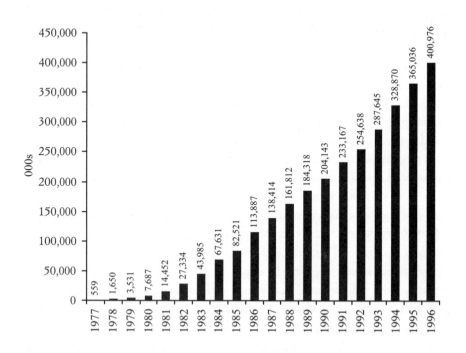

Sources: *Screen Digest* (1986c: 228; 1991b: 129; 1992: 132; 1993: 132; 1995: 179; and 1997b: 160).

Figure 3.2 Estimated World VCR Population (1977–96)

VCR population stood at 50,000 in Western Europe, 75,000 in North America and 43,000 in the Far East (*Screen Digest*, 1986c: 228). With data unavailable for many countries, these figures offered only a partial account of the world VCR population. At the end of 1982, the VCR population totalled approximately 25,250,500 VCRs, based on available data and estimates from other countries for which figures were not reported (*Screen Digest*, 1983a: 90) (see figure 3.1). Western Europe (9,350,000 units), the Far East (7,180,000) and North America (5,725,000) had become the leading regional markets, with over 88 per cent of VCR sales. The Middle East (1,003,000), Latin America (940,000), Australasia (577,500), South-west Asia (275,000) and Africa (200,000) remained at the fringes of the market. Mirroring the volume of regional sales, national markets in North America, Western Europe and the Far East showed the highest levels of VCR adoption.

Alongside sales volumes, a further measure of VCR adoption was the penetration of VCRs, based on the total number of units sold as a proportion of total television households (TVHHs), indicating the density of VCR ownership in national territories. *Screen Digest* estimated significant levels of VCR penetration in the UK (22.2 per cent), Netherlands (14.5 per cent), Taiwan (16.2 per cent), Japan (22.8 per cent) and West Germany (15.6 per cent) (1983a: 91). But the highest penetration levels were in the Arab Gulf states. Over half the total television households in the United Arab Emirates (UAE) (62.4 per cent), Kuwait (62.5 per cent) and Oman (50 per cent) owned VCRs. Despite the high penetration of VCR ownership, these countries, however, only accounted for modest proportions of the world's video population.

By the end of the 1980s, the VCR had become a globally popular item of media technology. According to *Screen Digest*'s estimates, in 1983 the world VCR population stood at 43,985m homes; at the end of the decade in 1989, that figure had reached 184,318m (figure 3.2). North America (63m), Western Europe (58.4m) and the Far East (33.2m) remained the regions with the highest numbers of VCR homes, accounting for over 84 per cent of the global total.

Market Dynamics and the Unknowable Video Audience

Production figures, export volumes, sales to dealers or penetration of TVHHs all provided different statistical prisms through which to estimate and measure the world VCR population. Yet the dynamics which shaped the global diffusion of the VCR presented problems to mounting authoritative data on the market. Faced with the limited availability of data and the rapid development of the market, at the start of the 1980s *Screen Digest* (1981b: 213) readily acknowledged that the size of the world VCR population was an issue on which the 'truth is no one really knows'. The unknowability of the VCR market did not result from limited data alone but rather was a consequence of the dynamics which shaped transnational flows of video hardware and software.

Trade or sales figures did not sufficiently document how re-exporting and the smuggling of VCRs between territories became key to flows of video hardware and therefore to the formation of the global video market. As Gladys D. Ganley and Oswald H. Ganley (1987: 21) observed, '[a]vailable statistics on VCR penetration are often guesses, for these machines frequently do not stay in the country to which they are shipped originally'. Re-exporting and smuggling operated beyond the eyes of organisations like the EIAJ, and the pervasiveness of these activities resulted in inconsistent and often implausible reporting. In Panama, for example, the Ganleys noted that according to different estimates, VCR penetration stood at 10 or 82 per cent. Export figures indicated how many VCRs were shipped to Panama, but these could not take into account how Panama was known to be the source for large numbers of VCRs smuggled into neighbouring Colombia.

Smuggling of VCRs across borders became endemic in many territories where governments imposed restrictions on the import of luxury goods or banned VCRs from fears concerning the circulation of subversive material. For example, in Mexico, as part of an austerity programme, in 1982 the government halted the import of VCRs and other luxury items. Over subsequent years, however, estimates of VCR ownership increased as machines were illegally imported from the US (pp. 21–2). Smuggling shadowed the legitimate market in VCRs but was not a rare or aberrant part of the video business. VCRs only became available in many territories because they were smuggled.

Export figures and sales data indicated how many VCRs were in circulation but these could not gauge the scale of the video audience at national or international levels. Measuring VCR penetration by the number of television households implicitly regarded the global video audience by the private unit of the family. However, as Hussein Y. Amin and Douglas A. Boyd (1993: 77–8) observed in a study of VCR adoption and use in Egypt,

> video consumption patterns in the Middle East should not be examined in a
> Western context. Similar to the use of radio and television receivers in the Arab
> world, there is a large amount of group VCR viewing by friends and extended family
> members. Not sharing one's media with others runs counter to Arab hospitality.

The TVHHs measure did not therefore account for contexts in which the video audience was not defined by the family.

A further difficulty with the TVHHs measure was that it failed to grasp how video was frequently used in venues outside the home for organised commercial entertainment. In India, for example, the widespread network of small-scale 'video parlours' – makeshift video theatres operating from converted restaurants – became venues where people could gather and pay to collectively watch films or other material (Agrawal, 1985: 14; Kumar, 1985: 18). In Guyana and India, gathering for video parties was also popular (Forsythe, 1983; Sarathy, 1983). Moreover, in major Indian cities, rough-and-ready cable systems were created by wiring a central VCR to apartments in a tower block, while VCRs were also installed on buses (Kumar, 1985: 18; Sarathy, 1983).

Knowing the market is essential for the video business; however, export and sales figures can only estimate the number of hardware units in circulation. Smuggling and re-exports problematised the task of accurately determining the distribution of video hardware. Furthermore, measuring the density of the VCR population by the penetration of TVHHs presumed a limited and misleading definition of the sociality of video consumption. It did not take into account how the diversity of practices in video consumption frequently spilled out beyond the home. These issues do not make analysis of the video market impossible but rather illuminate something of the dynamics which have generated the global dispersal of video media. They reveal the gap between knowing the scale of the video population (in terms of the number of video units in circulation) compared to the size and conduct of the video audience.

NATIONAL VIDEO MARKETS

Global diffusion of video was supplied through the internationalisation of VCR production and cross-border flows – whether legally or illegally – of hardware. As a commercial and leisure product, the VCR was subject to economic and cultural factors which influenced levels of adoption and patterns of use.

In a study of eighty-one countries, Joseph D. Straubhaar and Carolyn Lin (1989) identified a series of factors influencing VCR adoption and use. Per capita GNP and the concentration or distribution of national income determined expenditure on a luxury item such as a VCR. Pricing of VCRs and import restrictions (i.e. taxes and import quotas or bans) also influenced the availability of VCRs. In Colombia, for example, where contraband goods contributed a large part to video sales, in 1983 VCR prices ranged between US$900 and US$3,000. With a minimum monthly wage of US$120 and an average of US$250, VCRs were priced way beyond what most Colombians could afford. As communications researcher Amparo Cadavid (1983) noted, in the Colombian context, video 'is purely a gadget for the very rich. But, like any new fashion, this very exclusivity generates its own impact. Video has status. Therefore, the demand for VCRs is increasing, often for the purpose of demonstrating the owner's wealth and prosperity.'

Although income and pricing determined access to VCRs, Straubhaar and Lin found that VCR adoption was not confined to rich industrialised nations alone. VCR adoption dispersed internationally, from wealthy high-income industrialised (e.g. Japan, UK, US, West Germany) or oil exporting nations (e.g. Kuwait, Saudi Arabia, UAE), to East European non-market economies and middle- (e.g. Brazil, Fiji, Malaysia) or low-income (e.g. China, Ethiopia, India) economies. Economic factors alone did not therefore satisfactorily explain adoption of the VCR.

Straubhaar and Lin considered how the availability of other media options and provision of diversity in media content by the media industries were also important to the international diffusion of the VCR. Video ownership was high in countries familiar with and rich in other electronic media, particularly television and radio. Straubhaar and Lin examined VCR ownership in relation to different models of broadcasting system (government-owned, public service or commercial), the number of TV channels available and diversity of programme content aired. Looking at conditions in different national markets, the study considered whether the VCR was predominantly used for time-shifting or watching pre-recorded cassettes, and if these options related in any way to possible restrictions on the diversity of media channels available or shortages in the supply of televised entertainment. The study therefore explored if restrictions in services and/or scarcity of entertainment content led to use of the VCR as a complement to, or substitute for, television. Generally, the study found patterns of VCR adoption broadly divided between high-income countries with developed broadcasting systems offering diverse content where VCRs were mainly used for time-shift recording, compared to middle- or lower-income countries in which VCRs were used to play pre-recorded cassettes as compensation for restrictions on media content, either as a result of government control or a restricted media economy.

The effect of these factors can be understood further by examining the conditions in which the VCR was adopted in Japan, Ethiopia, Israel and the Arab Gulf states.

Japan – The Pioneer Market

After Sony and JVC had led research and development on the VCR, Japan became the pioneer market for the new medium. Sony's SL-6300 and LV-1801 Betamax models went on sale in Japan during May 1975 and in October, Matsushita introduced the VX format with the VX-100. A year later, JVC entered the format wars by launching VHS on the domestic market. In Japan, VCRs were introduced in a national context which combined high per capita income with an abundant television economy. By the 1980s, broadcasting in Japan was divided between Nippon Hōsō Kyōkai (NHK) and 102 commercial companies (Usami, 1988: 71).

At the end of 1976, the first full year of VCR sales, an estimated 40,000 homes owned a recorder. Seven years later, in 1983, the VCR population reached 8.9m homes after VCRs had been adopted by nearly a third of all TVHHs (*Screen Digest*, 1983b: 211). According to a 1982 survey of consumer durables by the Economic Planning Agency of the Japanese government, VCRs were the third most popular consumer electronics device after the audiocassette player and TV sets. The average cost of a VCR that year was ¥200,000 (Kabira, 1983). With the growth of the VCR market, Japan soon witnessed the consequences of the format war as Betamax quickly lost ground to the JVC format: by 1984, VHS accounted for 80.4 per cent of the market (Usami, 1988: 72).

Although videodisc failed to make any significant impact in the US, disc formats gained a respectable share of the market in Japan. After launching its videodisc format in the US, MCA introduced Laservision to the Japanese market in October 1981, and in April 1983 JVC followed with its own disc format, VHD/AHD. To support the introduction of VHD, JVC released 200 disc titles, priced at between ¥3,800 and ¥14,400 each (*Screen Digest*, 1983a: 92). Feature films accounted for the majority of releases. Rather than domestic productions, the catalogue mainly included classic and recent releases from Western Europe, the USSR and US. A range of music, documentary, sport and instructional titles were also available. As the videodisc market developed, sales of Laservision players outstripped VHD: by 1985, an estimated 490,000 Laservision machines had been sold, compared to 320,000 VHD units (*Screen Digest*, 1986c: 251). In 1990, the videodisc population was estimated to stand at 2.8m, around 7 per cent of TVHHs (*Screen Digest*, 1990a: 275).

Videocassette software was for sale or rental through a range of outlets, including record and video shops, department stores, supermarkets, camera shops, bookshops and mail order. However, the most widespread retail network for video sales was through electrical appliance shops. In the mid-1980s, there were approximately 70,000 of these shops in Japan: 'In every town, no matter how small, there are always rice dealers, drugstores, fishmongers, greengrocers, and the electrical appliance shop' (Usami, 1988: 72). Around 30,000 were owned by Matsushita, while Sony operated 15,000.

Japan's video software market displayed certain characteristics which distinguished it from other territories with large VCR populations. Elsewhere, video rental quickly took off as a popular practice but in Japan the video rental business remained virtually non-existent during the first half of the 1980s. According to a survey of VCRs in Japanese homes conducted by NHK in December 1984 only around 1.7 per cent of Japanese VCR owners watched pre-recorded software, with the majority preferring instead to use their machines for time-shift recordings (p. 82). Although sales of VCRs far exceeded videodisc players, in the mid-1980s the software market saw discs surpass sales of pre-recorded cassettes. Figures from the Japanese Video Association for the financial year 1984/5 indicated the value of disc sales reached over US$142.9m compared to US$125.9m for cassette sales and US$4.8m in cassette rentals (p. 80). In the cassette market, feature films and soft-core pornography accounted for the largest number of titles on the market, and together films and pornography were responsible for 43 per cent of sales (p. 81). With discs, however, the market was overwhelmingly swayed towards music titles. In 1984/5, music titles on videodisc accounted for over 83 per cent of sales. This trend arose after karaoke had become a popular form of participatory entertainment in the 1970s and videodisc players became widely used in homes and bars to provide video images as accompaniment for the singing of karaoke performers.

In terms of the installed base of video homes and sales of video software, Japan emerged as the world's second largest video market after the US. In 1989, the estimated Japanese video population had reached 24.8m, or 65.4 per cent of TVHHs, compared to 57.2m homes in the US and 13.4m homes in the UK, the third largest market (*Screen Digest*, 1990b: 250–1). Japanese consumers spent US$2,248m on renting videos and US$1,125m on sell-through titles in 1989. In the US that year, US$7,200m was spent on rental and US$2,300 on retail, and UK consumers spent US$927 on retail and US$500 on retail (*Screen Digest*, 1990a: 276).

Compared to the first half of the decade, video rental in Japan boomed during the late 1980s, peaking in 1988. The rental business was mainly made up of small owner-operated stores, but from the start of the 1990s these began to go out of business as large rental chains entered the market. Supermarket chain Nagasakiya developed its network of Sunhome Video outlets and US video chain Blockbuster opened its first Japanese store during July 1991 in the west Tokyo suburb of Hachiōji. During the development of the Japanese rental market, horror and pornographic titles had proved the most popular categories, but Blockbuster Video-Japan imitated the practice of the main US chain by excluding adult material and stocking children's and mainstream hit feature films (Terazono, 1991).

Ethiopia's Video Elite

The formation of the video market in Japan, where time-shift use exceeded the watching of pre-recorded cassettes, supports Straubhaar and Lin's (1989) findings that in high-income countries with multiple and diverse television services and content, the VCR was adopted and used to record from, not to replace, television. Similarly, the situation in Ethiopia confirms the conclusion that in low-income countries with limited television services, the VCR was adopted as a substitute for television.

At the start of the 1980s, Ethiopia's communication infrastructure was extremely limited. Among the population of 31m, only one-quarter of a per cent owned telephones and just over 1 per cent had radio receivers (Coleman, 1983). Television penetration was even lower, at a little over one-tenth of a per cent, with ownership concentrated among the rich and expatriate communities. Broadcast coverage reached only 6 per cent of the country and the Ethiopian Television Service offered limited provision, transmitting twenty-six hours of programming in any week.

VCR adoption was also low: rough estimates placed the installed base at only 300 VCRs, all owned by the wealthy and expatriates. Among these elite groupings, the VCR was used to supplement the limited television service. Indications suggested in the average week, VCR households may spend between one and five hours watching the local television service, but four to fourteen hours viewing imported pre-recorded cassettes. Most of these imports were from Europe and the US, with cassette exchange and copying widely practised between individuals.

Israel's Alternative Television Service

In Israel, which Straubhaar and Lin banded among upper-middle-income economies, the dearth of television services also created a strong incentive to adopt the VCR and use it to expand the television programming repertoire.

By 1982, the average cost of a VCR in Israel was in the region of £1,500, or two to three months the average net salary (Katz, 1983: 55). Despite the expense, video had quickly become a popular form of entertainment in the country. With the Israel Broadcasting Authority only providing a single television service, many Israelis tuned into the English-language service from neighbouring Jordan for a second television channel. In this context, the VCR proved popular as an alternative television service.

> Video is also a kind of second channel, offering choice to those who feel that choice is needed, or, more exactly, to those who feel that choice must be offered simultaneously rather than sequentially, and it must be offered on the tube itself rather than via other arts and activities. Thus, the popularity of video in Israel ... has something to do with the ostensible diversity of choice which it represents.
> (p. 55)

While imports made up half the programming on the national television service, an estimated 95 per cent of pre-recorded video material was imported, mainly in the form of foreign films and US or UK television programmes (p. 56). The VCR therefore supplemented the restricted television economy.

Video in the Arab Gulf States

As already indicated, early in the development of the global video market the Arab Gulf states had some of the highest levels of VCR penetration in the world. Following the oil crisis of 1973, oil income supported ambitious development plans in the region, which drew large numbers of expatriate workers from other Arab countries, Asia, Europe and the US (Boyd, 1987: 548). Oil wealth also provided the means to support expenditure on consumer luxuries. State-run broadcasting ran limited television services, restricting the diversity of content available. In this context, Arab nations not only had the economic means to buy VCRs but also the demand for additional sources of programming among the large migrant workforce.

Kuwait was representative of the reasons why Arab states saw high densities of VCR ownership from the earliest years of the global video market. By the early 1980s, oil had provided high levels of per capita income, while the climate limited opportunities for outdoors recreation and state-run broadcasting limited the types of programming available. Since the Iran revolution of 1979, Kuwaiti broadcasting had become increasingly conservative in response to Islamic fundamentalist pressures. This, however, left a high demand for forms of entertainment which were not provided by television, particularly among the expatriate community who made up over the half the country's population (Barakat, 1983).

While consumer video did not take off in most parts of the world until the introduction of Betamax and the VHS, in Saudi Arabia small numbers of the Sony CV-2000 were bought in the late 1960s and from 1972, U-matic recorders were imported (Boyd, 1987: 546–7). One Saudi Arabian minister referred to his country as 'the first video tape society' (quoted in Boyd and Straubhaar, 1985: 11). By the time Betamax came onto the Gulf market in 1976, Sony already had a strong network of dealers in the region. Sales of VHS machines from JVC, Hitachi and Matsushita's Panasonic brand, however, quickly overtook Betamax. Television broadcasting in Bahrain, Kuwait, Oman, Qatar and the UAE operated on the German PAL standard, while Saudi Arabia used the French SECAM system. Many Saudis had therefore bought multi-standard television sets to receive programming from their neighbours. Conscious of the potential market in the region, Japanese manufacturers began producing multi-standard VCRs explicitly for the Gulf (Boyd, 1987: 548).

Multi-standard VCRs not only increased the options for off-air recording beyond national borders but also provided a platform on which to play imported pre-recorded cassettes. Alongside commercially produced cassettes, some entre- preneurs organised networks for recording programming from American and British television for export to the Gulf. Demand for Western and Egyptian films also created a major market for pirated recordings. Singapore was identified as the source for many illegal pirate masters, which were shipped to Kuwait for duplication and then distribution (p. 550). Piracy in the region was believed to account for as much as 80 per cent of the software market.

As suggested earlier, re-exporting resulted in misleading estimates of the scale and density of VCR ownership across international territories. At the start of the 1980s, the high penetration levels of VCRs in the Arabian Gulf could partly be explained by the large volume of VCRs acquired by expatriate workers, who then returned home with their purchases. As most Gulf states did not apply taxes for consumer electronics goods, expatriates could buy VCRs at lower prices than in their home countries (Boyd and Adwan, 1988: 160). Through these routes, VCRs from the Gulf were re-exported to Egypt, India, Jordan, Pak- istan, the Philippines and Thailand.

REGULATING VIDEO

Unlike television or radio systems, the activities of the global video market were not dependent on government licence or large-scale capital investment in the insti- tutional conditions of production and dissemination. The porous trade in video hardware and software therefore could operate outside systems of media regulation and control. For O'Regan (1991), video was thus a decentralised medium: 'video's reproducibility, transportability, and the domestication of the apparatus of projec- tion has favoured the VCR's quite radical decentralization both within exhibition (the home) and distribution at the point of sale (the rental outlet and sell-through structures)' (p. 119). For Ganley and Ganley (1987: 94–115), the decentralising effect of the VCR held political potential, as video recordings could be passed between individuals, bypassing institutionally organised channels of communi- cation. This was particularly important in countries where government placed heavy controls over the press and broadcasting systems, and restricted or censored media content. In such contexts, VCRs not only provided a means for the decentralised exchange of communication but also gave viewers access to prohibited content. For example, following the 1983 assassination of the Philippine opposition leader Benigno S. Aquino Jr, in which the military and the government of President Ferdi- nand E. Marcos was implicated, copies of a Japanese television documentary and US newcasts on the killing were rumoured to have been smuggled into Manila on video- cassette and used to produce an alternative account of the incident (Trumbell, 1983).

However, although VCRs had the potential to be used as tools of democratic communication, more frequently the decentralised freedom of video served commercial rather than political aims. Widespread international piracy was the most direct outcome of this. Despite its porosity, or rather as a direct response to its decentralised character, video was subjected to centralised mechanisms of national regulation aimed at halting and controlling inflows of VCRs and cassettes. As the examples of the USSR, Iran and the UK show, forms of political, religious or moral regulation were consequently implemented at national levels to obstruct access to video.

Soviet Attempts to Halt the Threat of Video

In the USSR, VCRs presented a threat to the highly centralised, government-controlled media system (Boyd, 1989). Although no official ban on video was implemented, large-scale importation of VCRs was not permitted. Instead, tourists, journalists, commercial envoys and diplomats smuggled Japanese-produced VCRs into the country (Temko, 1983). As a mechanism of ideological control, imports of Western films and other forms of media content were deemed subversive and banned, although copies were also smuggled into the country and replicated. A network of underground video cinemas also emerged, showing illegal films. The newspaper *Sovietskaya Kultura* articulated government opinion when it warned 'video is used to enslave man spiritually. The big monopolies see technical novelties, first of all, as new means for manipulating people's thoughts' (quoted in *Business Week*, 1984). After a raid on a Black Sea café found illegal cassettes, *Komsomolskaya Pravda* reported that the place was a den for the 'three s's – sex, supermanism and sadism', where 'tapes were run with a special garnish – vile slander against our history and contemporary politics' (quoted in Schmemann, 1983).

To protect against the perceived threat of video, in November 1982 a new border law was introduced which classified video recordings among items to be checked by customs officers when looking for 'information that could harm the country's political or economic interests, state security, public order or the population's health or morals' (quoted in Schmemann, 1983). VCRs and cassettes, however, continued to be smuggled in. In the early 1980s, small numbers of imported VCRs were sold through 'commission stores' (state-run second-hand shops) selling at prices in the region of 3,500 rubles (approximately US$4,900), and for higher prices on the black market. With the average monthly wage standing at 180 rubles, in the early 1980s video was a medium which could only be illicitly enjoyed by the Soviet elite or by the public through the underground cinemas network (Owen, 1983; Schmemann, 1983; Temko, 1983).

Although pornography was banned, illegal 'Swedish tapes' costing up to 500 rubles proved the most popular category of video material. Eventually, these were supplanted as illegally imported Western feature films and other forms of filmed entertainment became available. *One Flew over the Cuckoo's Nest* (Milos Forman, 1975, US), *The Deer Hunter* (Michael Cimino, 1978, US), *Apocalypse Now* (Francis Ford Coppola, 1979, US), *Last Tango in Paris* (Bernardo Bertolucci, 1972, It/Fr), *A Clockwork Orange* (Stanley Kubrick, 1971, US), *Straw Dogs* (Sam Peckinpah, 1971, UK/US) and *The Godfather* were reported to be among the most wanted films in Moscow in the early 1980s (Schmemann, 1983; Taubman, 1985).

As the Soviet authorities were unable to stem the growth of the underground video industry, they introduced measures aimed at bringing the video business under the control of the state. To counteract imports of Japanese and other foreign-made machines, in May 1984 the Soviet electronics monopoly Electronika began to produce the USSR's own VCR with plans to begin exports to four other East European countries in the future. Through its factory at Voronezh, Electronika made its own model, the VM-12, test-marketing it in a small area of southern Russia. Although the VM-12 was developed by reverse-engineering, copying a Japanese VCR, it operated by a different technical standard, preventing its use for showing films from the West. However, the venture failed. The Voronezh plant could only produce in very small numbers and complaints were made about the quality of the machines (*Business Week*, 1984). Costing approximately US$1,500, the VM-12 was priced beyond the resources of the average consumer and, arguably, preventing the machine from playing imported programming removed the very reason why Soviet consumers wanted VCRs. Initiatives were also launched to create a video software market under the jurisdiction of the state. The State Committee for Cinematography set up a video rental programme, starting in May 1984 with the opening of the first video rental stores. These were stocked with authorised ideologically acceptable films from the USSR (Taubman, 1985).

Elsewhere in the Eastern Bloc, similar measures aimed at controlling video were introduced by Bulgaria, Poland, Czechoslovakia, Hungary and the German Democratic Republic (GDR) (Ganley and Ganley, 1987: 120–3).

Video and the Islamisation of Film Culture in Iran

Flexible recording media played a key role in the Iranian revolution of 1979 which toppled the pro-Western government of the Shah, as audiocassettes became a decentralised channel for the dissemination of oppositional opinion (Sreberny-Mohammadi and Mohammadi, 1994). Following the revolution, a series of measures were introduced aimed at instilling a fundamentalist Islamic culture as the foundation for the new theocracy. In this context, cinema was considered as both a threat and a tool. Since the first years of the twentieth century, critics in Iran had viewed cinema as a Western import which threatened the Muslim society (Naficy, 2004: 27). Before the revolution, Ayatollah Ruhollah Khomeini had contributed to these criticisms, branding cinema as a cause of prostitution, corruption and political dependence on the West (p. 28). On his return to Iran in the aftermath of the revolution, however, Khomeini also praised the capacity for cinema and television to be a channel for education. Khomeini's divided opinions were characteristic of wider ambivalence in the Islamic Republic towards cinema, which was regarded as both Western danger and valuable ideological tool. Cinema was not necessarily judged to be a threat, only the wrong type of cinema. Video played a role in this ideological project, for the Jehad for Reconstruction, which was entrusted with aiding the reconstruction and development of rural Iran, used videocassettes together with theatre, cinema, audiocassettes, photographs and posters to disseminate its messages (p. 42).

In the early years of the post-revolutionary era, the Ministry of Culture and Islamic Guidance (MCIG) was formed and entrusted with instilling a programme for the promotion of Islamic culture. As part of this process, imports of Western films were gradually reduced and domestic films subject to rigorous censorship. Regulations introduced by the MCIG in June 1982 aimed to purify the cinema by instilling Islamic values. According to these regulations, films needed a permit to be shown in cinemas or on video, and could be banned if they threatened Islamic principles and beliefs (pp. 36–7).

These measures contributed to the Islamisation of film culture in Iran but this did not result in a complete closing of Iran to imports: foreign films which satisfied the MCIG's regulations were imported and granted permits to be shown theatrically, including films from the US and Western Europe. Films on video were subject to the same regulations, yet those without permits, including pornographic titles, were still imported and circulated on videocassette. As Hamid Naficy (2004) suggests, despite the programme of Islamisation, the government had a contradictory policy towards video:

> From the beginning, the Islamist government had a love-hate relationship with video, fearing that it would undermine the 'Islamic culture' it was propagating. As a result, it frequently vacillated, alternately banning, curtailing, ignoring or grudgingly allowing video cassettes and VCRs. This in turn encouraged a burgeoning but fluctuating black market in major cities. (p. 54)

As in the USSR, a black market for videocassettes therefore emerged in post-revolutionary Iran despite, or as a response to, efforts by authoritarian government to control video entertainment. In both cases, black marketeering did not deliver subversive strikes against government control but instead served commercial rather than political purposes.

Britain and the 'Video Nasties' Phenomenon

In Britain, the regulation of video took an explicitly moral line. The video business took off very quickly in the UK and by the early 1980s Britain was the third largest video market in the world after the US and Japan. When the video market was first formed in the late 1970s, it was largely unregulated. Since 1912, a system for regulating and censoring film content had existed in Britain, with films receiving certification from the British Board of Film Censors (BBFC) prior to theatrical release. No similar framework, however, applied to the new medium of video recordings. Video therefore provided an outlet for films which had not received classification for theatrical release, and films with cuts imposed for showing in cinemas could also be released uncut on cassette.

Legislation for the regulation of video emerged after a series of developments fuelled a moral panic over the effects of violent content on video. In 1982, the Advertising Standards Authority upheld complaints from trade body the British Videogram Association (BVA) and the public against the video distributors Go Video and VIPCO for the grisly content of campaigns run to promote video releases of *Cannibal Holocaust* (Ruggero Deodato, 1980, It/Colombia), *Lager SSadis Kastrat Kommandantur* (*SS Experiment Camp*) (Sergio Garrone, 1976, It) and *The Driller Killer* (Abel Ferrera, 1979, US) (*Screen Digest*, 1982b). From May 1982, articles started to appear in some national newspapers protesting at how the unregulated market allowed children easy access to video titles which contained graphic violence. A leading voice here was the right-wing *Daily Mail*. After publishing the headline 'We Must Protect Our Children *Now*', in February 1983 the *Mail* launched its Ban the Sadist Videos campaign. The crusade received the backing of Mary Whitehouse, a high-profile moral campaigner and spokeswoman for the media lobby group the National Viewers' and Listeners' Association (NVLA). As Julian Petley (1984) observes, in the panic which followed, the absence of any clear definition to describe the films concerned resulted in 'the term "video nasty" [becoming] synonymous with the term "horror film"' (p. 70).

As the panic spiralled, the issue spurred a range of responses and actions from police, government and the video industry. The BVA commissioned the BBFC to establish a working party of experts in media regulation, child care and psychology to devise a voluntary classification system for video. On 14 April 1983, the BVA and BBFC introduced their classification code. A new body, the Videograms Standards Council (VSC), was formed to administer the code, and the BBFC was entrusted with awarding certificates for new releases. Video dealers were required to register with the BVA, and any who broke the terms of the code would be penalised by the withholding of supplies from the major film producers and distributors who made up the BVA membership. But as the scheme remained entirely voluntary, it failed to satisfy campaigners for stricter control of home video.

Meanwhile, the London Metropolitan Police Obscene Publications Squad made a report to Sir Thomas Hetherington, the Director of Public Prosecutions (DPP), recommending the prosecution of video distributors under the Obscene Publications Act (OPA), which previously had only applied to pornographic materials. At hearings in July and September 1982, the distributors of *Cannibal Holocaust, The Driller Killer, I Spit on Your Grave* (Meir Zarchi, 1978, US) and *SS Experiment Camp* were ordered to forfeit copies of these titles under section three of the OPA, and notice was given that any future prosecutions would be given a criminal trial with threat of imprisonment.

Pressure mounted for government to pass legislation regulating video. In their build-up to the 1983 general election, the Conservative Party promised in their manifesto to 'respond to the increasing public concern over obscenity and offences against public decency, which often have links to serious crime' by introducing legislation 'to deal with the most serious of these problems, such as the dangerous spread of violent and obscene video cassettes' (Conservative Party, 1983). After the party won with over 61 per cent of seats in the House of Commons, in July 1983 Conservative MP Graham Bright presented a private member's bill calling for legislation to prohibit the sale or rental of videos which did not meet the approval of a central censorship body. After progressing through Parliament, the bill became law when the Video Recordings Act (VRA) was passed in July 1984.

According to the VRA, the Secretary of State designated an authority to classify videos, and it became an offence to supply, or offer to supply, unclassified video works, with fines of up to £20,000 for anyone committing such an offence (HMSO, 1984). Allowing for certain exempted works, the Act required all videos commercially released in Britain to be classified. From August 1985, the BBFC was entrusted with the task of classifying new releases, together with a deadline of 1 September 1988 to retrospectively classify the huge backlog of over 12,000 titles already available on cassette. The Board had the power to award or withhold classification and to impose cuts. Classification was made according to the following categories:

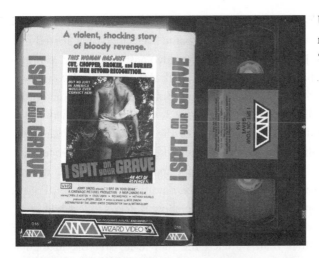

Unclassified original releases of notorious 'video nasties'

Uc   Universal – particularly suitable for unsupervised children

U   Universal

PG   Parent Guidance – general viewing but some scenes may be unsuitable for young children

15   Suitable only for persons of 15 years or over

18   Suitable only for persons of 18 years and over

R18 Restricted to distribution in licensed premises – no one under 18 to be admitted. (BBFC, 2006a)

As these changes came into effect, the BBFC changed its name to the British Board of Film Classification so as to reflect the Board's primary role.

The VRA introduced one of the most rigorous schemes for regulating video content anywhere in the world. However, the panic over video only abated for a few years in Britain. In 1993, the spectre of the video nasties returned as press speculation implicated the film *Child's Play 3* (Jack Bender, 1991, US) in two separate murder cases. When two-year-old Jamie Bulger was killed by a couple of boys aged ten, allegedly a copy of *Child's Play 3*, which was classified as 18 by the BBFC, was found in the home of one of the assailants and it was also claimed that aspects of the killing bore copycat resemblance to violence represented in the film. After teenager Suzanne Capper was abducted, it was alleged that her killers watched the film over the days they tortured her. Police investigations failed to produce any evidence to show Bulger's killers had seen the film, and while it emerged that Capper's killers had listened to music from the film's soundtrack rather than watched the film itself, still the incidents renewed outcries over the effects of violent videos on children and other members of the public. Press coverage used the incidents to assert that the effects of violent videos were obvious (Petley, 1994). But as Guy Cumberbatch (1994; 486) observed during these debates, '[i]n the mounting campaign against video violence the problem it represents has been assumed rather than demonstrated. The issue has taken on the characteristics of a modern mythology relying essentially on superstition for its credence'.

At this time, the Criminal Justice Bill was passing through Parliament and the Liberal Democrat MP David Alton, supported by the Movement for Christian Democracy, called for amendments to the bill to strengthen the regulation of video (Petley, 1994: 191). When the Criminal Justice and Public Order Act (CJPOA) became law in 1994, it made a series of changes to the VRA. Fines for supplying films which breached classification were increased and convictions could result in imprisonment. For categories of exempted works, new restrictions were placed on depictions of the techniques used to commit criminal offences. Further criteria were also added for the BBFC to apply when judging the suitability of recordings. Matters of 'special regard', including the representations of criminal behaviour, illegal drugs, violence and sexual activity, were to be judged for the harm caused to the viewer or by the viewer's behaviour on society (Morton, 1994: 45–6). In light of these new tests, the Video Recordings (Review of Determinations) Order 1995 was introduced as a supplement to the 1994 legislation, allowing the BBFC to review earlier decisions and reclassify works when judged necessary (BBFC, 2006b).

DVD – RE-ENERGISING THE GLOBAL VIDEO MARKET

By 1996, the year DVD was launched in Japan, the VCR population was still expanding, although the amazing growth seen in the early 1980s had inevitably disappeared (figure 3.2). DVD therefore emerged as the catalyst to drive the global market for video hardware into a second wave of significant growth.

DVD and the Global Market for Video Hardware

From March 1997, DVD players went on sale in the US and the following year the technology was rolled out across Western Europe. By the end of 2003, there was an estimated 189.6m DVD households worldwide, rising to 272.7m in the following year. Meanwhile, VCR households were declining (figure 3.3). At the end of 2004, DVD hardware had penetrated 26 per cent of worldwide TVHHs, while VCR homes declined to 35 per cent (*Screen Digest*, 2005d: 337). Meanwhile, VCD remained the most popular video platform in the emerging markets of the Asia-Pacific: in 2004, there was an estimated 106.7m VCD households in these territories, compared to 93m DVD homes and 73.6m VCR homes. China accounted for 64m of those VCD homes (p. 340).

Phenomenal sales in North America and Western Europe led to claims that DVD had rapidly become the fastest-selling technology in the history of consumer electronics. Across the leading Western European nations (UK, Germany, France, Spain and Italy), within six years the penetration of DVD hardware in television households had reached levels which it had taken between eleven and fourteen years for the VCR to achieve (*Screen Digest*, 2005b).

Following the pattern of the VCR market, early DVD ownership was heavily concentrated in North America and Western Europe. At the end of 2003, 69.2 per cent of the world DVD homes were in these regions, while in the Asia-Pacific the three mature markets (Australia, New Zealand and Japan) accounted for 8.1 per cent. Latin America represented 3.7 per cent, while Central and Eastern Europe had the lowest levels of DVD ownership, with just 1.5 per cent of the world total (table 3.2). These proportions were reflected in the penetration of DVD hardware: while nearly half of TVHHs in North America were believed to own a DVD player or recorder, and over a third of television homes in Western Europe, in Latin America and Central/Eastern Europe penetration levels stood at 10 and 4 per cent respectively (*Screen Digest*, 2004: 337). In just a few years, DVD hardware had formed a market heavily concentrated in the main industrialised nations.

Consumer Spending on Video Software

Similar trends could be found in the software market: in 1997, total consumer spending on video software (combining retail and rental of DVD, VHS and VCD) totalled US$31bn, but by 2003 it had reached US$50bn and a year later stood at nearly US$58bn (*Screen Digest*, 2004: 333, and 2005d: 333). Worldwide spending on DVD outstripped VHS for the first time in 2003: that year, 52.8 per

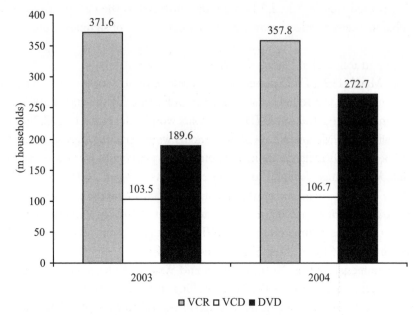

Source: based on data reported in *Screen Digest* (2005d: 338–40).

Figure 3.3 Global Installed Base of Video Hardware (2003–4)

	2003	2004
Asia-Pacific		
Australia and New Zealand	3.7	5.4
Japan	10.4	16.2
Other Asia-Pacific	48.6	71.4
Europe		
Eastern Europe	2.5	5.5
Western Europe	58.2	83.8
Americas		
North America	59.9	78.8
Latin America	6.3	11.6
Total	189.6	272.7

Source: based on data from *Screen Digest* (2005d: 338–40).

Table 3.2 Global DVD Population (2003–4) (millions)

cent share of total worldwide consumer spending was on DVD retail and 18.2 per cent on DVD rental, giving DVD a total share of 71 per cent; this compared to 17 per cent VHS rental and 10.3 per cent VHS retail (27.3 per cent total share). A further 1.6 per cent went on VCD retail and 0.1 per cent for VCD rental (*Screen Digest*, 2004: 333). A year later, DVD retail had increased its share of consumer spending to 61.9 per cent, while DVD rental accounted for 21 per cent (*Screen Digest*, 2005d: 334). Meanwhile, VHS expenditure declined to 10.9 per cent rental and less than 5 per cent on retail (table 3.3). As these figures indicate, DVD units not only displaced VHS as the most popular video software option but also the global market shifted towards spending on retail rather than rental, reversing the trend seen since the growth of the VHS market.

DVD caused a boom in the worldwide video market, but by 2005 this seemed to be over. For the first time since DVD went on the market, worldwide consumer expenditure on video software declined. According to estimates from *Screen Digest*, compared to the nearly US$58bn spent in 2004, during 2005 consumer spending decreased to US$51.8bn (2006: 365). This was due to three factors. Spending on DVD actually increased by 5 per cent in 2005 but as expenditure on the format had grown by 32 per cent the year before, signs were that growth was decelerating. Second, it was well known that VHS was rapidly becoming obsolete, but as VHS spending fell by 62 per cent to US$3.4bn, the decline was happening more quickly than predicted and low growth in DVD spending could not compensate for this fall. Finally, falling prices had helped

	DVD		VHS		VCD	
	Retail	Rental	Retail	Rental	Retail	Rental
Asia-Pacific						
Australia and New Zealand	51.6	39.2	3.5	5.7		
Japan	56.3	13.7	1.6	28.4		
Other Asia-Pacific	46.4	0.7	1.3	7.1	43.2	1.3
Europe						
Central and Eastern Europe	39.6	17.5	27.6	15.3		
Western Europe	72.9	16.7	7.0	3.4		
Americas						
North America	59.9	26.0	4.6	9.5		
Latin America	40.8	32.5	8.8	17.9		
World	61.9	21.0	4.8	10.9	1.3	0.04

Source: compiled from *Screen Digest* (2005d: 334).

Table 3.3 Worldwide Consumer Spending on Video Software (2004) (%)

stimulate DVD retail and so attracted consumers to the format during its introductory years, but with average prices for retail DVD standing at US$17.60 in
2004 and US$16.30 the year after, concerns were expressed in the industry that
price increases were needed if consumer expenditure was to rise again.

In terms of consumer spending, the US became the largest single-territory
market for video software. In 2005, the US was responsible for US$24,915m or
48 per cent of the world total for consumer spending on video software. Japan
came a long way second with US$6,408m (12 per cent) (table 3.4). Together,
the top five territories alone accounted for nearly 80 per cent of the world total
spending on video software; the top ten accounted for 91 per cent. Aside from
Japan and Australia, all these territories were located in North America or Western Europe. In these territories, with the exception of Japan, spending on DVD
retail and rental accounts for shares of between 92.7 to 98.8 per cent. The

		Spending (US$m)	Share Spent On DVD (%)	Proportion of World Total (%)
1	USA	24,915	93.8	48.1
2	Japan	6,408	84.1	12.4
3	UK	4,973	96.8	9.6
4	Canada	2,483	93.3	4.8
5	France	2,465	98.6	4.8
6	Germany	2,099	97.1	4.1
7	Australia	1,347	96.4	2.6
8	Spain	917	97.2	1.7
9	Italy	880	92.7	1.7
10	Netherlands	623	98.8	1.2
11	Brazil	477	94.9	0.9
12	Sweden	429	91.8	0.8
13	Norway	424	97.2	0.8
14	Mexico	407	94.3	0.8
15	Belgium	398	99.3	0.8
16	Denmark	337	98.6	0.7
17	Switzerland	310	99.4	0.6
18	South Korea	224	74.1	0.4
19	Ireland	223	92.5	0.4
20	China	132	52.5	0.3

Source: adapted from *Screen Digest* (2006: 371).

Table 3.4 Leading National Markets for Video Software (2005)

porosity of video means software can get anywhere, but nevertheless it must be recognised that today the notion of a 'world' video market actually means the concentration of spending on DVD by a few territories predominantly clustered in two regional blocks.

While these figures represent the legitimate market in video software, the introduction of DVD had also resulted in massive rises in commercial piracy. This situation will be discussed later in Chapter 6.

Efforts to Build the DVD Market in Japan

Japan had been the pioneer market for the VCR and it once again took this role with the introduction of DVD. At the start of November 1996, DVD was launched in Japan when, on the same day, Toshiba released its SD-3000 DVD player, priced at ¥77,000 (US$690), and Matsushita brought out its DVD-A100 and A300 players, priced at ¥79,800 and ¥98,000 (US$715 and US$875) respectively. Players also went on sale that day in South Korea, where Samsung released its DVD-860 model, retailing at US$1,100 (*Screen Digest*, 1996: 276).

Initially, sales were far slower than had been anticipated. By the end of 1998, an estimated 300,000 to 500,000 players had been shipped to retailers, suggesting that the format was finding difficulty breaking out from the narrow niche of early adopters to the larger mainstream market (*Screen Digest*, 1998b: 255). A crucial factor hampering the launch of the new format in Japan was the lack of available DVD software titles. When the first players went on sale, only forty-six to sixty-seven DVD titles were available to Japanese consumers (*Screen Digest*, 1996: 273). By the end of 1997, the first full year DVD was on the market, there were still only an estimated 200 titles available, approximately half of which were pornographic, and by late 1999, 456 titles were available (*Screen Digest*, 1997c: 252, and 2000c: 348).

Several factors accounted for the lack of available software. A prolonged dispute between screenwriters and producers over royalty payments in the first years DVD was in the market prevented the release of many domestically produced titles. Foreign productions therefore accounted for over half the available titles, but with copy protection issues still to be resolved, most of the major Hollywood film companies were not releasing on the format. On 20 December 1996, Warner Home Video did publish its first four DVD titles in Japan: *Point of No Return* (aka *The Assassin*) (John Badham, 1993, US), *Blade Runner* (Ridley Scott, 1982, US), *Eraser* (Chuck Russell, 1996, US) and *The Fugitive* (Andrew Davis, 1993, US). However, the other Hollywood majors did not immediately follow Warner's lead. Frustrated by how the dearth of software was hampering sales of players, some hardware manufacturers turned to licensing and distributing films from the Hollywood majors. For example, in December

1997 the electronics company Pioneer began releasing titles under licence from Universal and in early 1998 reached a deal to license forty titles from Disney (*Screen Digest*, 1997a, and 1998b: 256).

Initially, the industry remained antipathetic towards the development of a DVD rental market, pushing the format instead towards retail sales. To promote DVD, in December 1997 Toshiba and Matsushita together invested ¥595.5m (US$4.56m) in software publisher Culture Publishers, a subsidiary of Culture Convenience Club and operator of Tsutaya, the largest video rental chain in Japan. A separate DVD division was created, with Toshiba and Matsushita owning equal 19.9 per cent shares and Culture Convenience holding the remainder. Also partnering in the venture was Gaga Communications, which had acquired the rights to forty-nine titles from Orion, the failing Hollywood producer-distributor, with plans to offer these for rental (Herskovitz, 1997). Sony's Picture Entertainment division, owner of the Columbia and TriStar film libraries, also announced that they planned to release titles for rental (*Screen Digest*, 1998a).

Growth in the installed base of DVD players improved from the second half of 1999 after cheaper models went on sale priced at ¥30,000–40,000 (US$280–375), approximately half the cost of earlier models. Home computers with DVD drives installed also became available. However, in March 2000, the launch of Sony's PlayStation 2 games console in Japan provided the most significant development. Following the introduction of the original PlayStation to the Japanese market at the end of 1994, Sony had challenged and eventually surpassed Nintendo to dominate the global video games market. Introducing the PlayStation 2 was therefore aimed at consolidating Sony's dominance. As part of the innovations included with the new model, the PlayStation 2 had DVD playback capability. Retailing at ¥39,800 (US$370), the PlayStation 2 combined the games console with a relatively cheap DVD player, and over the first two days PlayStation 2 was on the market, shipments to retailers reached nearly 1m units. Research during May 2000 by business information publisher Nihon Keizai Shimbun reported that 53 per cent of PlayStation 2 owners had bought up to five DVD titles since acquiring the console (*Screen Digest*, 2000c: 347).

Compared to the situation in the wealthy regions of North America and Western Europe, where DVD had been on the market for a shorter period of time, DVD hardware received a slow start in Japan. In 1999, Japan became the first territory to see the launch of DVD recorders, giving consumers the same functionality previously enjoyed with the VCR. Sales of DVD recorders began to drive growth in the hardware market, and by the end of 2003, six full years after the format went on sale in the territory, an estimated 10.4m homes in Japan owned a DVD player or recorder. This represented 22 per cent penetration of

TVHHs in the country compared to the 37.4m households who owned VCRs (79 per cent penetration) (*Screen Digest*, 2004: 337–8). DVD ownership therefore remained a long way behind the installed base of VCR owners. By the end of 2005, 21.4m homes in Japan owned a DVD player or recorder, representing 44 per cent of TVHHs. When compared to other leading industrialised nations, this was still relatively low, for by that time penetration rates had reached 73 per cent in the US, 72 per cent in the UK and 66 per cent in Australia. One reason given for this situation was that many Japanese consumers were using PlayStation 2 consoles as DVD drives rather than buying dedicated stand-alone players (*Screen Digest*, 2006: 372). As the country also had the highest average price (US$36.35) for a retail DVD anywhere in the world, Japanese consumers still hired many discs, although DVD retail did account for 64 per cent of total consumer spending on video software during 2005.

Dividing the World – Regional Coding

As part of their contribution to the development of DVD, the Hollywood majors insisted on the division of the global market for DVD into eight regions (table 3.5). By encoding discs to play only in restricted geographical markets, the majors could maintain the same patterns of staggered territorial releasing which structured worldwide theatrical exhibition. Regioning also protected distributors who licensed titles on a territorial basis and prevented sales in a territory where the distribution rights had not been sold. Furthermore, dividing the international market was also intended to present obstacles to the distribution of pirated copies around the world.

From the initial launch of DVD, hardware manufacturers and retailers in Hong Kong challenged regioning. They disabled zoning controls because they believed consumers would never buy DVD players if they were unable to play US or Japanese discs (Rayns, 2000). Distributors of DVDs in Hong Kong followed by omitting regional coding, resulting in region-free discs on sale not only in Hong Kong but in other countries as well. In this context, breaking the regioning controls was regarded as necessary to the dissemination and survival of the new medium.

Many other gaps also appeared in the regioning system. Purpose-built region-free or multi-region players immediately went on the market and single-region players could be 'chipped' (physically modified) or 'hacked' (through a special sequence of commands from the remote control) to play discs from any region (Harper, 1999: 20; Luh, 2001). Circumvention of regional coding was particularly prevalent in Europe, as bypassing the regioning system enabled consumers to play Region 1 DVDs available from the US, where titles were released earlier and often with better packages of extras (*Video Week*, 1998c). As regional cod-

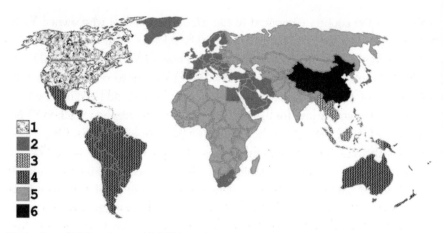

Regioning: dividing the world DVD market

ing detection was mandatory for DVD players but optional for discs, some distributors released region-free discs, classified as Region 0 (Leeds, 2003: 67).

For consumers, there were clear benefits to be gained from bypassing the regioning system. As distribution rights meant certain titles could be easily available in some territories and not others, by privately importing from foreign retailers, consumers could obtain titles unavailable in their own domestic market. Ironically, the DVD format itself actually encouraged and made possible parallel imports. As suggested in the previous chapter, DVD extras provided

Region	Territories
1	Canada, US
2	Western and Eastern Europe, Middle East, Egypt, Japan, South Africa
3	South-east Asia, East Asia (including Hong Kong)
4	Australia, New Zealand, Pacific Islands, Central America, Mexico, South America, Caribbean
5	Former Soviet Union, Indian Subcontinent, Africa, North Korea, Mongolia
6	China
7	Reserved
8	Special international venues (airplanes, cruise ships, etc.)

Source: adapted from Sendit.com (2005).

Table 3.5 The DVD Regioning System

one of the main attractions of the format. Between different territories, distributors put out different issues of the same title, with in some cases a foreign edition being supplemented by a richer and more generous array of extra features than was available on the local edition. The search for better packages of extras therefore encouraged consumers to look abroad. With the increased storage capacity of DVD, the inclusion of subtitling options and different language tracks also meant imported DVDs could be easily watched between regions.

Aside from the bypassing of technological controls, DVD regioning was also undermined by the rise of online retailing. Through online shopping, consumers could easily browse the availability and content of international editions and buy discs from other regions. Some online retailers – e.g. asianmv.com or hkflix.com – even specifically targeted parallel imports (p. 66). To counter loopholes in the regioning system, from late 2000 Warner Home Video and Columbia TriStar Home Entertainment introduced Regional Coding Enhancement (RCE), an additional layer of protection aimed at preventing Region 1 discs playing on multi-region and region-free players (Luh, 2001). Although RCE only affected some models of player and could be bypassed, it demonstrated a continuing commitment on the part of the Hollywood majors to impose controls segmenting the global market.

Regioning was intended to prevent the free-flow of DVD software between international territories. It was in many ways a new technological response to the mobility of video. However, the various mechanisms for bypassing regional coding, and the widespread willingness of consumers to use these precisely to circumvent the regioning system, demonstrated how the porosity of video persisted into the digital age.

VCD IN EAST ASIA

Due to the format's technological limitations (see previous chapter), VCD never captured a major market after it was launched in the US. Yet VCD became a popular video platform in East Asian territories. An enormous market for VCD emerged in China and the strong demand for Chinese-language films and television programmes on VCD led to the widespread adoption of the format in other Asian territories, including Hong Kong, Indonesia, Singapore and Taiwan (*Screen Digest*, 1997c: 251–4). In 2000, while VCR homes were believed to have reached 116m, an estimated 64m homes in the Asia-Pacific owned VCD players, representing 12 per cent penetration of television households across the region. The number of VCD homes in the region peaked at 81m in 2004 before falling to 77m the following year (*Screen Digest*, 2006: 371). Elsewhere in the Asia-Pacific, in Japan, Australia and New Zealand mature markets for VCRs already existed and VCD had no impact (*Screen Digest*, 2001: 374). VCD therefore established a base in markets left undeveloped by the VCR boom.

VCD provided the means for easy, low-cost duplication and the format fuelled a surge in the production of pirate and counterfeit discs. Large volumes of illegal recordings were sold in China, Hong Kong, Indonesia and Taiwan (see Chapter 6) alongside legitimate recordings. In his study of the VCD market in Hong Kong, Darrell Davis (2003) observes that VCDs have a ubiquitous presence, selling not only through major retailers such as Blockbuster, HMV and Tower Records but also in street markets. VCD became a popular medium in Hong Kong after 1996, when Japanese dramas or 'dorama' were recorded from satellite television, provided with Chinese subtitles and then imported and consumed by Hong Kong youth. With the growth of the market, VCD became a platform for a diverse range of audiovisual content, from feature films and television programmes to pornography, opera, documentary, karaoke and instructional titles.

Noting how the popularity of VCD in East Asia continued after the arrival of DVD, Davis regards VCDs as developing a distinctive and separate video market:

> VCDs are a 'glocal' technology . . . pervasive in Asia-Third World and all but invisible in North America, Western Europe and Japan. . . . they look like DVD and work like DVD. . . . But their versatility, de-territoriality, and above all, affordability are all pitched at specific local and ethnic markets. . . . VCDs could be regarded as the 'poor man's DVD', except that their widespread embrace fudges distinctions between high-tech, high-price DVD and their poor cousins. (p.166)

Following Davis's argument, it is a mistake to regard VCD as simply a precursor to DVD or an inferior version of DVD. Rather, the significance of VCD results from how it has represented an alternative popular video technology existing beyond the industries and markets which have cultivated the global dominance of the VCR or DVD. As Davis argues, 'VCDs in Asia undermine the distinctive technological and geographic identity – and superiority – carved out for DVD by manufacturers and media conglomerates' (p. 166).

VCD, DVD and SVCD in China

VCD was introduced to China through the karaoke market. According to China's largest electronics manufacturer, Xiamen Xiaxin Electronics (XXE), by November 1997 ownership of VCD players had surpassed VCRs in Chinese homes, with an estimated 50m VCD players in the country compared to 20m VCRs (*Screen Digest*, 1997c: 253). Local manufacturers dominated VCD hardware, producing 86 per cent of players in the country. Aggressive price-cutting rapidly reduced the price of players to as low as US$120, half the cost of a VCR.

By the end of 1997, over 10,000 VCD titles were on sale in China and the Ministry of Radio, Film and Television estimated software sales had reached 100m discs per annum.

In the late 1990s, post offices provided the main infrastructure for the VCD rental business. Chinese films and programmes made up the majority of VCD titles and local distributors were the leading suppliers. A few foreign titles were available and Warner Home Video became the first US distributor to supply VCD titles: the Hollywood distributor released fourteen initial titles, with *The Bodyguard* (Mick Jackson, 1992, US) and *The Fugitive* proving early hits. On average, local titles cost US$1 each, while Warner titles were priced at US$3–5.

DVD was introduced to China in 1997. Consumers were already familiar with the idea of watching video on disc and backwards compatibility ensured that existing VCD discs could run on DVD players. Compared to the limited DVD releases in Japan, the large number of legal and illegal VCD titles available meant that the Chinese market was already supplied with a wealth of software titles. Software providers, in particular the Hollywood majors, were keen for DVD to catch on in China, for they believed that the complexities and costs involved with DVD reproduction would stem the rampant piracy which resulted from VCD in the territory. China was therefore potentially better prepared than most other territories for the adoption of DVD. However, DVD faced a difficult entry to the Chinese market. DVD players were too expensive for consumers and problems arose from a shortage of software titles. As the Region 6 coding was reserved for China alone, Chinese DVD players could not easily play imported discs, and while VCDs could run on DVD players, pirated VCDs frequently presented problems. Due to the supremacy of VCD, it was difficult for DVD to initially find a foothold. Three years after the original basic VCD standard was introduced, it was estimated that the format had been adopted by 5 per cent of television households in the Asia-Pacific. DVD, however, had penetrated less than 1 per cent of television homes in the region over an equivalent period (*Screen Digest*, 2001: 376). By 2005, however, DVD accounted for over half of the US$132m spent by consumers on video software that year (table 3.4) (*Screen Digest*, 2006: 371).

Simultaneous with the introduction of DVD, government backing for a competing local format also caused some confusion in the market. In September 1998, the Chinese government endorsed the new Super VCD (SVCD) as the official Chinese format. SVCD had been developed by a committee of manufacturers supported by the government. Jukka Aho (2001) suggests that the government's intentions were to prevent the dependency of the domestic electronics industry on a standard developed and controlled by the foreign interests of the DVD Forum. Most DVD players in the Chinese market were produced by domestic manufacturers, who had to pay licensing fees to the foreign owners of DVD patents. These became a contentious issue, as many Chinese manufacturers considered the fees to be excessive. Development of SVCD was therefore not only a matter of national pride, 'an opportunity to flex some technical muscle, and to send a message to the outside world that China has enough critical mass to . . . ignore foreign entertainment standards it does not want to conform to', but it was believed that the home-grown standard could also put pressure on the DVD Forum to lower licensing fees for the Chinese territory.

Initially, three projects embarked on creating an enhanced VCD standard (Aho, 2001; Brent, 1998). Under the instruction of the Chinese Ministry of Information Industry (MII), the China National Committee of Standards worked at developing SVCD. Meanwhile, Philips, Sony, Matsushita and JVC formed the Video CD Consortium to develop their own second-generation video CD format, High-Quality Video CD (HQ-VCD), based on the original White Book standard. However, US company C-Cube Microsystems, a subcontractor in China supplying MPEG decoder chipsets for VCD players, worked with Chinese hardware manufacturers and in May 1998 launched Chinese Video Disc (CVD).

Angered by what they regarded as foreign interference by C-Cube, and faced with the prospects of seeing their attempts to create a national standard being surpassed, the Chinese government agreed to back the HQ-VCD Consortium on the understanding that elements from both HQ-VCD and SVCD would become integrated in a single standard. Yet with the major VCD manufacturers already backing and producing under the CVD standard, the Department of Science and Technology together with the Ministry of Information Industry brokered an agreement across the various parties enabling compatibility between CVD and SVCD. The resulting standard retained the SVCD name but also became known as ChaoJi VCD.

SVCD also received the backing of domestic hardware manufacturers keen to protect the share of the market they had won through the production of VCD players. Using the same MPEG-2 compression standard as DVD, but with lower resolution, SVCD offered sharper pictures than VCD but was incompatible with the earlier standard. DVD delivered better-quality images and the addition of extras but SVCD players were priced considerably lower than DVD machines: SVCD players cost up to US$150 compared to prices of US$250 or higher for DVD (*Screen Digest*, 1998b: 256).

SVCD went on sale at the end of 1998 and by 1999 an estimated 7m SVCD players had been sold, far lower than government expectations. Lack of available software impeded adoption – by 1999, only 100–200 legitimate titles were available – and it was believed that the absence of copyright protection for the SVCD standard indicated the presumption and official acceptance that pirated software should largely supply the market. Yet many illegal producers appeared unwilling to change over their operations from VCD to the new format, thereby limiting the range of available software (*Screen Digest*, 1999: 296). Sales of SVCD remained confined to Asia and players were released commercially in China, Hong Kong, Malaysia, Thailand, Singapore and India. Consequently, despite government backing for SVCD, the Chinese market remained strongly committed to VCD.

Licensing fees for DVD continued to be a cause for complaint among domestic manufacturers, and the Chinese government tried again to nurture a domestic standard by launching Enhanced Video Disc (EVD) in November 2003. While EVD failed to capture a market, interest in the format was revived towards the end of 2006 as Chinese manufacturers, disgruntled by the issue of licensing fees, placed their support behind EVD and announced they would halt DVD production by 2008. The timing of these developments followed the launch by Sony and Toshiba earlier in the year of the new high-definition DVD formats Blu-ray and HD-DVD in foreign territories. While not immediately available in China, inevitably these formats are destined for the national market, and so for Chinese manufacturers EVD represents the opportunity to unite and free themselves from the burden of licensing fees paid for foreign patents as DVD moves into its next generation. Yet if the SVCD example is anything to go by, EVD may be a bold but short-lived initiative.

CONCLUSION

As the adoption and use of VCRs spread beyond the industrialised world and to developing nations, so the technology was regarded by some commentators as another symbol of Western cultural imperialism. As Christine Ogan (1985) commented, 'the VCR has taken on a value in developing countries. It is the value of the content imported ... from the West' (p. 2). The same could be said of DVD. But as critics of the cultural imperialism thesis have frequently noted, such conclusions are largely based on assertion rather than evidence. Equally, whether considering the VCR, DVD or mass communications in general, the complexity of responses which greets media technologies and artefacts mean they can never be simply accepted as direct transmitters of cultural values.

Certainly, there is a hegemonic structure to the global video business. The axis of Japanese hardware and Hollywood software has influenced technological development and transnational conditions of supply in the market. Economic factors have also ensured that the video market has become unevenly distributed between high-, middle- and low-income economies. Yet the destinies of video media are not fixed at the point of design, production or circulation. VCRs and cassettes, and now VCD or DVD players and discs, have achieved global ubiquity because of their mobility and flexibility. The dencentralising porous character of video media has resulted in hardware and software becoming filtered into multiple contexts of commerce, use and consumption which continually transform the value, utility and meaning of video media.

4

Hollywood Home Entertainment: Controlling and Profiting from Video Software

Alongside Japan's technological leadership in consumer electronics, the Hollywood film industry is the other key influence in the global video business. Since the establishment of the VCR as a mass consumer medium in the late 1970s, Hollywood has remained the largest supplier of popular filmed entertainment for home video in the North American and international markets. Hollywood's influence is not confined to providing content for video software: as discussed in Chapter 2, MCA, the parent of Universal, was instrumental in the development of Laserdisc, and the Hollywood corporations played a crucial role in bringing about industry agreement on a unified standard for DVD. As the next chapter shows, those same companies are now playing a key role in launching the next generation of video formats and online delivery systems.

Over successive decades, 'Hollywood' has stood not only for a place – the geographic and industrial agglomeration at the centre of the film business in the US – but also for the oligopoly of major media corporations whose presence extends across the world into networks of distribution and production for films and television programming. Today, the Hollywood film industry is owned by a consolidated core of diversified media corporations. The film and television operations of these companies are subsumed under labyrinthine divisional structures. These media conglomerates not only operate in film production and distribution but also in other sectors of the media industries, including newspaper and book publishing, recorded music and music publishing, video games, cable channels, network television and online services. So, although the leading Hollywood companies are often labelled 'studios', this is something of a misnomer for organisations whose operations extend well beyond the function of making films which is conventionally understood to be the work of a studio. They are integrated financier-producer-distributors and as they dominate the film business not only in the US and overseas, collectively they represent 'the majors'.

When the VCR was launched in the mid-1970s, six companies dominated Hollywood: Columbia, MGM, Paramount, 20th Century-Fox, Universal and

Warner Bros. As members of the trade organisation the Motion Picture Association of America (MPAA) and its overseas arm the Motion Picture Association (MPA), these companies were able to mount a collective voice to lobby the US or international governments and other agencies to promote and protect their interests. The market for home video in the US emerged during a period of significant change for the Hollywood film industry. During the 1970s, as MGM cut back on production and its assets were bought, broken up and progressively sold off, the company lost its place among the majors. With the launch of Home Box Office (HBO) in 1972, pay-cable television also broke the 'bottleneck' of the three national networks (Hilmes, 1990), opening new channels for delivering filmed entertainment to the home and providing the Hollywood majors with additional outlets for their product. Most significant in the reshaping of Hollywood, however, was the process of conglomeration. A wave of conglomeration had started in the 1960s when the major film companies were bought by larger corporations who folded Hollywood film production and distribution into their widely diversified portfolios of assets. In the 1980s, however, as media and communication markets represented greater potential for growth than other business sectors, so these conglomerates divested themselves of various assets, leaving the Hollywood companies part of conglomerate structures with portfolios more tightly concentrated on media and communication operations (Prince, 2000).

Further changes in ownership occurred from the mid-1980s and into the 90s. News Corporation took over 20th Century-Fox in 1985 and four years later Time Inc. acquired Warner Bros. Paramount was sold to the television syndication company Viacom in 1994 and the following year Disney acquired ABC/Capital Cities. Links between Hollywood and the Japanese electronics industry were also formed as Sony bought Columbia in 1989. A year later, Matsushita acquired MCA, the parent company of Universal, which subsequently changed hands twice more before it was bought in 2004 by GE, which integrated Universal with their ownership of the NBC network. Meanwhile, after reversing the fortunes of its film operations, from the mid-1980s Disney came to occupy a place among the major companies in Hollywood. A new producer-distributor, DreamWorks, was also launched in 1994 with ambitions of joining the majors. As a result of these developments, today six companies dominate the Hollywood film industry, each of which are owned by a larger parent company: Walt Disney Studios (the Walt Disney Company), Columbia Pictures, which is part of Sony Pictures Entertainment (Sony), 20th Century-Fox Film Corporation (News Corporation), Paramount Pictures (Viacom, which in 2006 also acquired DreamWorks), Universal Pictures (NBC-Universal) and Warner Bros. Pictures (Time Warner).

Video therefore emerged as a medium for popular entertainment against the background of changes which shaped the modern Hollywood film industry. While the VCR opened up an entirely new window for Hollywood films, the stance of the majors towards video was deeply contradictory. On the one hand, Hollywood resisted and rejected video. Certain companies complained that home video recording presented a threat which infringed copyright, while there was a strong consensus across the whole of Hollywood that video rental prevented rights holders from sharing in revenues from rental transactions. Hollywood therefore greeted video with suspicion. On the other hand, as the video market boomed during the 1980s, video rental and retail emerged as the main revenue stream for Hollywood, surpassing earnings from the theatrical box office and all television windows. And so, by the end of the decade, Hollywood had learnt to welcome video.

Janet Wasko (1994: 129) accurately describes the contradictoriness of these responses when she regards Hollywood as adopting a 'schizophrenic attitude towards video'. This chapter focuses on this contradictory response. After discussing the formation of the video business in the US, the chapter outlines how Hollywood resisted and then embraced video. Although it is correct to see Hollywood as divided over how to deal with the arrival of video, the twin responses of rejecting and welcoming the new medium were both focused on the same issue: how could video be controlled to generate profits? Hollywood did not want to reject video totally – it simply wanted to find ways of making video lucrative. The story of Hollywood's relationship to video is therefore the tale of how Hollywood took control of video to make it profitable.

THE FORMATION OF THE VIDEO BUSINESS IN THE US

After Betamax was launched in Japan, Sony introduced the format to the US in 1976 and RCA brought VHS onto the US market in 1977. Japan was the leading producer of VCRs and by the end of the 1970s, Japanese homes represented the largest national VCR population in the world, yet by the early 1980s, the US had emerged as the largest consumer market for video hardware. Research studies arrived at conflicting accounts of VCR penetration. According to Nielsen Media Research, by 1985 an estimated 23m homes in the US owned a VCR, penetrating 27 per cent of television households (TVHHs) (table 4.1). The Electronics Industries Association (EIA) placed the figure higher at 35 per cent of TVHHs (Klopfenstein, 1989: 25). From the late 1980s, a large volume of sales were accounted for by replacement VCRs, as consumers exchanged their original machines for newer models.

As the VCR population grew, economies of scale saw the factory price of a VCR unit fall, resulting in significant reductions in average retail prices: when

Betamax was introduced in 1976, the average factory price stood at US$862.30, while the retail price averaged US$2,300. By 1985, the factory price was down to US$401.88 and retail prices averaged US$450 (p. 28). US manufacturers aligned with the respective formats. Machines were not manufactured in the US but American companies sold them under their own labels: Zenith, Toshiba, Sears and Sanyo supported Betamax; RCA, Matsushita's Panasonic label, Magnavox, GE, Quasar, JVC, Curtes Mathes, Sylvania, Admiral and Philco were behind VHS (see Chapter 1).

By 1979, VHS was already showing signs of having won the format war: in a sixteen-city survey by Media Statistics Inc., VHS accounted for 57.2 per cent of VCRs in use (Nulty, 1979: 112). Matsushita's OEM arrangement with RCA and

	TV Households	VCR Households	VCR Penetration
	(m)	(m)	(% TVHHs)
2005	110.2	97.7	88.7
2004	109.6	98.9	90.2
2003	108.4	98.4	90.8
2002	106.7	97.6	91.5
2001	105.5	96.2	91.2
2000	102.2	88.1	86.2
1999	100.8	85.8	85.1
1998	99.4	84.1	84.6
1997	98.0	80.4	82.0
1996	95.9	78.8	82.2
1995	95.4	75.8	79.5
1994	94.2	72.8	77.3
1993	93.1	71.7	77.0
1992	93.1	70.4	75.6
1991	92.0	67.5	73.3
1990	93.1	65.4	70.2
1989	92.1	62.3	67.6
1988	90.0	56.2	62.2
1987	88.6	45.8	51.7
1986	87.4	32.5	37.2
1985	86.1	23.5	27.3
1984	85.3	15.0	17.6
1983	84.2	8.3	9.9
1982	83.7	4.8	5.7
1981	81.9	2.5	3.1
1980	78.0	1.9	2.4

Sources: Nielsen Media Research data reported in MPA (2002: 27; and 2006f: 27) and MPAA (1998).

Table 4.1 VCR Penetration in the US (1980–2005)

many other major domestic electronics manufacturers ensured that VHS prevailed as the dominant format. *Video Week* reported that Betamax was accounting for only 17 per cent of the market in 1984 and two years later that proportion had fallen to only 5 per cent. Similar estimates by *Television Digest* reported that the VCR market was divided 45/55 per cent between Beta/VHS in 1979 but the imbalance grew to 2/98 per cent by 1986. In 1987, the year before Sony announced it was commencing VHS production, Betamax was believed to hold a mere 1 per cent share of the US market (Klopfenstein, 1989: 28). Alongside its broad base of support among US electronics companies, VHS became the dominant format because of the longer recording time which RCA insisted on, together with lower average retail prices and a greater number of titles available on pre-recorded cassettes. Videodisc systems from MCA, Magnavox and RCA were the product of home-grown engineering but these came and went without making any impact on the direction of the hardware market (see Chapter 2).

During the 1990s, the growth in VCR sales slowed but significant increases still occurred in the number of homes owning VCRs. In 1990, Nielsen Media Research estimated 65.4m households owned VCRs, penetrating 70 per cent of TVHHs; by 2000, that figure had increased to over 88m, representing 86 per cent of TVHHs (table 4.1).

Video Entrepreneurs

As the installed base of VCRs grew and the format battle was worked out, other commercial developments opened up a complementary market for the rental and retailing of pre-recorded videocassette software in the US. Sony, JVC, Matsushita and a smaller number of other VCR manufacturers were at the core of the video hardware business but these companies had no involvement in the software side of video. The formation of the software market, however, brought a large array of audiovisual producers and distributors, video duplicators, video rental outlets and retailers of entertainment products into the video business. Video software therefore expanded the number and range of participants who counted as part of the video business. While the long-standing power of the Hollywood oligopoly dominated the theatrical film business, the formation of the video software industry took place largely without the involvement of the major film companies. Instead it was small-scale entrepreneurs with little experience of working in media industries who saw fresh commercial opportunities in the new medium of the VCR.

In the late 1970s, with the VCR population still largely confined to early adopters, pornography became the predominant form of film material available on pre-recorded cassette in the US. At the start of the decade, an extensive network of adult theatres already existed for showing pornographic features. With the commercial success of *Deep Throat* (Gerard Damiano, 1972, US), followed by *Behind the Green Door* (Artie and Jim Mitchell, 1972, US) and *The Devil in Miss Jones* (Gerard Damiano, 1973, US), hard-core feature films were surpassing Hollywood features at the box office. However, this new visibility for pornography was met with moral and legal reaction aimed at outlawing the theatrical presentation of hard-core films (Lewis, 2002). Consequently, video arrived at just the right time for the adult industry as porn moved out of the theatre and into the home. Pornography dominated the emergent software market in the early 1980s. Nearly all adult titles were video transfers of theatrically released X-rated films. As video became so successful for the adult industry, it provided the final nail in the coffin of the adult theatre business.

With the arrival of the VCR in the late 1970s, producers, distributors and exhibitors of adult films represented one grouping of early video entrepreneurs as they became the first large-scale suppliers and retailers of titles on videocassette. Arthur or 'Art' Morowitz, for example, had started producing and distributing X-rated features in the 1960s, before buying a chain of mainly adult theatres. In July 1978, he began selling X-rated films on cassettes in the lobby of one of his theatres, priced at US$99.50. After these sales proved popular, in 1979 Morowitz opened his store, Video Shack, next door to an adult theatre at 49th Street and Broadway in Manhattan. Adult titles were placed on sale alongside mainstream films. Building on the success of his first store, Morowitz began expanding to other sites, with Video Shacks in the Upper East Side of Manhattan, Paramus, NJ, and Scarsdale, NY (Schwartz, 1981).

As the video market grew during the 1980s, pornography began to lose its place at the forefront of the video software business. Video provided the makers of adult films with a new low-cost production technology, and videotape soon replaced film as the preferred medium of the adult industry. For example, in 1986, adult films could be made on video for as little as US$5,000–10,000 each and that year around 1,600 adult titles were released (Kristof, 1986). However, this had the effect of swamping the market with a glut of poor-quality material. Outside the adult industry, as more producers and distributors, including the Hollywood majors, began to release films for the video market, consumers were also offered an ever-increasing number and variety of popular films and other categories of mainstream entertainment. As the choice of titles broadened, pornography became just one category among a diversifying set of options for video entertainment.

Morowitz's enterprise was representative of what became the general destiny of adult entertainment during the founding years of the software market. Initially, adult titles comprised the majority of sales at Video Shack but as more mainstream titles became available, so sales of adult titles declined. With the general difficulties of defining pornography, it was impossible for the video rental business to accurately gauge just how large the adult market was, but one estimate in 1978 judged that adult titles accounted for up to 70 per cent of rentals and sales, with rental transactions exceeding sales of retail units by an estimated ratio of 12:1. By the early 1980s, however, that share had fallen, with differing estimates placing pornography at anywhere between 20 and 50 per cent of the market (*New York Times*, 1982).

While adult entertainment played a central role in establishing the video software business in the US, other entrepreneurial ventures were directed towards bringing more mainstream film entertainment to consumers. A first step toward the full entry of the Hollywood majors into the video software market came after Andre Blay arrived at an agreement with Fox to release the company's titles through his company Magnetic Video Corporation (MVC). Since 1969, Blay had built a successful business in the Farmington Hills suburb of Detroit for distributing and servicing audio and video equipment. Prior to entering video retail, Blay sold 8-track tapes and low-budget records through direct mail marketing and was involved in duplication and audio production. To explore the possibility of launching a business for selling feature films on cassette, Blay wrote to all the Hollywood majors enquiring about licensing films for video retail. Only Fox replied with positive interest and a contract was signed in July 1977. Blay paid Fox an advance of US$300,000, plus a minimum of US$500,000 a year against a royalty of US$7.50 for each cassette sold. Fox offered Blay a list of 100 pre-1972 titles, previously sold to network television. Blay was permitted to choose fifty titles from the list, on which he could hold non-exclusive rights for three years (Klain, 1977; Lardner, 1987: 172). Blay's first selections included *Patton* (Franklin J. Schaffner, 1970, US), *The French Connection* (William Friedkin, 1971, US) and *M*A*S*H* (Robert Altman, 1970, US). Tapes went on sale through retail outlets priced at US$49.95. MVC also experimented by launching a direct mail division, the Video Club of America, which for a one-time membership fee of US$10 entitled members to purchase tapes for 20 per cent below the list price. Expanding the sources of supply, MVC made deals with other distributors, including Viacom, Lew Grade and Avco Embassy (Lardner, 1987: 174). A little under a year after the start of retailing, due to the success of the venture, in November 1978 Fox announced it would buy out MVC for US$7.2m cash (*Variety*, 1978). Fox used the company to form its own video distribution subsidiary while retaining Blay to head the operation.

Schemes for renting films to watch in the home had existed in the US since the Home P-K and Pathéscope (see Chapter 1), but film rental boomed with the VCR. George Atkinson, a small businessman in Los Angeles, is often credited as the founding figure of the video rental business. Through his company, Home Theater Systems, Atkinson had been distributing Super-8 films for parties when he began buying videocassettes in 1977 to rent through his LA store. Renters joined a video club for US$50 a year and rented films for US$10 per day. After helping a further store owner to establish his own business in Pasadena, Atkinson began to franchise his rental store concept, building a chain of Video Station outlets. Video rental was a easy business to enter. New businesses could be set up quickly with a relatively small capital outlay in the region of US$10,000 to buy a modest inventory of 200 Beta and VHS cassettes. Video rental therefore prompted a wave of entrepreneurial activity as hundreds of first-time business people opened small stores:

> Americans from every imaginable walk of life cracked open their nest eggs, re-mortgaged their homes, and put the arm on their parents, siblings, and in-laws in order to become the proud proprietors of Video Castles, Connections, Corners, Hutches, Huts, Palaces, Patches, Places, Shacks, Sheds, Sources, Spots and Stations. (Lardner, 1987: 180)

In its founding years, the video software business in the US therefore developed outside the conventional film industry. Video provided a field of entrepreneurial activity as the adult entertainment industry and small-scale entrepreneurs established the rental and retail infrastructure which brought pre-recorded cassettes to US consumers.

HOLLYWOOD'S RESISTANCE TO VIDEO

For the first few years after the introduction of the VCR, the Hollywood companies withheld their films from video. Fox's licensing of films to Magnetic was uncharacteristic of the attitude among the majors. They had two main reservations about video. From the 1950s onwards, the majors had witnessed the impact which the popularisation of television had on the theatrical box office and they feared video would have a similar deleterious effect on the value of filmed entertainment. With the VCR, it was possible that films aired on television could be recorded, duplicated and then possibly sold. Releasing films on cassette also increased the chances of illegal copying.

A further cause for concern was the legal obstacle of the 'first sale doctrine' which the majors believed shut them out from participating in revenues from rental turns. Coming into effect during the same year as the VCR was introduced in the US, the *1976 Copyright Act* played a decisive role in clarifying the legal status of home recording and was important in determining the conduct of the video rental market. Before revision in 1976, the original *1909 US Copyright Act* allowed anyone who purchased a copy of a copyright work to then transfer or dispose of that copy as they wished. As the rights of the original owner ended when the copy was initially sold, this part of the Act became known as the first sale doctrine. When the Act was revised, the same principle was extended to include anyone who lawfully owned the copy, regardless of whether it was purchased or not. According to section 109 of the 1976 Act, 'the owner of a particular copy . . . is entitled, without the authority of the copyright owner, to sell or otherwise dispose of the possession of that copy' (US Copyright Office, 2003: 22).

As rental became a crucial part of the video software business, the first sale doctrine drove a barrier between film distributors such as the Hollywood companies and the public circulation of their properties on cassette. Since the early twentieth century, film exhibition in the US had relied upon a business model whereby distributors held the rights to exploit film properties in the market and leased prints to exhibitors in return for an agreed proportion of the box office. Distributors therefore participated in a share of revenues from each ticket transaction. Due to the first sale doctrine, however, video retail and rental could legally operate by a different model. Rights holders, for example film distributors, sold duplicated cassettes to wholesalers, who then sold on the cassettes to retailers and rental outlets. This two-step process was more in line with practice in the recorded music business than the film industry and it meant that the rights holder only received revenues from sales of cassettes to wholesalers and not when those cassettes were subsequently sold to retailers or rentailers. Even if cassettes were sold directly to retailers and rental outlets, the distributor could only expect revenues from the first sale. With retail sales, this was not an issue, because a distributor would not expect to see any return beyond the wholesale price. In the video rental business, however, cassettes were used to generate further revenues. Unlike the leasing of prints for theatrical exhibition, video rentailers owned the cassettes they bought and were free to use those tapes for whatever purpose they wished. Cassettes could be hired by customers over repeated rental 'turns' but distributors were not entitled to share in those transactions.

As the video business matured and Hollywood became the largest supplier of film titles to the market, the major companies were unable to bypass the first sale doctrine and regarded rentals as lost revenues. In response to these issues, Hollywood therefore launched a two-pronged attack against video. Starting in 1976, Universal embarked on a prolonged legal action against Sony aimed at blocking use of the VCR for home recording. Other major Hollywood distributors also attempted to implement business models which would allow them to share in the revenues from rental transactions.

Universal vs. the VCR

Universal, together with Disney, quickly assumed a combative stance against the VCR, taking Sony to court by claiming that the introduction of the VCR infringed copyright. When Betamax was launched on the US market, Sony had hired advertising agency Doyle, Dane and Bernbach (DD&B) to promote the new technology. DD&B ran a campaign focused on the time-shift possibilities of the VCR, with ads announcing 'What in the world are we doing to ourselves? Our lives are being governed to too great an extent by TV schedules' (quoted in Wasser, 2001: 83). Later, RCA would market its VHS SelectaVision machines with the slogan 'Now you can have the best television. Whenever you want it', and Zenith's VCRs were promoted with copy promising 'Now you can make the TV schedule fit your schedule' (quoted in Shales, 1977). Each campaign hailed the time-shift function of the VCR for the greater control it granted to the viewer, but that control conflicted with the interests of rights holders to protect the circulation and use of their works. Once recorded, a film or television programme could be freely passed between members of the public, copied and maybe sold. Equally, in the context of the commercial model on which US broadcasting was based, home recording and time-shifting liberated but also diverted audiences from the highly organised schema of the schedules, which were aimed at drawing viewers to advertising: instead of recording and watching ads, viewers could stop and start recordings to omit ads or otherwise ignore these by 'zipping' through them when watching on playback. As Frederick Wasser (2001: 87) notes, the 'VCR was allowing the audience to become nomadic, upsetting the billion-dollar industry devoted to pinning it down'.

While these possibilities were potentially issues for broadcasters and all holders of copyrighted works shown on television, only Universal and Disney were quick to take action against what they saw as the threat of home recording and time-shifting. As Wasser points out, both companies had particular interests in combating home recording (p. 4). Universal was not only one of the major Hollywood film producer-distributors but was also a division of MCA, a diversified media conglomerate which was a leading producer and distributor of television programming in the US. MCA/Universal had a strong interest in protecting works broadcast on television because the company earned more revenues from television sales than any of the other Hollywood majors. Universal was not entirely against home video, only the VCR. MCA initiated the DiscoVision venture (see Chapter 2) and so wanted to see a video business built only around pre-recorded software without the home-recording facility which the VCR permitted.

In the late 1970s, Disney was still one of the smaller companies in Hollywood but after diversifying in the mid-1950s into television production and theme parks, revenues from filmed entertainment diminished in their importance for the company. Nevertheless, to a large extent the identity of Disney and its diversified operations still rested on the legacy and value of the classic animated feature films produced by the company over several decades. To protect the longevity of its animated features and address new generations of child audiences, Disney had established the practice of periodically re-releasing its classics to theatres at intervals of several years before withdrawing them from circulation. By withholding films from the market, Disney could engineer and cultivate demand over successive generations of children, but this system could not work if those films were always and widely available on cassette.

In November 1976, at the Federal District Court of the Central District of California, the co-plaintiffs filed a suit for copyright infringement against Sony as the manufacturer of VCRs, together with DD&B, a number of Betamax retailers and William Griffiths, an individual Betamax user who allegedly had used his machine to make copies of programmes recorded from television (Bettig, 1996: 159). At the time the case was heard, the Copyright Act had only recently been revised. Section 106 of the 1976 Act protected exclusive rights over copyrighted works, granting the rights to reproduce, prepare derivative works, distribute and publicly perform or display works (US Copyright Office, 2003: 16). Section 107, however, limited these rights: 'the fair use of a copyrighted work ..., for purposes such as criticism, comment, news reporting, teaching ..., scholarship, or research is not an infringement of copyright' (p. 18). To assess fair use, the Act set out four considerations: the purpose and character of the use; the nature of the copyrighted work; the amount of the work copied; and the economic impact of copying. Particular uses of copyrighted works were therefore permitted without the authorisation of the owner or payment of compensation. Universal and Disney claimed that off-air recording did not qualify as fair use according to the four tests but represented an infringement of copyright. Sony, the plaintiffs argued, was contributing to that infringement by manufacturing the technology which made taping possible. In filing the suit, Ronald Bettig describes Universal and Disney as seeking 'relief in the form of damages, an equitable accounting of profits, and an injunction against the manufacture and marketing of the Betamax VCR within the United States' (1996: 159).

In October 1979, Judge Warren Ferguson ruled against the plaintiffs. In reaching this decision, Judge Ferguson accepted that home taping was fair use, as recording was conducted by individuals and families in private for the convenience of watching entertainment in the home. As Sony did not directly oversee use of VCRs, Judge Ferguson also ruled that the company could not be held liable for contributory infringement (p. 160). Two years later, the decision was reversed by the Court of Appeals, who ruled that video recording of television broadcasts did not satisfy the tests for fair use and so should be considered an infringement of copyright. Sony in turn appealed this decision, taking the case to the Supreme Court, which in January 1984 voted to overturn the appeal court's decision and support the original ruling. The Supreme Court decided home taping was an instance of fair use because it satisfied the four tests: recording was for non-commercial purposes; copyright owners had already sold their works to broadcasters for showing to audiences for free; copying the entirety of a work was traditionally accepted under the fair use doctrine; and copyright owners had failed to demonstrate the economic harm of recording (pp. 176–7).

Following the Betamax case, home recording could not be outlawed. Video was set to stay and the Hollywood majors would have to accept it. Instead of stopping video, the question therefore became how could video be most effectively controlled and turned into a source of profit?

Attempts to Manage Rentals

Once established, the video software business in the US saw rental revenues exceeding sales. Frustrated by what they saw as lost revenues from rental transactions, between 1979 and 1985 the Hollywood companies introduced four key strategies aimed at controlling the rental market (Wasser, 2001: 110–16). Fox had included an anti-rental provision in their original 1977 contract with Magnetic, and other companies followed suit, but by 1981 these contractual prohibitions were phased out, as they proved impossible to enforce. A second option involved establishing partnerships with retailers to form rental networks or otherwise to lease tapes to outlets. Between 1979 and 1982, Paramount created a partnership with the photo service chain Fotomat for renting tapes through the company's national network of kiosks, but as customers had to advance-order tapes through a catalogue for collection the next day, the venture lost out to conventional rental outlets where customers could browse and immediately take a tape. Meanwhile, in 1980 Disney introduced a scheme for leasing tapes to rentailers and similar plans were established the following year by Warner, Fox and MGM (Lardner, 1987: 192–6; Wasser, 2001: 111–12). While the detail of these plans differed, each involved rentailers paying the major distributors to lease tapes for periods of weeks or months, during which time the tape could be rented out for repeated turns.

These schemes were popular with the majors because the distributor retained ownership of the leased stock, imitating the form of accepted practice found in theatrical exhibition. Rentailers, however, were unhappy with the terms set by the majors, together with the additional paperwork involved with administering the leasing plans and the fact that leasing prevented them from owning their inventory of tapes, which represented a major asset for rentailers. In some cases, the terms set demanded payment of 50 per cent of rental revenues to the distributor. As the rental business was still at an early stage of development and based mainly on small family-run companies, many rentailers regarded the terms imposed by the majors as preventing them from running a profitable business (Wasser, 2001: 112). Warner, in particular, antagonised rentailers by proposing to recall titles currently on sale so that they could be reissued for rental only (Lardner, 1987: 194). To protect their collective interests against the power of the majors, at the Consumer Electronics Show in January 1982 rentailers formed the Video Software Dealers Association (VSDA) and Video Software Retailers of America (VSRA), which later merged as the VSDA (p. 199).

Rather than giving the majors a share of the rental market, the leasing plans served to bring rentailers together as a collective body to oppose the schemes, and by 1982 these plans had been withdrawn. Although the majors backed off, they still continued to harbour hopes of introducing a scheme which allowed them to participate in the rental business, and the leasing schemes of the early 1980s prefigured the revenue-sharing arrangements which became widely accepted during the late 1990s (see next chapter).

As a third option, the majors unsuccessfully lobbied Congress through the MPAA for an exemption from the first sale doctrine. As the Hollywood companies could not therefore participate in rental transactions or bypass the first sale doctrine, as a final strategy they fell back on the only remaining option – raising the price of cassettes. Towards the end of 1981, Paramount placed surcharges of up to US$10 on cassettes (Wasser, 2001: 115–16).

HOLLYWOOD EMBRACES VIDEO

At the same time as the Hollywood majors were actively trying to stop home recording and bring the video rental business under their control, they were also establishing their own operations to handle video distribution. Between 1977 and 1981, all the majors entered video distribution in three different ways. Fox's 1977 agreement with Magnetic was based on a form of subsidiary distribution: Fox supplied the films, Magnetic did the distribution. In 1978/9, Warner became the first of the major Hollywood companies to launch its own in-house video division, followed over the next year by Columbia, Paramount and Disney. In 1981, MCA/Universal was still embroiled in its lengthy battle against home recording but this did not stop it from establishing a video division that year. A third option involved the formation of a distribution partnership for video. Fox formed its own video division out of Magnetic and in 1982 this was folded into a partnership with CBS. Previously, in 1980, Metro-Goldywn-Mayer had linked up with CBS for video distribution, but after the company acquired United Artists in 1982 the partnership with CBS was dissolved as MGM/UA formed its own video distribution operation. After running its own division for two years, in 1981 Columbia formed a partnership with RCA. In 1991, both the CBS/Fox and RCA/Columbia ventures were dissolved as the relevant Hollywood companies set up their own divisions (Prince, 2000: 102; Wasser, 2001: 95–6).

Sell-through

After Hollywood failed in its efforts to control video rental, the majors began to actively promote a consumer market for video sales (Bettig, 1996: 179–80). Key to this promotion was the reduction of retail prices to stimulate consumer sales. At the start of the 1980s, the price of cassettes remained high, averaging in the region of US$80 to US$90 per unit. Among the majors, Paramount led the initiative to reduce prices and encourage high-volume consumer sales. When the company released *Star Trek: The Motion Picture* (Robert Wise, 1979, US) on video in 1980, cassettes sold at the high price of US$79.95. Two years later, with the video release of *Star Trek II: The Wrath of Khan* (Nicholas Meyer, 1982, US), Paramount experimented by reducing the retail price to US$39.95. After *Star Trek II* sold 290,000 units, Paramount released further titles at the same price, including *An Officer and a Gentleman* (Taylor Hackford, 1982, US), *Flashdance* (Adrian Lyne, 1983, US) and *Raiders of the Lost Ark* (Steven Spielberg, 1981, US). Warner and independent distributor Embassy followed Paramount's example, and after Disney lowered prices even further to US$29.95, at the end of 1984 Paramount and Warner subsequently ran campaigns with cassettes priced at US$24.95.

Setting different pricing levels divided video retail. As Wasser (2001: 134) notes, the Hollywood majors introduced a system of 'two-tiered pricing':

	Rental				Sell-through		
	Distributor	Units (000s)	List Price (US$)		Distributor	Units (000s)	List Price (US$)
Platoon	HBO	350	99.95	*Top Gun*	Paramount	2,850	26.95
Karate Kid II	RCA/Columbia	300	79.95	*Lady and the Tramp*	Disney	2,000	29.95
Lethal Weapon	Warner	280	89.95	*Crocodile Dundee*	Paramount	1,800	29.95
Dirty Dancing	Vestron	280	89.98	*Star Trek IV*	Paramount	1,500	29.95
Golden Child	Paramount	275	79.95	*An American Tail*	MCA/Universal	800	29.95

Source: compiled and adapted from *Video Store* magazine data reported in Nmungwun (1987: 178–9).

Table 4.2 Two-tiered Market: Sales of Top Rental and Sell-through Priced Titles in the US (1987)

Journeying into sell-through. Cover for Paramount Home Video's 1982 US release of *Star Trek II: Wrath of Khan*

Videocassettes are either list priced at the high $90-plus or at low prices ranging from the break-even price of $8 through the $30 range, most typically between $15 and $25. The rental stores are free to buy low-priced tapes and consumers free to buy high-priced ones. However, it is generally the case that only rental stores will invest so much money in the high-priced tapes and will have less interest in the low-priced tapes, since part of the audience for such tapes will have already purchased them and will not be renting those titles.

This strategy had the effect of creating two categories of tape: high-priced tapes intended for sale to rentailers and lower-priced titles targeted at consumers. This latter category became known in industry parlance as 'sell-through' tapes.

Sell-through pricing encouraged mass volume sales. In 1987, for example, the top sell-through title, *Top Gun* (Tony Scott, 1986, US), sold nearly 3m units at the list price of US$26.95, compared to the 350,0000 units of *Platoon* (Oliver Stone, 1986, US), the top rental title, priced at US$99.95 (table 4.2). But as nearly 60 per cent of pre-recorded cassette sales in that year were for titles priced at US$60 or higher, compared to 32 per cent in the US$10–30 range, rental-priced cassettes accounted for the majority share of the market (figure 4.1). Two-tiered pricing was significant, for it not only represented the acceptance of the video market by Hollywood but also demonstrated that the majors were try-ing to steer the market in a direction which would most favour their interests.

The Value of Video

For the Hollywood majors, promoting sell-through had the objective of steering the market in a direction which would make up for the revenues 'lost' to dis-tributors by rental transactions. However, the results of this strategy were mixed. Following the introduction of two-tier pricing, from 1984 onwards the volume of sell-through cassettes surpassed rental-priced sales. In 1986, a decade after the introduction of the VCR, 46m sell-through cassettes were shipped to dealers, against 21m rental-priced units. A decade later, in 1996 over 600m sell-through cassettes were sold, compared to 40m rental units (table 4.3). However, although more sell-through than rental-priced units were sold, rental turns

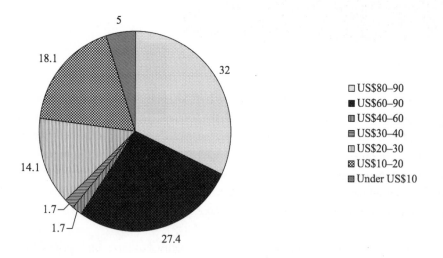

Figure 4.1 Pre-recorded Cassette Sales by Price Level (1987) (%)

accounted for the larger share of consumer spending on video. According to the research by *Video Store* magazine, in 1986 consumers in the US spent US$3.3bn on video rental, compared to US$0.8bn on sell-through spending. By 1993, rental spending had reached US$7.6bn, against US$5.2bn for sell-through purchases (data reported in Monush, 1995: 697). Sell-through was therefore accounting for an increasing proportion of total consumer spending on video (41 per cent in 1993 against 20 per cent in 1986) but, overall, rentals continued to represent the largest share of spending on video.

As the Hollywood majors did not participate in rental transactions, the growth of sell-through had a significant impact on the revenues returned to distributors. In 1989, distributor revenues from video rental totalled US$1.8bn, compared to US$1.55bn from sell-through, proportionally 54/46 per cent. Two years later, sell-through exceeded rental revenues for the first time: rental revenues totalled US$1.8bn, against US$1.9bn from sell-through (49/51 per cent). A year later, rental revenues stood at US$2.15bn, while sell-through had reached US$2.55bn (46/54 per cent) (author's analysis of *Video Store* data reported in Monush, 1993: 663, and 1994: 692).

As the 1980s progressed and the software market matured, the video distribution divisions of the majors consolidated their dominance. Collectively, Disney's Buena Vista, CBS/Fox (later Fox Video), MCA/Universal, Paramount, RCA/Columbia (later Columbia TriStar) and Warner accounted for 58.5 per cent of total revenues to distributors in 1988, and by 1992 that share had increased to 81.6 per cent (analysis of *Video Store* magazine data reported in Monush, 1991: 610, and 1994: 692).

Video Releasing

Video created a new exhibition window for Hollywood features and contributed to extending the life cycle of Hollywood films. Initially, a film would open in theatres and then four to six months later it would be released in the domestic market on videocassette. Eight months after the theatrical release, the film appeared on US pay-per-view (PPV) cable for a window of two months before moving to subscription television (STV) channels four months later, where it would be shown for twelve to eighteen months. Network broadcasts would fall between two years and thirty months after the theatrical release, and finally, five years after opening in theatres, the film entered syndication, where it would be licensed, usually as part of a package, to independent television stations or cable systems for showing in local markets (Austin, 1990: 321; Blume, 2006: 335; Waterman, 1985: 230). This basic sequence of release windows was further complicated by distribution to overseas markets. It was common for the Hollywood majors to initially open a film in theatres across the domestic market of the US

	Rental	Sell-through	Total
2005	14.9	33.7	48.6
2004	33.0	115.7	148.7
2003	53.2	240.2	293.4
2002	73.6	407.5	481.1
2001	86.2	539.6	625.8
2000	99.4	565.0	664.4
1999	86.2	561.0	647.2
1998	57.0	626.4	683.4
1997	39.9	635.5	675.4
1996	40.4	600.1	640.5
1995	38.7	483.7	522.4
1994	36.5	398.4	434.9
1993	35.8	326.9	362.7
1992	33.3	264.1	297.4
1991	31.6	232.0	263.6
1990	32.3	209.5	241.8
1989	31.0	172.9	203.9
1988	30.0	116.6	146.6
1987	26.7	76.5	103.2
1986	21.0	46.0	67.0
1985	15.2	25.7	40.9
1984	10.0	11.3	21.3
1983	6.0	5.9	11.9
1982	3.5	3.0	6.5
1981	2.1	1.5	3.6
1980	2.0	1.0	3.0

Sources: Adams Media Research data reported in MPA (2002: 28; 2003: 30; 2004b: 30; & 2006f: 29) and MPAA (1998).

Table 4.3 Sales of Rental-priced and Sell-through Cassettes to US Dealers (1980–2005) (million units)

and Canada, and then wait a few weeks or months before rolling the film out internationally. No uniform sequence of release dates existed for international distribution and instead the opening of a film in different territories could be spread over six to nine months, with the video release coming six months later. However, these intervals are indicative only. In the case of *Top Gun*, the US video release in March 1987 came ten months after the film opened in theatres (figure 4.2). This was followed eight months later with the pay-cable premiere and the film received its first network screening eighteen months afterwards.

Although a film may only be exhibited for a limited period of time in the theatrical and various television windows, unless the distributor had the policy of systematically withdrawing titles, then once a film was released on video it was available for purchase or rental over many years. Video therefore not only added to the outlets through which films could be sold but also extended the period in which films remained in commercial circulation.

Video releasing became integrated into the economic logic of what Harold Vogel (2001: 83) describes as '[s]equential distribution patterns':

> films are normally first distributed to the market that generates the highest marginal revenue over the least amount of time. They then 'cascade' in order of marginal-revenue contribution down to markets that return the lowest revenues per unit time. . . . Sequencing is always a marketing decision that attempts to maximize income, and it is generally sensible for profit-maximizing distributors to price-discriminate in different markets or 'windows' by selling the same product at different prices to different buyers.

Before the arrival of video or television, theatrical film exhibition had instituted sequential distribution through the systems of first-run and subsequent-run theatres established in the US and international territories. With the introduction of television and later video, this system survived but was spread across different media technologies instead of the stratified structure of theatres: video and the PPV formed the 'second-run' window for films, while pay-cable, network and syndicated television provided the subsequent runs.

Television transformed the life cycle of films but distributors continued to prioritise the domestic box office as the major source of revenues. Video, however, challenged this logic. According to estimates by the investment company Smith Barney, in 1984 a Hollywood film earned for the distributor US$1.50 from each ticket sale at the theatrical box office, US$0.25 per household from pay-TV and US$0.05 a household through network TV (cited in Austin, 1990: 334). Sales of a rental-priced videocassette with a wholesale price of US$50.00 were, however, believed to net US$5.80 per unit to the distributor. Video sales became an increasingly important revenue stream for the majors and other film distributors. At the start of the 1980s, video sales counted for a very small proportion of the total revenues from all exhibition windows. In 1980, video was the source for US$280m, or a mere 7 per cent of total worldwide revenues for the American film industry. This compared to US$2,094m (or 52 per cent of revenues) from the domestic and international theatrical box office (Vogel, 2001: 62). By 1990, nearly 39 per cent

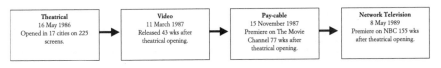

Sources: BiB (2004b: F-1542), *TV Guide* (1987: A-68; 1989: 138), *Variety* (1986).

Figure 4.2 *Top Gun*: Sequenced Release Windows in the US (1986–9)

of revenues came from video, against 25 per cent from the box office (figure 4.3).
As these proportions remained roughly similar over the following decade, video
was established as the main revenue stream for the Hollywood film companies.

This trend did not occur at the expense of the theatrical box office. As Wasser
(2001: 153) notes, video did not reduce or 'cannibalise' potential revenues
which may otherwise have been earned through other windows. Video became
the largest slice of an expanding size of pie, as rental and sell-through contributed to increasing total revenues from all sources.

Video releasing did not displace the precedence of the theatrical window, and
the economic importance of the box office did not diminish. To support major
releases for the theatrical window, the Hollywood majors mounted huge
advance promotional and publicity campaigns to build expectation prior to the
theatrical opening. While further marketing would go into promoting the film
for its video release, this expenditure only ever represented a fraction of the
spending made on promotions for the theatrical release. Although apparently
contradictory – spending less money to market a film for the most lucrative
release window – the value of theatrical marketing is not confined to selling tick-

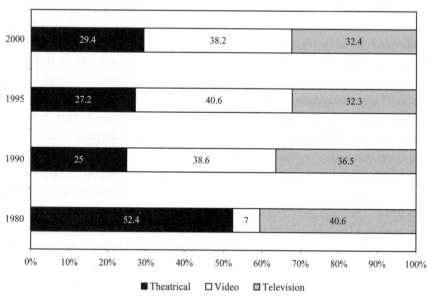

Sources: author's analysis based on data from Vogel (1990: 52; 1998: 55 and 2001: 62)

Notes: Values represent the proportion of revenues from combined domestic and international markets.
'Theatrical' combines revenues from the domestic and international box office.
'Television' combines revenues from sales of feature films to pay-cable, network TV, syndication and overseas TV, and for sales of made-for-TV-
films.

Figure 4.3 Worldwide Revenue Sources for Hollywood Films (1980–2000) (%)

ets at the box office alone. Theatrical releasing still commands the largest marketing expenditure for Hollywood, as the opening of films in theatres provides the up-front hype that raises the public visibility of a film and carries it through subsequent windows, including video.

Video Money and Blockbuster Production

Video provided Hollywood with new sources of revenue, but the increasing value of the video market was paralleled by dramatic increases in the costs of producing and marketing major Hollywood films. Video did not cause the price of film-making to rise, but increasingly the majors had to rely on video revenues to offset the economics of producing and marketing films in Hollywood.

According to the Hollywood vernacular, production costs are frequently referred to as 'negative costs' (i.e. the expenditure involved with producing the first completed negative of the film). Marketing or distribution expenditure combines the costs involved with duplicating *prints*, together with buying *advertising* space or time, and consequently is known as 'P&A'. During the 1980s, as the video software market was established and expanded, expenditure by the Hollywood majors on producing and marketing films nearly trebled. In 1980, for films produced by members of the MPAA that year, negative costs averaged US$9.4m. With P&A expenditure of US$4.3m to support a North American release, the average cost of making and then releasing a film in the domestic market totalled US$13.7m. By 1990, combined negative and P&A costs had risen to an average US$38.8m per film and escalated to US$82.1m ten years later (table 4.4).

Outstripping the rate of inflation, these figures marked the dramatic increase in the costs of producing and distributing films by Hollywood. Production of

	Average Negative Costs	Average P&A Costs	Average Combined Negative and P&A Costs
	(US$m)	(US$m)	(US$m)
2005	60.0	36.2	96.2
2000	54.8	27.3	82.1
1995	36.4	17.7	54.1
1990	26.8	12.0	38.8
1985	16.8	6.5	23.3
1980	9.4	4.3	13.7

Sources: MPA (2002: 16 and 19; 2005: 18 and 19).

Table 4.4 MPAA Companies Average Film Production and Distribution Costs (1980–2005)

costly 'spectaculars', 'blockbusters' or 'event' movies has been a well-established tradition in Hollywood, yet the escalation of negative and P&A costs demonstrates how during the 1980s, the majors further focused their efforts on making and selling a few major productions. In a circular logic, blockbuster production increased costs through expenditure on staging large-scale spectacle and the hiring of costly stars to draw in mass audiences, but to attract that audience the majors needed to raise their investment through mounting extensive domestic and international marketing campaigns. As the blockbuster mentality took hold in Hollywood, the film market therefore became ever more focused around the performance and profitability of a few hit titles.

Like all film industries, Hollywood faces the challenge of trying to sell products which customers do not really need. As audience tastes can also never be securely predicted, stars and generic formulae serve as ways of trying to prefigure popularity. Yet as film history has continually shown, slavishly repeating the combination of factors from one hit film does not automatically guarantee success on another occasion. As blockbuster production has increased investment in the making and marketing films, then greater losses have become an ever present possibility, leading to common claims that the film industry is a risky business. Janet Wasko (2003: 222), however, rejects such notions:

> [I]s the film business actually a risky business at all? A common assumption is that Hollywood films rarely return their investments at the box office and companies survive from the successes of a few blockbuster films. This assumption, however, belies the fact that box office receipts are not the only source of income for film commodities. ... theatres are only the beginning of a chain of windows or markets where little additional investment is needed, but more income and, not infrequently, extensive profits are produced.

Contemporary blockbuster production has occurred within the context of video and cable opening new exhibition windows and revenues streams for films:

> For the film industry, more distribution outlets have translated into less risk. Videocassette, DVD, and cable release have provided especially lucrative rewards for films that do well in theatres, as well as giving 'legs' to films that have not performed well in theatrical release. Moveover, globalization and privatization have opened international markets that further reduce the risk of distributing these indefinitely exportable products. (p. 222)

Strategically video distribution has provided a form of protection, possibly the most important form of protection, against the risks of contemporary film production.

As Wasser (2001: 169–71) notes, from the early 1980s onwards, theatrical rentals alone could not cover rising negative costs. According to Wasser's analysis, in 1980 rentals from the theatrical releasing totalled US$1,235m, or over 98 per cent of the estimated US$1,260m spent by the Hollywood majors on producing films that year, while video revenues were equivalent to only 1 per cent. By 1993, however, box-office rentals covered as little as 46 per cent of total negative costs, while video revenues had risen to levels where they could cover over 93 per cent (p. 171). As Wasser comments, '[h]ome video's increasing importance gave studios the courage to increase production budgets beyond the capacity of the US theatrical rentals' (p. 169). Video was therefore not only providing Hollywood with a new source of income but more importantly had also become an essential source of income to support the inflated economics of blockbuster production.

Video Hits

Hollywood not only took the dominant share of distributor revenues from the video sales but films from the majors also defined mass popularity in the market. Looking at the top-ranked titles priced for the rental market between 1989 and 1991, among the biggest-selling rental-priced titles, the majority fell into two categories (table 4.5):

- Family adventures and comedies: e.g. *Back to the Future II* (Robert Zemeckis, 1989, US), *Big* (Penny Marshall, 1988, US), *Coming to America* (John Landis, 1988, US), *Crocodile Dundee II* (John Cornell, 1988, Aus/US), *Dick Tracy* (Warren Beatty, 1990, US), *Ghostbusters 2* (Ivan Reitman, 1989, US), *Kindergarten Cop* (Ivan Reitman, 1990, US) and *Look Who's Talking* (Amy Heckerling, 1989, US).
- Action features: e.g. *Another 48 Hours* (Walter Hill, 1990, US), *Backdraft* (Ron Howard, 1991, US), *Days of Thunder* (Tony Scott, 1990, US), *Die Hard* (John McTiernan, 1988, US), *Die Hard 2* (Renny Harlin, 1990, US), *The Hunt for Red October* (John McTiernan, 1990, US) and *Tango and Cash* (Andrei Konchalovsky, 1989, US).

Films orientated towards a family audience reigned in the video charts. As Robert C. Allen (1999) notes, the growth of the video market during the 1980s coincided with the second boom in births witnessed in the US since the end of the Second World War. By 1964, the original post-war 'baby boom' had petered out, but from 1977 to 1995 a further explosion in births became the 'echo boom' (p. 110). Until the late 1970s, young people aged thirteen to twenty-five, the original baby-boomers, formed the core of the regular moviegoing audience.

	Title	Distributor	Estimated Units Sold
			(000s)
1991	*Terminator 2*	LIVE	675
	Dances with Wolves	Orion	652
	Ghost	Paramount	595
	Silence of the Lambs	Orion	525
	Die Hard 2	CBS/Fox	505
	Dick Tracy	Buena Vista	475
	City Slickers	New Line	463
	Kindergarten Cop	MCA/Universal	460
	Backdraft	MCA/Universal	420
	Days of Thunder	Paramount	412
1990	*Look Who's Talking*	RCA/Columbia	420
	Back to the Future II	MCA/Universal	390
	Born on the Fourth of July	MCA/Universal	385
	Driving Miss Daisy	Warner	375
	The Hunt for Red October	Paramount	372
	Another 48 Hours	Paramount	368
	Dead Poets Society	Buena Vista	365
	Back to the Future III	MCA/Universal	363
	Tango and Cash	Warner	360
	Bird on a Wire	MCA/Universal	355
1989	*Rain Man*	MGM/UA	455
	Crocodile Dundee II	Paramount	407
	Big	CBS/Fox	399
	Coming to America	Paramount	398
	Ghostbusters 2	RCA/Columbia	396
	Cocktail	Touchstone	385
	Die Hard	CBS/Fox	374
	Twins	MCA/Universal	360
	Working Girl	CBS/Fox	310
	Beaches	Touchstone	305

Sources: *Video Store* magazine market research data reported in Monush (1991: 609; 1992: 629; and 1993: 663).

Note: Estimates are for sales in Canada and the US combined based on the volume of units sold to dealers up until the pre-order cut-off date.

Table 4.5 Top Rental-priced Videocassette Titles Sold in North America (1989–91)

After 1980, however, the baby-boomers grew out of the primary moviegoing demographic (p. 117). As the 1980s progressed, the number of teenage and young adult moviegoers declined, while birth rates increased, and the video business looked to place itself in relation to this changing composition of the film-consuming audience:

The home video rental and sales industries ... positioned themselves in relation not to the baby-bust generation ... but to the two generations on either demographic side: the post-twenties baby-boomers and their 'echo boom' children. These two age cohorts, joined together in the industry's imagination around the glowing (video) hearth of the middle-class home, would emerge as 'the family' audience that would drive the video industry and transform the film business in the early 1990s. (p. 118)

For Allen, the changing audience gave rise to the production and popularity of the 'cross-generational family film'. Films like *Back to the Future II*, *Crocodile Dundee II*, *Kindergarten Cop* and *Look Who's Talking* were too knowing and smart to be simply regarded as kids' films. These were movies with the potential to appeal equally to the echo boom kids and the grown-up baby-boomers, and as they were released on cassette they defined popular video entertainment for all the family.

By addressing pre-teenagers, home video cultivated an audience for whom the VCR and not the theatre represented the familiar experience of film consumption: 'Just as the baby boom overlaps almost exactly with the diffusion of television technology and maturation of broadcast television as an institution and cultural form, the echo boom also has its defining technology, the VCR' (p. 111). Echo boomers represented the first generation of film consumers to grow up with the VCR, and as the older members of that generation have aged, so their offspring have readily accepted the family 'tradition' of using video as the prime window for consuming films.

In the early 1990s, a major video release would sell between 350,000 and 650,000 copies for rental. A hit video title would be expected to achieve over 10m rental turns nationwide. In 1993, the top ten video rental titles scored between 11.2m and 15.7m rental turns. To qualify as a sell-through hit, a title

		Rental[1]				Sell-through		
		Distributor	Average Store's Rental Turns	National Rental Turns (m)			Distributor	Units Sold (m)
1	A Few Good Men	Columbia TriStar	446	15.7		Aladdin	Buena Vista	22.4
2	Under Siege	Warner	404	14.0		Pinocchio	Buena Vista	8.8
3	A League of Their Own	Columbia TriStar	380	13.4		Home Alone 2	Fox Video	7.5
4	Unforgiven	Warner	378	13.3		Free Willy	Warner	5.5
5	Last of the Mohicans	Fox Video	368	12.9		Homeward Bound	Buena Vista	5.4
6	The Bodyguard	Warner	364	12.8		Dennis the Menace	Warner	3.1
7	Single White Female	Columbia TriStar	344	12.1		Teenage Mutant Ninja Turtles 3	New Line	2.9
8	Sneakers	MCA/Universal	331	11.6		Once Upon a Forest	Fox Video	2.0
9	Forever Young	Warner	324	11.4		Tom & Jerry	LIVE	1.8
10	Scent of a Woman	MCA/Universal	318	11.2		Miracle on 34th Street	Fox Video	1.8

Sources: *Video Store* Magazine Market Research data reported in Monush (1995: 695)

Notes: Rentals were tracked for the first four months after release.

Table 4.6 Top 10 Rental Priced and Sell Through Titles in the US (1993)

had to sell in excess of 5m copies (table 4.6). When Buena Vista released the Disney animated feature *Aladdin* (Ron Clements and John Musker, 1992, US) in October 1993, it proved a phenomenal hit and on the strength of the film's video performance alone the company quickly made a sequel, *The Return of Jafar* (Toby Shelton and Alan Zaslove, 1994, US), produced solely for the video market (reported in Monush, 1995: 692). After *The Return of Jafar* became a hit in its own right, selling over 16m units worldwide, Disney began producing its 'video premieres' as direct-to-video sequels for the company's most popular modern animated hits, including a second *Aladdin* video sequel, *Aladdin and the King of Thieves* (Tad Stones, 1996, US) (Ferguson, 1999).

Video-as-Event – Marketing *E.T.*

In theatrical exhibition, the heavy marketing placed behind blockbuster productions frequently aimed towards cultivating the widespread awareness necessary to make the opening of a film into a national event. As video money became increasingly important to supporting blockbuster productions, in certain cases marketing also achieved the task of making the video into a major national event. It was this trend which made *E.T. The Extra-Terrestrial* (Steven Spielberg, 1982, US) into the top video hit of the 1980s after the film sold 15m units when released on cassette in 1988. *E.T.* was Steven Spielberg's fifth feature film as director. Spielberg had already established his reputation as a popular director with *Jaws* and *Raiders of the Lost Ark*, and *E.T.* further contributed to making him the most commercially successful director in the history of cinema. Amblin Entertainment, Spielberg's production company, made *E.T.* for Universal Pictures, who distributed the film internationally. Universal released *E.T.* in North America on 11 June 1982 before rolling it out internationally, starting in European territories during December that year. By the end of its theatrical run, the film had made US$395m at the North American box office and over US$300m internationally. With these ticket sales, many industry commentators hailed *E.T.* as the biggest-grossing movie of all time.

E.T. appeared in theatres when the Hollywood majors were still attempting to control the rental market and prevent home recording. Most feature films found their way to video within six months of their theatrical release, but in the case of *E.T.*, Universal delayed putting the film out on video for over six years, and there was a further three years' wait before it was broadcast on network television. Universal offered no clear explanation for withholding the video release, but the most often cited reason was that Spielberg refused to let the film become available on video. Whatever the reason for the delay, the history-making box office from the film generated prolonged anticipation of an eventual video release. When MCA Home Video therefore eventually announced in May

1988 that *E.T.* would be available on video from autumn that year, the news was widely welcomed by video retailers.

Before MCA/Universal's release of *E.T.*, Disney had been responsible for the biggest hits on video. *Lady and the Tramp* (Clyde Geronimi, Wilfred Jackson and Hamilton Luske, 1955, US) was released in 1987, with a list price of US$29.95, and broke sales records after over 3m units were shipped to retailers. On 4 October 1988, just a few weeks before *E.T.* came out on video, Disney released *Cinderella* (Clyde Geronimi, Wilfred Jackson and Hamilton Luske, 1950, US), retailing at US$26.99. With pre-orders of 4.3m units, *Cinderella* immediately became the biggest-selling title to-date and by the end of the year, 7.2m units had been sold (Parisi, 1988d: 4). Before *E.T.*, MCA's previous highest-selling title had been the animated feature *An American Tail* (Don Bluth, 1986, US), which had sold just 1.5m units (Weinstein, 1988).

Box-office reputation and a major marketing campaign stimulated huge interest in the video release of *E.T.* MCA scheduled the release for Thursday 27 October 1988. Coming just a few days before Halloween, the timing of the video release linked to the film's narrative: E.T. lands on earth shortly before Halloween. The hype around the release led to huge volumes of advance orders. A deadline of 29 September was set for retailers to make pre-bookings, and by the start of that month orders had reached 10,016,147 for the US market and 662,155 in Canada. After allowing maybe 500,000 sales for rental purposes, sell-through copies of *E.T.* reached approximately 20 per cent of the 50m-plus VCR homes in North America (Parisi, 1988b: 1). To fulfil these volumes, MCA exhausted the capacity of video duplicators. Not only were duplicators unable to produce all the copies required to completely fulfil the advance orders but also orders for other titles released around that time (Blowen, 1988). Distributors also complained that advance orders for *Cinderella* and *E.T.* had reduced orders from video stores for other films, including *Above the Law* (Andrew Davis, 1988, US/HK), *Biloxi Blues* (Mike Nichols, 1988, US) and *Sunset* (Blake Edwards, 1988, US) (Harmetz, 1988a).

MCA mounted a US$25m promotional campaign and stimulated demand among consumers by giving *E.T.* a low retail price of US$24.95. To cultivate an air of exclusivity and urgency, the film was withheld from the PPV window, while the announcement was made by the distributor that the video release would only be available for a limited period until spring 1989. Limited releasing broke from the convention employed by most distributors, including MCA, of putting films out indefinitely on video. Instead, with *E.T.* MCA imitated Disney's practice of putting its films out on video for short periods before withdrawing them. Disney used this strategy to stimulate mass sales over short periods. It also preserved the value of its film properties, particularly important for titles aimed at child audiences, for by withholding them from the market the appeal of films could be protected for future generations.

Prior to the release, drinks manufacturer Pepsi Cola agreed a deal with MCA for a joint marketing campaign. Pepsi had included an advert on the video edition of *Top Gun* but Spielberg refused to allow any similar advertising on the *E.T.* cassettes. The drinks manufacturer therefore supported the release with a campaign which involved the production of special 'mini-film' commercials for network and cable television. Further promotions saw Pepsi also giving away 100,000 free copies of the film through consumer sweepstakes. Finally, Pepsi contributed to lowering prices by offering a $5 rebate scheme: after buying certain Pepsi products, including Pepsi, Diet Pepsi, Mountain Dew and Slice, consumers could obtain a mail-in coupon. When posted with proof of purchasing the video, the consumer was reimbursed, reducing the eventual price paid for the video to US$19.95 (Parisi, 1988c: 8).

After the mass popularity of *E.T.* in theatres, MCA were concerned that the video release would provide rich pickings for commercial piracy. In the build-up to the video release the distributor therefore took a series of measures to prevent the reproduction and sale of illegal copies (Harmetz, 1988b). Macro-vision, the mechanism for disrupting the copying of pre-recorded tapes, was

Video blockbuster: MCA Home Video's 1988 VHS release of *E.T.*

included on tapes as standard protection, and legally reproduced copies could be identified by the inclusion of a hologram of the Universal logo on the cassette case. MCA also went to the lengths of having stock stored in warehouses with special security guards. To try and prevent widespread piracy overseas, MCA chose a uniform day-and-date for the North American and international release of *E.T.* on video, dubbing the film into a dozen languages for international territories. The video release of *E.T.* on 27 October 1988 therefore created a global event as the film became available simultaneously across the world's major markets for filmed entertainment.

Advance promotions generated enormous hype around the release, leading retailers to placing mass volume pre-orders and consumers pre-paying to reserve copies. Once the film was available on cassette, the promotional efforts received additional free publicity as news stories abounded of consumers queuing at video stores before opening to get copies on the first day of release (Parisi, 1988a). Alongside the huge volume of sales, stories also frequently reported cases of retailers unable to satisfy consumer demand due to shortages in supply from duplicators. Heavily promoted in advance of its release to encourage large pre-orders, the retailing of *E.T.* in turn further contributed to the excitement as the hype moved from anticipating the availability of the film to the drama of its unavailability due to excess demand.

Calculated on the recommended retail price of US$24.95, the 15m copies of *E.T.* shipped to retailers in 1988 generated over US$374m in sales. As MCA was believed to be selling cassettes for US$15 per unit wholesale, it is reasonable to estimate that video sales of *E.T.* returned US$225m to the distributor before duplication and marketing costs. This compared to the US$187m in rentals (not gross box office) which were returned from the film's initial theatrical release (*Variety*, 1983: 13). *E.T.*'s widespread appeal as a family adventure, together with its prior box-office reputation, extensive marketing and limited releasing, contributed towards making the release of the film on video into a national and international event. Part of the eagerness which greeted the release was also a result of MCA withholding the film from television, and it was not until 28 November 1991 that *E.T.* finally received its US network premiere on CBS (BiB, 2004a: F-458). With *E.T.*, MCA therefore gave a video release the same form of calculated event marketing used to sell major blockbuster films in the theatrical window.

SYNERGIES

During the vertically integrated studio system of the 1930s and 40s, the major Hollywood companies concentrated on the production, distribution and exhibition of films. Although some had developed connections with the radio and recorded music industries, or had experimented with early television, Hollywood represented a collection of companies focused on the business of film. In 1962, Universal was bought by the Music Corporation of America (MCA), a leading talent agency and major producer of television programming. The MCA/Universal deal not only strengthened links between Hollywood and broadcasting but also started off a succession of changes in ownership which formed the first wave of conglomeration in Hollywood. Before the decade was over, Gulf and Western added Paramount to its diversified portfolio of assets and Warner Bros. changed hands twice. A further wave of ownership changes occurred during the 1980s as Coca Cola bought Columbia, Fox was sold to News Corporation and Time Inc. acquired Warner. In the case of Fox and Warner, these companies immediately became components of large established media conglomerates.

As these changes brought the major Hollywood film producers and distributors under the same corporate parentage as companies who owned diversified media assets in other sectors, so 'synergy' became one of the buzzwords of the modern Hollywood (Brodie and Robins, 1994). Synergy entered corporate jargon in the 1980s to describe instances where an acquisition or partnership created possibilities for interaction between complementary business operations, offering the potential for those operations to make higher gains than either could achieve independently. As Mark L. Sirower (1997: 5) comments, '[t]he common definition of synergy is 2 + 2 = 5'. Such opportunities are not achieved between companies but between different divisions or arms of the same company. Synergy is believed to offer the company a better payoff than just good marketing, because interactions between different operations or products create a *syn*thesis of marketing en*ergy*(ies). For the cultural industries, Keith Negus (1997: 85) suggests, 'synergy provide[s] the corporation with opportunities for extending the presentation of and gaining the maximum exposure and revenue from specific cultural products and people'.

Sony and Matsushita Buy Hollywood

From the range of potential synergistic relationships formed by the cultural industries, Negus includes hardware–software synergies, relationships between 'the text and the technology' (p. 85). As part of the second wave of conglomeration in Hollywood, hardware–software synergies were formed between the consumer electronics industry and the majors. On 27 September 1989, Sony agreed a deal to pay US$3.3bn in cash and assume US$1.3bn in debt to buy Columbia Pictures Entertainment (CPE) from Coca Cola (Kipps, 1989a). The logic of synergy was driven by belief in the gains which could be achieved through drawing together electronic hardware with entertainment software.

Sony had previously shown interest in forming close alliances with the entertainment industries two decades before, when in 1968 the company established a partnership with the major music label CBS, forming Sony/CBS Records. A year before the Columbia deal, in February 1988, Sony eventually bought CBS Records for US$2bn. To avoid losing ground to its main competitor in the consumer electronics business, Matsushita quickly followed Sony's example, and on 29 December 1990 paid US$6.6bn for 97 per cent of stock in MCA Inc., owners of Universal's film and television operations.

With their moves into Hollywood, Sony and Matsushita both acquired extensive film libraries which could be transferred to, and exploited on, videocassette. Sony gained CPE's two film divisions, Columbia Pictures and TriStar Pictures, with a combined film library of 2,770 titles. Other acquired assets included a 45 per cent interest in the Burbank Studios (shared with Warner), CPE's international theatrical distribution network and the 820 screens of the Loews Theaters chain. A 50 per cent share in the joint venture RCA/Columbia Pictures Home Video also gave Sony access to valuable software for supporting the adoption of the 8mm video format, which Sony had begun promoting as an alternative to VHS (Stewart, 1989).

Video alone did not, however, justify these corporate manoeuvres. Although Columbia's film operations were seen as the core of the Sony deal, other key assets were equally important. Arguably, the real value of the deal lay not in Columbia's film properties but in television, as the company was the industry leader in the syndication market (Nathan, 2001: 185). Columbia TriStar Television Group held the rights to 23,000 episodes of 260 series, including the hit *Who's the Boss?* (1984–92). In Matsushita's case, the company not only acquired Universal Pictures and the MCA Television Group but also the music companies MCA Records and Geffen Records, a 49 per cent investment in the exhibition chain Cineplex Odeon, publishing division Putnam Berkley Books, the Universal Studios theme parks in Florida and Hollywood, and a 50 per cent interest in USA Networks.

Marrying Hollywood entertainment with consumer electronics seemed a perfect match with rich synergistic potential. Sony and Matsushita made the machines for presenting home entertainment, while Columbia and Universal held the rights to large libraries of film and television properties for showing on televisions or VCRs. By linking hardware and software, 'Sony [had] a role in almost every step of an entertainment property's life – from producing a movie and its soundtrack album, playing them in its theatres and then selling them to the home video and audio markets' (Farhi, 1989).

With the VCR format wars only recently ended and Sony commencing VHS production, many commentators believed Betamax had lost out because VHS was supported by a wider range of software titles. 'Sony learned a lesson when they tried to sell Betamax. ... They discovered that you can have the best hardware and no one will want it if the software's not there' (Liz Buyer, analyst with Prudential Bache, quoted in Farhi, 1989). '[I]f Sony had owned a studio to support its Betamax format for video-cassette recorders in the 1970s, it might not have been forced to cede the market to the rival VHS format' (Wagstyl, 1989). This view overestimated the importance of software, for it was JVC and Matsushita's OEM strategy which ultimately decided the VCR wars (see Chapter 1). However, the hardware–software synergies created by the Sony/Columbia and Matsushita/MCA deals appeared a perfect and inevitable fit. As well as offering revenue streams in their own right, potentially films and television programming could also be used as the software to support the introduction of any innovations in video and television hardware in the future. Even if software had not decided the VCR wars, Sony and Matsushita were hedging their bets that it could become a deciding factor in any future competition between technologies.

The logic of these synergistic mergers was perfectly encapsulated by one commentator when he remarked, 'Columbia Pictures Entertainment will fit into the Sony Corp.'s future plans as easily as a videocassette slides into a VCR' (Kipps, 1989b: 5). In reality, however, both acquisitions resulted in problems for all parties concerned. On paper, the uniting of hardware and software seemed straightforward but as both Sony and Matsushita found out, it was not so easy to make the parts work together in any profitable way. Sony's purchase of Columbia raised widespread criticisms that Japan was taking over Hollywood, bastion of American popular culture. For its critics, the deal was the latest case of the encroaching threat of Japanese business in the US. Shortly after the deal was agreed, a *Newsweek* (1989) poll registered that over half of respondents regarded Japan's trading policy with the US as unfair and that Japanese economic power presented a greater threat to the US than the military power of the Soviet Union. Sony was cautious to avoid the political fall-out from the Columbia deal, and so guaranteed operational autonomy and appointed US management to steer the film, television and music operations. Matsushita followed suit. However, the grand plan of hardware–software interaction proved hard to realise (Griffin and Masters, 1997). Columbia and TriStar were reorganised as Sony Pictures Entertainment, but as a series of expensive films failed at the box office and major outlays were paid to hire an expensive management team, five years after taking over the companies, Sony announced that it was reducing their value by US$3.2bn (Sterngold, 1994).

Similar problems beset Matsushita. In the early 1990s, Universal's film and television divisions both suffered several flops. Corporate differences were also revealed in the divergence of management philosophy between Hollywood and

Japanese business (McDougal, 1998: 494–6). These problems were compounded as the Japanese economy entered a steep recession, and on 9 April 1995 80 per cent of MCA was sold for US$5.7bn cash to the Canadian spirits and beverages company Seagram. Matsushita retained the remaining 20 per cent. Rather than achieving the seamless synergy of hardware and software, Sony and Matsushita both struggled to understand and adapt to the commercial demands of the US entertainment business.

Other links between the consumer electronics industry and Hollywood did, however, have consequences for the video business. In 1991, Toshiba bought a share in Hollywood when it formed a partnership with the Japanese trading company C. Itoh to buy a 5.7 per cent stake in Time Warner Entertainment (TWE), the film, television and music group of Time Warner (Bruck, 1994). This deal was more modest than the acquisitions completed by Sony and Matsushita, and was driven by interest in TWE's cable operations rather than software properties (Sanger, 1991). Following this deal, Toshiba was able to draw on Warner as a partner in the competition between rival formats which led to the development of DVD (see Chapter 2), and which became important to the settling of industry agreement over a unified standard between the consumer electronics industry and the Hollywood majors. Later, Toshiba also drew on Warner for support as a new war loomed between competing high-definition DVD formats: Warner aligned itself with Toshiba's HD-DVD, while Sony used the Columbia library to help the launch of Blu-ray (see next chapter).

Viacom, Paramount and Blockbuster

At the height of the classic Hollywood studio system in the 1930s and 40s, the major companies dominated the film market because they were vertically integrated: by owning operations in film production, distribution and exhibition, the majors controlled the means to make, sell and show films. While control of the whole supply chain was vital to this dominance, the most important element of this structure was the ownership of theatres for the exhibition of films. Theatres represented the interface between the industry and moviegoing public. Although the majors did not own the majority of theatres in the US, they did own most of the leading first-run houses, the most profitable venues. Following the Paramount case in 1948, all the majors signed consent decrees agreeing to sell off their exhibition holdings. This led to structural change in the US film industry as exhibition was divorced from production and distribution.

Sony and Matsushita's attempts to achieve synergy between video hardware and film and television software could be regarded as in their own way attempting to seek a form of vertical integration, as companies responsible for manufacturing the exhibition technology of the VCR acquired operations involved with the making and distribution of entertainment content. While taking a different form, the same process of integration was the objective of Viacom's purchase of the Blockbuster video rental chain in 1994. David Cook and his associate Kenneth W. Anderson opened the first Blockbuster video store on 19 October 1985 in Dallas. At that time, the video rental business was still characterised by small family-owned operations, offering a relatively limited range of new hit films, where titles were not displayed in the store but had to be requested from behind the counter. Blockbuster transformed the video rental business by introducing new business practices. At the Dallas store, 6,500 titles were available on 8,000 cassettes. Due to the demand on space made by this volume of stock, cassettes boxes had to be openly displayed on shelves in the store. This necessity saw Blockbuster imitating the bookshop environment in which customers are free to browse titles. Cook had a background in information technology and was able to computerise inventory control and checkout, streamlining transactions by installing barcodes on cassettes and membership cards.

Cook began to build Blockbuster as a chain, opening more wholly owned stores and licensing the Blockbuster concept to franchises across the US. Early in 1987, Waste Management, Inc., the world's largest refuse-processing company, headed by H. Wayne Huizenga, paid US$18.5m for 60 per cent of Blockbuster stock. With the backing of the new parent company, Blockbuster embarked on an acquisition programme, buying other chains to become the leading outlet for video rentals in the US. From 1989, the chain also began expanding overseas, opening stores abroad and forming franchise agreements (DeGeorge, 1996; Rourke and Rothbird, 2000).

After Viacom bought an 81 per cent stake of Blockbuster for US$8.4bn in January 1994, the acquisition not only gave the television syndicator a major foothold in the video business but also provided an extra advantage to beat off a rival bid from shopping channel QVC in the battle to acquire Paramount Communications, owner of Paramount's film and television operations. In February 1994, Viacom paid US$9.85bn to purchase a 74.6 per cent stake in Paramount (Greene, 1994; Noglow and Robins, 1994). Viacom now owned a producer and distributor of content for release on video, while also controlling the largest international chain for the rental of cassettes. Although the other Hollywood majors did not share in rental transactions, with these deals Viacom could gain revenues from all stages of the video value chain: Paramount was a key supplier to rentailers, while Blockbuster stocked tapes from all the Hollywood majors, including Paramount.

By the late 1990s, however, the video software business was turned around as the popularity of DVD steered the market strongly towards sales over rentals (see next chapter). Blockbuster remained the dominant player in the rental business but as the company's profitability was hit, in September 2004 Viacom spun off the rental chain by selling its shares to the public. Like the Sony/Columbia and Matsushita/Universal deals, Viacom's attempt to integrate Hollywood with the video business seemed a beautifully simple idea in theory, but in practice the holy grail of synergy proved more elusive.

CONCLUSION

Home video introduced a whole new exhibition window for films. Initially, the video software market in the US was established through the efforts of independent entrepreneurs, but as video grew in popularity the major Hollywood film companies entered and then dominated that market. Although the majors fought against the VCR and tried to manipulate the rental market, at the same time they were also doing everything necessary to become a part of the business growing around the new medium. Hollywood accepted video once revenues from sales to rentailers and consumers became not only a valuable but also an essential revenue stream for films. Hollywood was suspicious of video but could also see its potential.

Although the recording capabilities of the VCR raised anxieties among Hollywood executives, the core issue here was not a matter of technology but of intellectual property rights. It is not films or television but copyright which is at the foundation of Hollywood. As Ronald Bettig (1996: 160) observes, 'the general logic underlying the copyright system drives copyright owners to seek compensation from all new forms of use'. Hollywood's initial ambivalence towards video was not the product of technophobia, an unreasoned fear of the newness of new technology, but rather the result of specific and well-grounded worries about how such technology may prevent the majors from protecting the copyrighted works which they owned. While the Hollywood majors had consolidated their control over the theatrical box office over a period of several decades, the introduction of a new exhibition technology like the VCR presented the film industry with challenges over the mechanisms for protecting the works to which they owned the rights. Rather than rejecting video, the majors wanted video on their own terms, which meant finding the best ways to control and exploit their copyrighted works in order to profit from home entertainment.

After the introduction of the VCR, the Hollywood majors failed to outlaw home recording or to secure a share in video rentals, but they did introduce two-tier pricing and created the popular sell-through market. By the end of the 1980s, Hollywood was therefore largely reconciled to video. Video distribution subsidiaries became an established feature in the divisional structures of the majors. Today, Buena Vista Home Entertainment (Disney), Paramount Home Entertainment, Sony Pictures Home Entertainment, 20th Century-Fox Home Entertainment, Universal Studios Home Entertainment and Warner Home Video are the six leading names in Hollywood's video business. Once video had become the key revenue stream for feature film entertainment, the majors were ready to welcome the arrival of DVD in the mid-1990s, and the following chapter looks at the involvement of Hollywood in the video business during the digital age. Even while Hollywood enjoyed the profits which came from videocassettes and DVD, at the same time video remained a thorn in the side for the majors, as widespread industrialised piracy made the protection of intellectual property the key issue defining Hollywood's relationship to video. Chapter 6 will therefore consider how Hollywood has remained embroiled in global battles to halt video piracy.

5

Videocopia: Shaping the US Market in the Digital Age

DVD players were launched in the US market on 24 March 1997. When DVD was introduced, approximately 82 per cent of television households in the US owned at least one VCR (table 5.1). According to industry estimates, by the end of 1997 approximately 300,000 DVD players had been sold to consumers. Over the next eight years, DVD sales in the US showed phenomenal rates of growth, so that by the end of 2005 DVD penetration had reached approximately 84m homes, over 76 per cent of television households. With this rate of adoption, DVD became the fastest-selling item in the history of the US consumer electronics market. Rapidly falling prices stimulated a mass market for the new technology: compared to US$390 in 1998, the average price of a DVD player had dropped to US$73 by 2005 (MPA, 2003: 32, and 2006f: 31). In the space of only a few years, DVD displaced the VCR and cassette among consumers as the popular home video technology.

This chapter concentrates on the US video market in the period since the introduction of DVD. Looking at developments between 1997 and 2006, the chapter examines how the Hollywood majors have been central to the shaping of the video market in the digital era. Although the leading film companies joined with the consumer electronics and information technology industry to place their full support behind the introduction of DVD, yet again Hollywood took a contradictory attitude towards the arrival of a new medium for home entertainment. While supporting DVD, some of the Hollywood majors also

	1995	1996	1997	1998	1999	2000	2001	2002	2003	2004	2005
Television Households (m)	95.4	95.9	98.0	99.4	100.8	102.2	105.2	106.7	108.4	109.6	110.2
VCR Households (m)	75.8	78.8	80.4	84.1	85.8	88.1	96.2	97.6	98.4	98.9	97.7
VCR Penetration (%)	79.5	82.2	82.0	84.6	85.1	86.2	91.2	91.5	90.8	90.2	88.7
DVD Households (m)			0.3	1.2	4.6	13.0	24.8	38.8	46.7	65.4	84.0
DVD Penetration (%)			0.3	1.2	4.6	12.7	23.6	36.4	43.1	59.7	76.2

Sources: Nielsen Media Research and Adams Media Research data reported in MPA (2003: 29; and 2006f: 27–8).

Table 5.1 VCR and DVD Households in the US (1995–2005)

backed the competing rival format of Digital Video Express (Divx) and nearly sparked a new format war. This chapter also reviews how the arrival of DVD eventually produced a huge windfall for the majors. In the same period, other changes were occurring which transformed the basis on which video rental and retail operated, following the introduction of revenue-sharing arrangements for video rental and the rising dominance of mass merchants as the primary outlet for sell-through video. Finally, the chapter outlines how the Hollywood majors were involved with the launch of competing high-definition DVD formats and how those companies also cautiously moved into online delivery of video entertainment via broadband.

HOLLYWOOD, DVD AND THE CHALLENGE OF DIGITAL VIDEO EXPRESS

Lack of consensus characterised the immediate response of the majors to DVD. Several of the leading Hollywood companies quickly announced they would release titles on the format, while others withheld their support. As the battle over home recording and video rentals had shown, the Hollywood majors greeted the VCR with attempts to forcefully control the circulation of filmed entertainment in the retail market and the home. This same preoccupation returned as Divx, a rival digital disc system to DVD with a conditional access mechanism, was launched in 1998. As the majors split their allegiances between DVD or Divx, Hollywood stood divided over the new digital media. Three months before the launch of DVD on the consumer market, at the start of 1997 Warren Lieberfarb, President of Warner Home Video, noted, 'Hollywood is behaving as it always behaves. ... It repeatedly finds itself caught in a difficult pregnancy as it tries to reconcile the arrival of a new media [sic] with its existing business' (quoted in Markoff, 1997).

Hollywood's Response to DVD

DVD promised to provide consumer electronics manufacturers with a rich new market in hardware sales. Warner and Columbia TriStar had close relations to the consumer electronics industry through Toshiba and Sony, and these companies immediately gave their support to DVD. At the Consumer Electronics Show in Las Vegas during January 1997, both Warner and Columbia announced they would be releasing their first titles on digital disc in March and April as the format went to market. Warner would also release titles for MGM and the Time Warner subsidiary New Line Cinema. Philips joined in the announcement by revealing that its subsidiary PolyGram Filmed Entertainment would also provide titles on DVD. As part of an initial run of thirty titles, Warners planned to release *Blade Runner*, *Casablanca* and *Doctor Zhivago* (David

Lean, 1965, US). Sony promised *Fly Away Home* (Carroll Ballard, 1996, US), *Jumanji* (Joe Johnston, 1995, US), *In the Line of Fire* (Wolfgang Petersen, 1993, US) and *Matilda* (Danny DeVito, 1996, US) among the first releases from Columbia TriStar (Markoff, 1997; Stalter, 1997). A list price of US$24.98 was set for these titles.

Meanwhile, DreamWorks, Disney, Paramount, 20th Century-Fox and Universal withheld their support. As Matsushita, one of the largest electronics manufacturers backing DVD, continued to hold a 20 per cent stake in Universal, the company's stand appeared unusual. While the Hollywood majors said they were cautiously waiting to see if DVD became a profit generator, speculation suggested they were holding out to be offered financial incentives to back the format (Weiner and Stalter, 1997: 51). Four months after the first players went on sale, in July 1997 Universal announced it too would start putting its films on DVD, beginning in November with the release of *Beethoven* (Brian Levant, 1992, US), *The Land before Time* (Don Bluth, 1988, US/Ir), *The Paper* (Ron Howard, 1994, US) and *The Shadow* (Russell Mulcahy, 1994 ,US) (Hettrick, 1997). Before the end of the year, Disney had added its support, releasing the company's first DVD titles for Christmas (Karon and Sandler, 1997).

Digital Video Express

Divx was developed in the context of this industry division. Digital Video Express was a joint venture between the computer and consumer electronics retailer Circuit City Store Inc. and the LA entertainment law firm Ziffen, Brittenham, Branca & Fischer. Forming the partnership Digital Video Express L.P., an initial investment of US$30m was made in May 1995 to develop Divx, with a further US$100m committed to the project in September 1997. Divx was launched in test markets on 8 June 1998 before receiving a national roll-out in October that year.

Although many commentators observed that the situation created a new format war, Divx was not really a format but an encryption system linked to a retail scheme. Divx used the same 120mm discs as DVD but integrated these with a retail system which was a peculiar hybrid of sell-through and rental video models: consumers bought discs, which they could own, but the cost of the initial purchase only allowed a limited viewing period, just as with video rental. In the system which Circuit City devised, discs were sold for US$4.49. A consumer could then take the disc home to watch at anytime but additional encryption coding ensured that from the moment a Divx disc was played for the first time, it could only be watched over the next forty-eight hours. Divx discs could be stopped, fast-forwarded and replayed, but the range of extras and special features which made DVD a popular format were not included.

Widescreen presentation, which became a standard feature for films on DVDs, was also not available and films were instead shown in pan-and-scan presentation. For an additional US$3.25, the disc could be renewed and unlocked to allow viewing for a further forty-eight hours, and if the consumer wanted to keep the film, then unlimited viewing was available at costs of US$14.99–19.99 per disc. Divx coded discs did not play on conventional DVD players, and so consumers were required to buy machines with the Divx feature; however, DVDs could then be played on these. Alongside the discs and player, consumers also had to register an account with Digital Video Express. Usage was recorded by the player, which contained an internal modem linked to a standard telephone line, through which the company could then monitor plays and take updates once or twice every month (Gilligan, 1998).

During its development, the Digital Video Express partnership promoted Divx as a form of DVD with enhanced features. At the centre of this appeal was the capacity which Divx allowed consumers to obtain digital-quality image and sound but at a lower price than DVD: rentals of DVD would not take off until late spring 1998 and discs were retailing at US$20–35. Divx offered DVD quality but at prices closer to the cost of renting VHS. Unlike video rentals, however, Digital Video Express emphasised that the consumer did not have to return the disc to a rental outlet and so was saved from incurring any late fees. Convenience therefore became one of the key selling points for the system.

Digital Video Express focused on promoting the benefits which Divx offered the consumer; however, the Hollywood majors saw several advantages which served their interests. While the Triple DES encryption coding was principally used as a way to limit the viewing period, it also offered high-level protection against illegal copying. Furthermore, Divx seemed to provide a solution to the problems of the first sale doctrine which had concerned the Hollywood majors since the growth of video sell-through and rental in the 1970s (see previous chapter). Apart from the cases where a consumer decided to pay and keep a film, the timed viewing control prevented the consumer from possessing the content, thereby avoiding the ownership issues caused by the first sale doctrine. If distributors simply wanted to withdraw a title, maybe to stimulate interest in a future release, then it could be quite easily taken out of circulation at the point of supply. Moreover, the system provided a form of revenue-sharing by allowing distributors participation in each transaction. Based on the US$4.49 list price, titles were sold at US$3 wholesale, half of which went to Hollywood distributors, who were also entitled to US$1.25 from each renewal (*Video Week*, 1998f).

Disney and Universal already supported DVD but by late 1997 they agreed terms to also release titles on Divx. Paramount and DreamWorks, meanwhile, had not committed to DVD and instead placed their support exclusively behind Divx. Fox had also withheld support for DVD and in February 1998 signed an agreement for Divx releases; MGM added its support two months later (Goldstein, 1998b; Hettrick, 1998a and 1998c). These distributors all agreed to give Divx titles the same day-and-date release as their VHS titles. With DVD already building a consumer base, securing agreements for the exclusive release of films on Divx was vital to establishing the system in the market. DreamWorks, Fox and Paramount all said they would not release on DVD in order to give Divx title exclusivity, while Disney, Universal and MGM said they would release on Divx and DVD simultaneously. To draw the support of the Hollywood majors, Digital Video Express offered financial inducements, committing to pay US$112m over five years in the way of upfront advances and minimum sales guarantees (Gilligan, 1998; Hettrick, 1998b: 85; *Video Week*, 1998b). While the majority of the majors lined up behind Divx, Warner and Columbia TriStar declared opposition to the system and stood by their exclusive commitment to DVD. This was unsurprising, as Toshiba and Sony were at the forefront of the consumer electronics manufacturers who had introduced DVD. Warner's Lieberfarb became the chief advocate of DVD and the most vocal critic of Divx, questioning the benefits of Divx and arguing that the system undermined the nascent DVD market by creating unnecessary confusion among consumers.

Further support for Divx came from hardware manufacturers. To produce the players, Digital Video Express initially agreed a deal with Zenith. Other hardware manufacturers followed: Thomson agreed to make players under its RCA and Proscan brands, and Matsushita produced players with the Panasonic label. JVC, Pioneer and Harman Kardon also offered their support. Video retailers were reluctant to support Divx, as the system threatened to damage the rental market, while electronics retailers were unhappy with stocking a product from which their powerful rival, Circuit City, had the most to gain. Only the San Francisco-based Good Guys chain of consumer electronics stores agreed to use their outlets for sales of Divx players and discs.

With limited support from retailers and the film industry still divided, plans to launch Divx were announced in the first quarter of 1998. Digital Video Express aimed to introduce Zenith-produced players supported by an initial catalogue of thirty titles from Disney, DreamWorks, Fox, MGM, Paramount and Universal. Two test markets were identified for the launch: Richmond, Virginia, home to Circuit City offices, and San Francisco, where Good Guys had an established presence.

As the launch of Divx neared, a series of announcements were made which promised to bring DVD rental closer to becoming a commercial reality. In April 1998, the month set for the launch of Divx, Blockbuster announced that it would be piloting DVD rental and Netflix.com was established as a new internet site offering consumers DVDs for rent through mail delivery. Warner also made a direct challenge to Divx, announcing in April that it would test a DVD rental programme in five areas, including Richmond and San Francisco, thereby placing it in head-to-head competition with the Divx launch (*Video Week*, 1998h). Warner's programme involved selling starter kits to rental outlets, which packaged together DVD players and Warner films on DVD. In the same month, Paramount, one of the earliest supporters of Divx, announced that it would also be adopting DVD. This left Fox and DreamWorks as the only major distributors still holding out to offer title exclusivity on Divx (Hettrick, 1998e). There was no clear reason given for this change of allegiance, but as Paramount was owned by Viacom, which also owned Blockbuster, the company's backing for DVD appeared to fall into line with supporting the video chain's rental plans.

The Failure of Divx

After the launch was pushed back two months, on 8 June Divx players and discs went on sale in five Circuit City stores in Richmond and thirty-eight Circuit City and Good Guys stores across San Francisco (*Video Week*, 1998d). Boston-based advertising company Arnold Communications prepared a campaign which hailed Divx as 'DVD and so much more'. Immediately, the system faced problems. Consumers were reluctant to pay US$499 for a Divx player, which cost around US$100 more than an entry-level DVD player. A catalogue of thirty titles had been planned for the time of launch but shipping difficulties meant many titles were unavailable. Supporting distributors also offered limited title exclusivity. Fox, Paramount and Disney provided several titles already available on VHS but scheduled for a DVD release later in the month, including *The Full Monty* (Peter Cattaneo, 1997, UK), *Clear and Present Danger* (Phillip Noyce, 1994, US) and *Flubber* (Les Mayfield, 1997, US). Meanwhile, MGM and Universal offered titles already available on both VHS and DVD, such as *Tomorrow Never Dies* (Roger Spottiswoode, 1997, UK/US) and *Liar, Liar* (Tom Shadyac, 1997, US) (*Video Week*, 1998e). As Richard Sharp, Chairman and CEO of Circuit City, said at the press conference accompanying the launch, 'we're a little title-challenged right now' (quoted in *Video Week*, 1998a).

Warner responded in July by lowering DVD costs with the introduction of three tiers of pricing: US$24.98, US$19.98 and US$14.98. It also announced that it would be rolling out its rental programme nationally and reducing the prices of its DVD starter kits for rental outlets (*Video Week*, 1998g). Ads jointly sponsored by Warner and software dealers appeared in New York, Los Angeles, San Francisco and Chicago newspapers, and although these did not refer directly to Divx, they did allude to its account management system with the picture of a hand holding a telephone cable accompanied by the statement 'Don't let anyone feed you a line' (Brinkley, 1998).

Around fifty new Divx titles were added each month, building up to the national roll-out in October 1998 across 700 retail outlets. However, the system failed to capture consumer interest: by June 1999, 200,000 Divx players had been sold and 1m discs, compared to 2m DVD players and 30m DVD discs. On 16 June 1999, just over a year after Divx was launched, Digital Video Express announced that it would be no longer registering new customer accounts. Only 494 titles were available on Divx by the time the venture folded, compared to 3,600 on DVD. Divx players still worked as fully operational DVD players and owners of Divx players could claim a US$100 rebate to bring their purchase into line with the cost of DVD players. A two-year phase-out period was scheduled until 30 June 2001, during which time discs could be watched and renewed. In closing down the business, Circuit City made an after tax loss of US$114m (Graser, 1999; Stroughton, 1999).

Sharp identified lack of support by the Hollywood majors and retailers as causes for the failure but there was a more substantial reason for the demise of Divx. As a closed system, Divx offered few benefits for consumers and none at all when compared to open DVD. Hardware costs were higher and pricing of the limited viewing period became uncompetitive as DVD rental was introduced. Without the added features or widescreen presentation, Divx actually seemed like DVD only less. Divx offered copyright holders such as the Hollywood majors greater control over video consumption but it was precisely that control which consumers rejected. As Mark Macgillivray of H&M Consulting observed, '[t]hese technologies, particularly in entertainment, tend to come to market because they can be brought to market rather than because customers want them to be brought to market' (quoted in Graser, 1999).

With the collapse of Divx, the path was clear for open DVD to become the digital disc standard. Back in August 1998, Fox had announced that it would start releasing on DVD for rental and retail from 3 November, starting with six titles, including *The Abyss* (James Cameron, 1989, US), *Home Alone 3* (Raja Gosnell, 1997, US) and *Hope Floats* (Forest Whitaker, 1998, US). Shortly afterwards, in September, DreamWorks also announced its first DVD titles, with *Mousehunt* (Gore Verbinski, 1997, US), *The Peacemaker* (Mimi Leder, 1997, US) and *Small Soldiers* (Joe Dante, 1998, US). By the end of 1998, all the Hollywood majors were releasing on DVD. A standard digital disc format or system and the united backing of the main software providers gave the market the stability and industry support necessary for making DVD a popular entertainment medium. In 1999, the DVD population in the US jumped, from 1.2m to 4.6m homes. By 2001, almost a quarter of television households owned a DVD player (table 5.1).

HOLLYWOOD FILM AND THE DVD BOOM

After the huge increases witnessed during the 1980s, growth in the video soft-ware market began to slow in the early 1990s. Video rental still accounted for the largest portion of consumer spending on video. According to estimates by *Video Store Magazine*, consumers spent US$9.8bn on video in 1990, of which US$6.7bn was on rental and US$3.1bn on purchasing cassettes. By 1993, total spending had reached US$12.8bn after rental spending increased to US$7.6bn against US$5.2bn on sell-through. Rental transactions increased from 3,230m in 1990 to 3,645m in 1993 (based on data reported in Monush, 1995: 697). DVD changed this, for after the format was introduced in 1997, it not only re-energised the entire video software business in the US, displacing VHS in terms of both the volume and value of sales, but also directed the market towards retail over rental.

The DVD Windfall

When pre-recorded videocassettes first appeared on the market, they were given high pricing levels aimed at rentailers. To encourage the establishment and growth of a large retail market for DVD, the Hollywood majors immediately started pricing DVD releases at comparatively low prices. Discs were cheap to manufacture and could be offered at prices which appealed to consumers. In the first year DVD was on the market in the US, Warner and Columbia were already setting some sell-through prices as low as US$14–US$18 per disc. Other discs were priced in the region of US$39.95. As Viacom regarded this strategy as a direct challenge to the rental market, which was dominated by its subsidiary Blockbuster Entertainment, the conglomerate's Paramount division withheld releasing any titles on DVD for over two years (Epstein, 2006: 214). As part of its challenge to Divx, when Warner Home Video launched its pilot rental pro-gramme in spring 1998, the distributor was charting new ground for the Hollywood majors who only began to offer their titles for DVD rental from late 1998 into 1999 onwards. However, low pricing had already established DVD as a sell-through medium and even after titles were offered for rental, DVD con-tinued to be predominantly a retail market. In 2002, six years after the format was launched in the US, the volume of DVD units sold for rental or retail sur-passed VHS sales for the first time: in 2001, combined VHS rental and retail units totalled 625.8m, compared to 351m DVD units; by 2002, VHS sales had declined to 481.1m, while DVD sales increased to 619.2m (figure 5.1). In 2005, sell-through DVD accounted for 1,292.6m of the total 1,341.2m VHS and DVD units sold to dealers for either rental or retail.

DVD offered generous profit margins for the major distributors and retailers. For example, a newly released DVD may retail for US$20, with a wholesale price

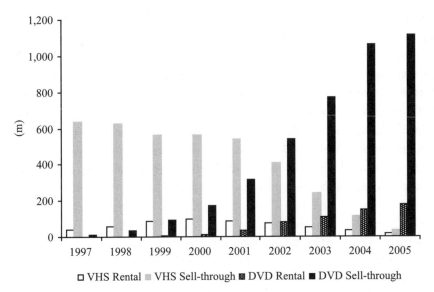

Sources: compiled from Adams Media Research data reported in MPA (2003: 30; 2004b: 30; and 2006f: 29).

Figure 5.1 The Rise of DVD: Sales of VHS and DVD Software Units to Dealers in the US (1997–2005)

in the region of US$17, providing the retailer with US$3. With manufacturing costs of US$2.50 per unit and US$2.50 for sales and marketing, the distributor would profit by US$12 (not counting returns) (Blume, 2006: 340). Older library or 'catalogue' titles would likely stay on the shelves for longer than new and recent releases, selling fewer units and usually at lower prices; however, for the retailer, the lower volume of sales was balanced by higher profit margins. In the case of an older title retailing at US$9.95, with a wholesale price of US$8, the US$1.95 profit represented over 24 per cent of the cost, compared to the US$3 or 17 per cent from US$18 for newer titles (Feingold, 2006: 413).

DVD not only revived the video software market but also made sell-through sales the biggest revenue generator from all distribution channels for the Hollywood majors. Sell-through DVD became the largest source of consumer spending on filmed entertainment across all distribution channels fed by the majors. Research agency Adams Media estimated that in 2004, a total of US$39.1bn was spent by US consumers on films across the theatrical box office, video retail and rental, pay-TV film channel subscriptions and on-demand services. Sell-through video – both VHS and DVD – accounted for the largest portion of this expenditure, with US$11.4bn or 29 per cent, of which DVD sales contributed 94 per cent. Rental, meanwhile, provided US$8.9bn or 23 per cent of total spending. Video retail and rental therefore accounted for over half of all expenditure on filmed entertainment. In comparison, the theatrical box office, the second largest source of spending, attracted US$9.6bn in ticket sales (24 per cent of total spending), while pay-TV subscriptions provided US$8.3bn (21 per cent) and on-demand services US$900m (2 per cent). From sales across all distribution outlets, US$17.2bn was returned to distributors as net revenues. Sell-through video not only accounted for half of the total revenues but also provided the highest returns. Approximately 80 per cent, or US$8.7bn, of consumer spending on sell-through video returned to distributors as revenues, compared to 25 per cent (US$2.2bn) from video rental and 47 per cent (US$4.4bn) through the box office (*Screen Digest*, 2005a).

A Hit-Driven Market

Feature films released by the Hollywood majors have continued to dominate the video market. Based on combined DVD and VHS sales, of the top twenty retail titles sold in 2004 and 2005, all were distributed by the Hollywood majors or by divisions of the same parent companies, such as Time Warner's New Line Cinema and Disney's Miramax (tables 5.2 and 5.3). When released on video, these films replayed the type of performance they had previously enjoyed at the theatrical box office, as most of the top twenty video releases had also featured in the top twenty at the box office in the years they were released. Like the theatrical box office, video retailing therefore cultivated a hit-driven market concentrated around a few dozen films from the majors in any year.

Looking further at the biggest sellers in 2004 and 2005, the top one or two titles on video stood out from even the other hits. In 2005, the top-selling title of the year, *The Incredibles* (Brad Bird, 2004, US), sold more than double the number of units than even the fifth-ranked title, *The Polar Express* (Robert Zemeckis, 2004, US). While their sales rankings were based on combined DVD and VHS units, if taking the DVD profit margin of US$12 per unit as a rough indicator, then *The Incredibles* returned in the region of US$209.3m to Disney, compared to the US$102m which Warner picked up from *The Polar Express*.

When it is considered that these titles were joined at the top of the video charts by films like *Shrek 2* (Andrew Adamson, Kelly Asbury and Conrad Vernon, 2004, US), *Madagascar* (Eric Darnell and Tom McGrath, 2005, US) and *Shark Tale* (Bibo Bergeron, Vicky Jenson and Rob Letterman, 2004, US), then it is clear that cross-generational family entertainment has remained at the forefront of defining popularity in the video market (see previous chapter). The other noticeable trend among the highest-selling titles was the preponderance of instalments from fantasy-adventure franchises, e.g. *Lord of the Rings: The Return of the King* (Peter Jackson, 2003, US/NZ/Ger), *Harry Potter: The Prisoner of Az-kaban* (Alfonso Cuarón, 2004, UK/US), *Spider-man 2* (Sam Raimi, 2004,

Title	Distributor	Units Sold (m)	Box-Office Gross (US$m)	Box-Office Ranking in Year of Release[2]
1 Shrek 2	DreamWorks	22.22	436.7	1
2 Lord of the Rings: The Return of the King	New Line	17.29	377.0	3
3 The Passion of the Christ	Fox	12.67	370.3	3
4 Harry Potter: The Prisoner of Azkaban	Warner Bros.	12.29	249.4	5
5 Spider-man 2	Sony	11.08	373.4	2
6 The Lion King 1½[3]	Buena Vista	9.16		
7 Elf	New Line	8.92	173.4	7
8 Brother Bear	Buena Vista	8.46	85.3	31
9 The Day After Tomorrow	Fox	6.70	186.7	6
10 Star War Trilogy[4]	Fox	6.20	n/a	n/a
11 The Matrix Revolutions	Warner Bros.	5.78	139.3	11
12 Kill Bill Vol.1	Buena Vista	5.66	70.1	40
13 Cheaper by the Dozen	Fox	5.59	138.6	30
14 American Wedding	Universal	5.49	104.4	23
15 The Bourne Supremacy	Universal	5.28	176.0	7
16 The Last Samurai	Warner Bros.	5.22	111.1	28
17 Shrek	DreamWorks	5.16	267.7	2
18 Aladdin – Special Edition[5]	Buena Vista	5.03		
19 Dr Seuss' The Cat in the Hat	Universal	4.91	100.4	27
20 Princess Diaries 2: Royal Engagement	Buena Vista	4.60	95.1	22

Sources: compiled from MPA (2005: 16 and 31) and D'Alessandro (2001, 2004 and 2005).

Notes:
1. Based on combined VHS and DVD units sales.
2. Films were released theatrically in 2001, 2003 or 2004. Where the release of films was carried over other years, box office ranking is for the year of original release only.
3. Direct to video.
4. Three-film box set of Star Wars (George Lucas, 1977, US), The Empire Strikes Back (Irwin Kershner, 1980, US) and Return of the Jedi (Richard Marquand, 1983, US).
5. Aladdin (Ron Clements and John Musker, US) was originally released theatrically in 1992. Box-office gross is not included, as value and ranking not comparable to 2004.

Table 5.2 Top 20 Sell-through Titles in the US[1] (2004)

Table 5.3 Top 20 Sell-through Titles in the US[1] (2005)

Title	Distributor	Units Sold (m)	Box-Office Gross (US$m)	Box-Office Ranking in Year of Release[2]
1 The Incredibles	Disney	17.44	261.4	4
2 Star Wars: Episode III	Fox	10.73	380.3	1
3 Madagascar	DreamWorks	10.28	193.1	9
4 Shark Tale	DreamWorks	10.06	160.8	9
5 The Polar Express	Warner Bros.	8.50	173.2	10
6 Meet the Fockers	Universal	7.31	279.2	8
7 National Treasure	Buena Vista/Disney	7.20	173.0	11
8 Cinderella[3]	Buena Vista/Disney	6.86		
9 Batman Begins	Warner Bros.	6.42	205.3	8
10 Ray	Universal	6.11	75.3	38
11 Mr & Mrs Smith	Fox	6.02	186.3	10
12 Charlie and the Chocolate Factory	Warner Bros.	5.81	206.4	7
13 War of the Worlds	DreamWorks	5.42	234.3	4
14 Bambi: Special Edition[3]	Buena Vista/Disney	5.39		
15 The Notebook	New Line	5.16	81.0	31
16 Robots	Fox	5.12	128.2	15
17 Troy	Warner Bros.	4.89	133.2	13
18 The 40 Year Old Virgin	Universal	4.71	109.1	19
19 Napoleon Dynamite	Fox	4.70	44.5	67
20 Fantastic Four	Fox	4.61	154.7	13

Sources: compiled from MPA (2005: 16; and 2006f: 14 and 30) and D'Alessandro (2005)

Notes:
1. Based on combined VHS and DVD units sales.
2. Films were released theatrically in 2004 or 2005. Where the release of films was carried over both years, box-office ranking is for the year of original release only.
3. Cinderella (Clyde Geronimi, Wilfred Jackson and Hamilton Luske, US) was originally released theatrically in 1950, and Bambi (David Hand, US) was first shown in theatres during 1942, before receiving re-issues in 1982 and 1988. Box-office grosses are not included, as values and rankings not comparable to 2005.

Table 5.3 Top 20 Sell-through Titles in the US[1] (2005)

US) and *Star Wars: Episode III – The Revenge of the Sith* (George Lucas, 2005, US), which again cater for a broad cross-generational audience.

In a market predominantly focused on video releases of films shown over the last twelve months in theatres, Disney's continuing strategy of mining its back catalogue to re-release animated classics on video media for new generations of children has remained a distinctive feature of the company's home entertainment policy. *Bambi* (David Hand, 1942, US), *Cinderella* and *Aladdin* all provided hit DVD titles for Disney in 2004 and 2005 without the benefit of any immediate theatrical re-release. After Disney's success with *The Return of Jafar* (see previous chapter), the distributor had continued producing its 'video premieres', but *The Lion King 1½* (Bradley Raymond, 2004, US) stood out as the only direct-to-video release to rank successfully among the sell-through hits.

Although most video hits usually follow on from a strong theatrical performance, box-office success is not a pre-condition of video success. In the case of *Napoleon Dynamite* (Jared Hess, 2004, US), the independently produced feature was picked up by Fox's speciality distribution division, Fox Searchlight. The film was released in US theatres from 11 June 2004, but with an unknown director and lead cast, Fox Searchlight only gave the film a limited release. Good word-of-mouth among cinemagoers, however, sustained the run for eight months and the film finally grossed over US$44m, coming 67th in *Variety*'s annual box-office rankings (D'Alessandro, 2005: 14). That same word-of-mouth then carried over to the film's performance on video: 20th Century-Fox Home Entertainment released *Napoleon Dynamite* on VHS and DVD from 21 December 2004, where it found a new audience to become the 19th highest sell-through title of 2005 with 4.7m units sold (table 5.3).

In the case of the Quentin Tarantino-directed feature *Kill Bill: Vol. 1* (2003, US), Disney's speciality production and distribution subsidiary Miramax Films produced the film and released it to theatres on 10 October 2003. By the end of the calendar year, it had grossed US$69.7m in North America and was placed 40th in *Variety*'s end-of-year rankings (D'Alessandro, 2004: 14). Continuing its run until late May 2004, *Kill Bill: Vol. 1* eventually grossed US$70.1m in total. With the film still finishing its run in theatres, on 13 April 2004 Miramax's video division released it on DVD and by the end of the year nearly 5.7m units had been sold, making it the 12th ranked title in the sell-through chart for that year (table 5.2). Although only a modest success in theatres, *Kill Bill: Vol. 1* became a video hit.

Part of this discrepancy could be explained by the niche logic of the speciality market, where the cultish auteur status of Tarantino appeals to a relatively small but loyal set of fan consumers. After their initial video release, Tarantino's earlier features *Reservoir Dogs* (1992, US), *Pulp Fiction* (1994, US) and *Jackie*

Brown (1997, US) had all appeared in special editions supplemented by additional DVD extras, catering for, but arguably also cultivating, a collecting mentality around the director's name. Equally, by co-opting the narrative conventions and visual style of Hong Kong action cinema, *Kill Bill: Vol 1* tapped into a specialised sector of the US film market where few Hong Kong imports gain a theatrical release and interested consumers must rely instead on VHS or DVD if they want to see titles.

TRANSFORMATIONS IN VIDEO RENTAL AND RETAIL

DVD took the US video business into the digital age. However, some of the most significant developments in the business could not be attributed to technology but rather the emergence of new models and channels for video rental and retail. From the late 1990s, these changes were evident in three ways: the introduction of revenue-sharing arrangements for video rental, the increasing importance of mass merchants for the sell-through market and the launch of online rental services. Hollywood again played a key role in shaping all these developments.

Revenue-Sharing

As discussed in the previous chapter, the first sale doctrine barred video distributors from participating in revenues from rental transactions. Although unsuccessful in attempts to force their leasing plans on rentailers in the early 1980s, the Hollywood majors continued to believe that they were entitled to a share of rental revenues. Distributors shared in revenues from tickets sold at the theatrical box office, and the majors wanted to see video rental adopt a similar model. Revenue-sharing therefore remained a goal for the Hollywood majors. Rentrak, a video wholesaler based in Portland, Oregon, had organised revenue-sharing deals with small rental chains from 1988, and in the late 1990s the matter of revenue-sharing became a hot topic for the video business as the Hollywood majors began to agree non-exclusive revenue-sharing deals with Blockbuster, the largest of the rental chains. Blockbuster did not pioneer revenue-sharing but it did apply such arrangements on a scale which transformed the whole rental business.

Blockbuster was the largest chain in the US. In the late 1990s, the chain commanded a 23 per cent share of the rental market, but in recent years the company's profits had fallen as part of the general decline in rentals as retail DVD dominated the video market. For rentailers, a widely recognised problem was shortages in the depth or number of copies stored at outlets. Wholesale pricing limited the volume of titles which could be bought: by the late 1990s, tapes still wholesaled at around US$50 to US$70, requiring rentailers to make large outlays when buying new releases in volume. With limited depth of copy, stores ran out of stock and customers frequently left without their chosen film or any film at all. While customers may select a different title from their first choice, one study indicated that customers rented on average 1.4 movies per transaction if their first choice was not available, compared to 2.4 movies per transaction when that choice was available (Jamgocyan, 1998).

Revenue-sharing arrangements provided a solution to this situation. Instead of paying the high rental price, rentailers could buy cassettes at prices between US$5 and US$10 per copy and in return pay a 45–50 per cent share of revenues to the wholesaler or distributor (Hindes, 1998: 9). Such arrangements benefited both rentailers and the major Hollywood suppliers. Rentailers were saved from making large outlays of capital to buy copies in volume, while distributors not only realised their aim of seeing income from each rental transaction but also could rely on a more continuous flow of income across the financial year, compared to the lump payments made when copies were bought in wholesale volumes. In this scheme, rentailers and the Hollywood majors shared in both the risks but also the rewards of the rental market.

After appointing the former 7–11 executive John Antioco as its new CEO in June 1997, Blockbuster began to experiment with revenue-sharing. Starting in November 1997, test trials were conducted in six markets before a national roll-out during 1998. Rentrak was already administering revenue-sharing transactions for 6,500 stores, which accounted for around 20–25 per cent of the rental market, and in March 1998 the wholesaler signed an agreement to monitor transactions at Blockbuster's 3,300 stores in North America. To feed the scheme, during 1998 Blockbuster secured a non-exclusive revenue-sharing agreement with Disney. Universal, MGM, Warners, Columbia-TriStar and Paramount followed but Fox held back from joining the scheme. To force the issue, Blockbuster reduced the volume of Fox titles it bought and the distributor eventually signed an agreement in February 1999 (Sweeting, 1999). Initially, all these arrangements were for VHS only and did not include DVD.

Revenue-sharing attracted criticisms concerning the impact of bulk buying on diversity. Increasing depth of copy reduced shelf space for other titles, with an impact on the variety or breadth of titles available. As this situation gave greater prominence to mass popular A titles from the Hollywood majors, these companies gained greater leverage than independent distributors when dealing with Blockbuster or other rentailers. For independent producers and distributors, whose films may get a limited theatrical release, the backend of the video market was very important for gaining revenues unavailable at the box office. Independents were disadvantaged, however, by revenue-sharing arrangements, for rentailers might delay returning the share of revenues for six months or longer instead of paying the higher wholesale price close to the time cassettes were delivered. This could seriously impede cashflow for producers and distributors who lacked the levels of finance enjoyed by the Hollywood majors. Furthermore, independent releases actually benefited from any shortages in the availability of A titles in rental stores, as consumers may select a less well-known title as an alternative to the hits from the majors (Hindes, 1998: 14).

Where revenue-sharing became a major area of contention was in disputes between independent rentailers against Blockbuster and the Hollywood majors. Blockbuster presented revenue-sharing as a programme aimed at serving the interests of consumers, but other rentailers criticised the scheme for strengthening Blockbuster's market share at the expense of smaller chains and outlets. Independent retailers complained that the major distributors granted Blockbuster unfair preferential terms. Conventionally, Rentrak's revenue-sharing scheme saw 55 per cent of revenues go to distributors, with 40 per cent retained by the rentailer and 5 per cent by Rentrak (Goldstein, 1998a). But at the annual meeting of the Video Software Dealers Association (VSDA) in July 1998, Antioco acknowledged that the company kept 50–60 per cent from some transactions (Sweeting, 1998). Concerns were also raised that as a result of revenue-sharing, Blockbuster could buy popular titles in huge bulk orders, creating overwhelming depth of copy while also allowing the chain to cut rental charges below the average.

At the VSDA meeting in July 1998, independent rentailers organised to form the Independent Video Retailers Group (IVRG) with the intention of taking legal action against Blockbuster (Goldstein, 1998a). Although the IVRG did not in the end bring action against Blockbuster and the major distributors, the cause was picked up by the Fairness Alliance of Independent Retailers (FAIR), which in July 1999 filed two lawsuits against Blockbuster and the majors under federal anti-trust and California state law. These suits rested on two assertions: a conspiracy charge that Blockbuster and the major distributors had colluded to prevent independent rentailers from engaging in revenue-sharing arrangements, and a price discrimination charge, according to which it was alleged that the Hollywood majors granted more favourable terms to Blockbuster.

After nearly two years of litigation, in March 2001 the US District Court in San Antonio, Texas, denied the plaintiffs' request to have the case heard as a class action, and the same decision was reached by the Los Angeles County Superior Court in January the following year. In the absence of class action certification, three individual plaintiffs pursued the case but without success. On 27 June 2002 at the federal court in San Antonio, Judge Edward Prado ruled in favour of the defence, dismissing the case after the plaintiffs failed to supply sufficient evidence supporting their allegations. In the other case, the Los Angeles Superior Court denied class certification in January 2002 and on 21

February entered a judgment in favour of the defence. In both suits, the defence was able to show that many independent rentailers had not attempted to secure revenue-sharing arrangements with the majors, and the conspiracy charge was weakened as the plaintiffs were unable to provide compelling evidence of collusion between the majors. Subsequently, in August 2003 the US Court of Appeals for the Fifth Circuit upheld the decision of the federal judge, while in November 2005 the California Court of Appeal affirmed the trial court's dismissal of the anti-trust and conspiracy claims. However, the Court of Appeal did reverse the dismissal of claims made under the California Unfair Practices Act, sending these back to the trial court (Viacom, 2005: I-28; Watson, 2005).

Whether the anti-trust and conspiracy claims were justified or not, after the introduction of revenue-sharing Blockbuster did consolidate its dominance of the rental market. Industry observers had predicted that the decline of the rental market would bring about the collapse of Blockbuster, yet by 2000 Blockbuster

	Up-front Fee[1]	Rentailer/Rentrak Split[2]	Minimum Transaction Fee	Sell-through Date[3]	Lease Term[4]
	(US$)	(%)	US$	(Days)	(Months)
First Look/DEJ	0	65/35	1.05	30	6
Lionsgate Home Entertainment	0	61/39	1.10	29	6
20th Century-Fox	1.25	61/39	1.25	30	6
Paramount/ DreamWorks	1.50	62/38	1.20	31	6
Sony Pictures	1.50	61/39	1.25	29	6
Warner (including HBO, New Line and TNT)	1.00	63/37	1.10	29	6

Source: Rentrak (2006)

Notes:
1. Or 'order processing fee': the amount paid by the rentailer per DVD or VHS copy including shipping.
2. The percentage division between the rentailer and Rentrak of each rental transaction. For example, on a 65/35 split for US$3 transaction, the rentailer would pay Rentral US$1.05. However, the amount paid to Rentrak is protected by a 'minimum transaction fee' which sets the least amount the rentailer is required to pay for each transaction. These fees vary between suppliers and fall in the region of US$1.05 to US$1.25.
3. The period of time which must elapse after the street date before any former rental DVDs and cassettes can be offered for sale. Usually 50% of inventory can be sold immediately after this time. Rentrak are paid a flat fee per copy – typically US$2.00 to US$4.50 for DVD, or US$1.35 to 2.00 for VHS – or otherwise a percentage is paid of 35–45%.
4. The length of time rentailers are required to keep at least one copy of the title available for rental. After this term expires, the remaining inventory can be returned or purchased.

Table 5.4 Rentrak: Supplier Terms (2006)

had increased its market share to 36 per cent (Blockbuster, 2000: 5). Concurrently, according to the VSDA, between 1998 and 2001 an estimated 2,500 independent video stores – approximately 10 per cent of the national total – closed (Schiesel, 2002).

Blockbuster's dominance of the rental market gave the chain the leverage to force terms with the majors, as was evident when Fox was cornered into joining the revenue-sharing programme. Blockbuster's tough negotiating power was regarded by the majors as having forced revenue splits down to unprofitable levels. This situation had the effect of souring the relationship between the majors and Blockbuster. On 31 December 2002, Disney sued Blockbuster, accusing the chain of improperly deducting US$55m in promotional and operations credits while failing to account for 'hundreds of thousands' of cassettes worth US$26m, prematurely selling 200,000 before their rental period had expired and selling 45,000 cassettes over the amount permitted by the five-year revenue-sharing agreement signed in 1997 (Sweeting, 2003b). Blockbuster finally settled in July 2005 with a payment of $18m to Disney but no new revenue-sharing deal was agreed.

Following the introduction of DVD, Blockbuster's position was undermined as the majors flooded the market with low-priced discs sold through mass merchants. Consequently, the majors began to let their revenue-sharing agreements with Blockbuster expire and priced all VHS titles for sell-through in order to promote the retail market (Amdur, 2004a: 4). Rentrak continued to administer revenue-sharing for the majors but films were offered on a title-by-title basis or on selected titles only with no formal output deal (Netherby, 2004). In 2006, Rentrak held deals with the major Hollywood suppliers DreamWorks, Fox, Paramount, Sony and Warner, together with independent distributors First Look/DEJ and Lionsgate. DVD and VHS units were offered for low upfront fees with splits varying between 61/39 per cent and 65/35 per cent in favour of the rentailer against minimum transaction fees of US$1.05–1.25. Units could be leased for up to six months or sold off after twenty-nine to thirty-one days (table 5.4).

Mass Merchants

Revenue-sharing had partly been a response to the flattening video rental market. As the US market became more focused on sales over rental, so discount mass merchant chains such as Wal-Mart, Target and Costco, along with consumer electronics chains like Best Buy and Circuit City, became the most important outlets for the video business.

By the late 1990s, Wal-Mart rivalled Blockbuster as the most powerful outlet for video in the US. At the start of 2004, Wal-Mart had over 3,500 stores in the

US, including its Supercenter, SAM'S CLUB and Neighborhood Market outlets. As one commentator noted, '[w]ith 100 million Americans shopping there each week compared with the 30 million who pay for a movie ticket, Wal-Mart is the largest distribution outlet in the film biz' (Learmonth, 2005: 1). While Blockbuster is a specialist video chain, Wal-Mart stocks general merchandise, selling DVDs under the same roof as apparel, bedding, books, electronics hardware, garden furniture, housewares, pharmaceuticals and toys. Wal-Mart built its status as the world's largest retailer on a reputation for low prices. DVDs were sold at bargain prices at close to cost or at a loss – in some cases as low as US$5 – to draw in customer traffic in the hope that shoppers may go on to buy other products while on-site. Outlets do not attempt to stock a diverse range of video titles: most are popular and family-orientated films in the top twenty chart together with a limited selection of bargain-priced catalogue titles. This strategy saw Wal-Mart gain a huge share of the sell-through market: in 2001, Wal-Mart accounted for 17.6 per cent of sell-through revenues and by 2002 that share had increased to 25 per cent (table 5.5) (Hazelton, 2004a: 12). According to a 2004 survey by the research company NPD, Wal-Mart was responsible for 37 per cent of all units sold, followed by Best Buy with 14 per cent and Target, Costco and Circuit City holding a combined 13 per cent share (Amdur, 2004b: 6).

As a non-specialist video retailer, Wal-Mart co-opted expertise by assigning a single Hollywood distributor as a so-called 'category captain'. This role was occupied for several years by Warner Home Video in an arrangement which gave the distributor access to confidential sales data from Wal-Mart in order to advise the chain on the types of product to stock. For Wal-Mart, the arrangement saved on management costs, while Warner obtained privileged information on a large segment of the sell-through market (Hazelton, 2004a: 13).

	Estimated No. Outlets	DVD Market Share (%)	DVD Sales (US$m)
Wal-Mart	2,849	25.5	2,200
Best Buy	578	9.8	851
Target Stores	1,145	9.2	805
Costco	304	7.3	631
Blockbuster	5,566	4.2	370

Source: adapted from *Video Store* magazine market research data in Hazelton (2004b).

Table 5.5 Leading Retailers for DVD Sales in the US (2002)

For the Hollywood majors, Wal-Mart offers the benefit of dealing with a single customer in order to sell a large volume of DVDs: in 2004, an estimated 39 per cent of Disney DVDs purchased in the US were sold through Wal-Mart. On the other hand, Wal-Mart's dominant market share gives the chain great buying power, putting the retailer in a position to gain broader influence in the video business. Wal-Mart refuses to stock any titles carrying parental advisory warnings and this policy is taken into account by distributors. As one executive from Warner Home Video commented, '[w]e will release certain products if [Walmart purchasing agents] say they are interested in them and not release certain products if they are not' (quoted in Hazelton, 2004a: 12–13).

Wal-Mart is also reducing the shelf life of DVDs by quickly rotating new releases from prime display spots once sales begin to diminish. Consequently, new DVDs make 60–80 per cent of their sales in the first three weeks, compressing the commercial life of discs and creating a situation similar to that found in theatrical exhibition, where the success of hit films depends on their performance in the first one or two weeks. As Bob Alexander, home entertainment analyst at Alexander and Associates comments, '[t]he fact that sales are compressed into those first three weeks actually reduces total sales. It's a big problem. You are actually shrinking the market' (quoted in Learmonth, 2005: 1). However, compressing the amount of time over which a hit title will make its highest volume of sales does not necessarily reduce total sales, and instead may stimulate an urgency to buy among consumers which actually raises sales. Wal-Mart's retail power allows the chain to leverage better deals with the majors than other retailers can obtain. However, as Wal-Mart has a reputation for forcing wholesale price cuts from suppliers, there is a concern in the industry that its budget-priced DVDs can generally force down prices across the market: 'Today's loss-leader ... could be tomorrow's new retail benchmark' (Amdur, 2004b: 6). In which case, mass volume sales do not compensate for an overall devaluing of the sell-through market. On the other hand, it could be claimed that DVDs are over-priced by distributors and other retailers anyway, and so Wal-Mart are actually forcing the market to set more realistic prices.

Online Retail and Rental

Aside from the bricks-and-mortar rentailer or retail outlets represented by Blockbuster and Wal-Mart, the growth in electronic commerce has made the internet a key channel for buying and renting video. In the 1990s, online retailers such as Amazon.com and Buy.com added VHS and DVD to their product range. In 2002, Amazon was selling more VHS and DVD units than any other online retailer, with an estimated US$301.9m in gross revenues (table 5.6). With online retailing, a more extensive range of inventory can be offered compared to the stock held at bricks-and-mortar stores. Amazon fulfils orders through its own huge warehousing and shipping operations, while Buy.com routes orders to the independent wholesalers Ingram Entertainment in Nashville and Baker & Taylor in Chicago (Sweeting, 2006b: 435).

Online rentals have also transformed the manner in which video enters the home. Netflix, headquartered in Los Gatos, California, introduced its innovative subscription scheme on 14 April 1998 (Hettrick, 1998d) before patenting it in 2003. Monthly subscription charges are set at different levels from US$4.99 to US$23.99, allowing customers to choose options to take out between one and eight titles at any time. Titles can be ordered online and despatched through the US mail, with pre-paid envelopes included for return. Late-return fees are eliminated and a distinctive feature for the Netflix operation is its online queuing system: customers can organise and prioritise a list of requests to be despatched once they become available and the customer has freed space from his or her current quota. As the number of rentals each month is unlimited under most options, the time taken to view and then return films is the only constraint on the volume of rentals. Several other online rental schemes have appeared, including cafedvd.com, dvdavenue.com and intelliflix.com among others, but Netflix has rapidly become the clear market leader. By summer 2006, Netflix offered in excess of 60,000 titles, boasting over 4.9m subscribers and shipping from thirty-nine regional distribution centres to reach 90 per cent of its customers with overnight delivery (Netflix, 2006).

Netflix, but also Amazon, are cited by Chris Anderson (2006) as examples of how e-commerce is creating the economic phenomenon which he terms 'the Long Tail'. Based on analysis of online services offering music downloads, books

	Products	Estimated Gross Revenue (US$m)
Amazon.com	DVD and VHS Sales	302
Netflix.com	DVD Rentals	154
Buy.com	DVD and VHS Sales	53
DVD.com	DVD Sales	49
Walmart.com	DVD and VHS Sales/DVD Rentals	48

Source: adapted from *Video Store* magazine market research data in Hazelton (2004b).

Table 5.6 Highest Grossing Online Services for VHS/DVD Retail and Rental in the US (2002)

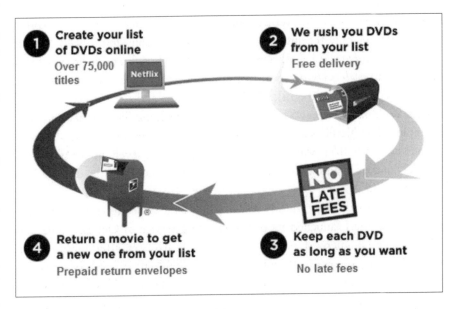

1 Create your list of DVDs online
Over 75,000 titles
Netflix

2 We rush you DVDs from your list
Free delivery

NO LATE FEES

4 Return a movie to get a new one from your list
Prepaid return envelopes

3 Keep each DVD as long as you want
No late fees

Online retailing: Netflix's business model

for sale or video rental, Anderson argues such services are better placed than conventional bricks-and-mortar outlets to meet the demand of niche markets for cultural goods. On a demand curve ranked by popularity, online services will show high levels of demand for a few 'hit' products yet there will also be widespread but low levels of demand for an abundance of other less popular goods, forming a 'Long Tail' for the curve. For Anderson, 'all those niches, when aggregated, can make up a significant market' (p. 10). Consequently, he concludes, '[i]f the twentieth-century entertainment industry was about *hits*, the twenty-first will be equally about *niches*' (emphasis in original, p. 16).

Undoubtedly, online retailers and rental outlets like Amazon and Netflix are in the business of hits on video, but the breadth of inventory which they can house in their warehouses exceeds anything which could be supplied by even the largest video retail or rental store. Online services supply the large market formed by cumulative niche tastes when other conventional retailers or rentailers cannot. According to Anderson's research, 21 per cent of Netflix's sales came from items which were not available in offline stores (p. 23). Hits are, of course, still important for online rentailers, but at the same time these services also diversify choice: 'You can find *everything* out here in the Long Tail ... Oh sure, there's a lot of crap here in the Long Tail' but '[w]hat's amazing about the Long Tail is the sheer size of it ... if you combine enough of the non-hits, you've actually established a market that rivals the hits' (emphasis in original, pp. 22–3). For this reason, at the start of 2007 Netflix could draw on its extensive inventory to offer subscribers not only the hits *King Kong* (Peter Jackson, 2005, NZ/US) and *Mission: Impossible III* (J. J. Abrams, 2006, US/Ger) but also more obscure titles like *La morte negli occhi del gatto* (*Seven Deaths in the Cat's Eye*) (Anthony M. Dawson [Antonio Margheriti], 1973, Fr/It/W. Ger) and *Let Me Die a Woman* (Doris Wishman, 1978, US). However even the Long Tail has its end. For example, while Netflix's stock is extensive, the infamous *Salò o le 120 giornate di Sodoma* (1975, It/Fr) was not available in Spring 2007, even though published on DVD in the US and while many other works were stocked from director Pier Paolo Pasolini.

Netflix's success drew the interest of other large concerns in the US video market. Wal-Mart launched its own competing service in October 2002 and Blockbuster commenced online rentals two years later after buying Film-Caddy.com. In keeping with company policy, Wal-Mart offered its service at lower subscription fees and a price war ensued. Although Wal-Mart's fees consistently undercut Netflix, by May 2005 the service had attracted fewer than 100,000 subscribers and was closed down. Wal-Mart's association with bargain prices had not met the consumer demographic of the online rental market: as one analyst observed prior to Wal-Mart's withdrawal, the 'people that go to Wal-Mart are not the people who are renting DVDs online right now' (cited in Hazelton, 2004b).

With two main players left, online video rental has seen some aggressive competition. Netflix filed a lawsuit against Blockbuster in April 2006 claiming that the chain had infringed the patent on its business model (Netherby, 2006e). As the price war has continued, Netflix and Blockbuster have driven down subscription charges, introducing options priced as low as US$4.99 and US$5.99, but leaving both parties struggling to see profits from their operations. Compared to the nearly 5m Netflix subscribers, Blockbuster's service is estimated to have a base of around 1m.

With the rental market eclipsed by expenditure on DVD retail, subscription schemes have now emerged as the most viable model of video rental. *Screen Digest* estimated that 'by the end of 2005, 7.5m US households were paying monthly subscription fees, about 5.5m online and 2m in-store. [This] new model generated US$1.4bn in spending during 2005, more than double the amount spent in 2004' (2006: 369).

HIGH-DEFINITION DVD

Revenue-sharing transformed the rental business and the arrival of DVD marked a second phase of significant growth in the video market. However, DVD had only been on sale for less than ten years when the video business was faced with the arrival of high-definition DVD, which was introduced to the market in the US during the second quarter of 2006.

Two circumstances motivated research and development into high-definition formats. The roll-out of DVD coincided with renewed interest by the broadcasting industries in high-definition television (HDTV). From the 1960s, Japanese broadcaster NHK had experimented with high-resolution television images. During the 1980s, NHK conducted demonstrations and test broadcasts with its high-definition TV system and separate tests were undertaken in Europe from the early 1990s. Both the Japanese and European projects were based on analogue technology and did not progress beyond the experimental stage. Interest in HDTV returned, however, in the 1990s with the introduction of digital methods of delivery, and broadcasts of digital HDTV began in the US towards the end of the decade. From December 2003, digital HDTV services were available in Japan and the following month the first European service began (Ochiva, 2006; *Screen Digest*, 1991a; Winston, 1996). Presentation of the full high-definition experience requires not only high-definition broadcasting and suitable hardware but also the availability of content produced to HD standards (*Screen Digest*, 2005c: 306). While DVD provided good-quality images and sound, it was a technology designed for standard-definition television. High-definition DVD is therefore aimed at providing a video storage medium for the next generation of television broadcasting.

A second factor leading the development was the slowing of growth in the DVD market. DVD had produced phenomenal revenues in a very short period of time with boom years of double-digit growth, but as discussed in Chapter 3, world consumer spending on video software was estimated to have declined by 5 per cent in 2005 (*Screen Digest*, 2006). At the end of 2006, as falling sales of DVD discs were reported at electronics retailers Best Buy and Circuit City, analysts predicated that the software market would continue to decline (Netherby, 2006f). Software suppliers were therefore eager to prolong the energy of the DVD boom and looked towards high-definition formats to sustain the momentum.

HD-DVD and Blu-ray Disc

After conceding to Toshiba over the original DVD format, Sony continued to pursue its own digital disc project with aims to create a high-definition standard for DVD. Other electronics manufacturers joined the project and in February 2002 Sony, together with Hitachi, LG Electronics, Matsushita, Pioneer, Philips, Samsung, Sharp and Thomson, announced specifications for their system, Blu-ray Disc. When Toshiba announced its own competing project, which gained the support of manufacturers NEC and Sanyo, the development of high-definition

DVD began to resemble the stand-off between Sony and Toshiba which had preceded the launch of standard-definition DVD. Toshiba's format, known as HD-DVD, won the endorsement of the DVD Forum in November 2003. In response, the nine manufacturers of the opposing camp, who were themselves members of the DVD Forum, formed the Blu-ray Disc Association as a collective body to promote the format.

While a new format war emerged, both sides were conscious that DVD itself was still a new and extant technology. The HD-DVD and Blu-ray projects therefore developed systems which were backwards compatible, allowing standard DVD to play on new high-definition machines. Both also employed blue laser technology to read discs instead of the red laser used in conventional DVD. However, in all other respects the two formats were entirely dissimilar. While both projects used the same 120mm-diameter discs as standard DVD, the thickness of discs differed between the formats. Both formats relied on expanded storage capacity to provide high-definition images: on a single-layer disc, Blu-ray held 25GB and 50GB on a double-layered disc, compared to the 15GB and 30GB capacity of HD-DVD. As a cost-effective measure, HD-DVD was designed to be produced on modified DVD pressing plants and Toshiba estimated that an HD-DVD unit cost no more than 25 cents extra to produce than a standard DVD, but manufacture of Blu-ray Discs involved a more complex and costly production process (Hazelton, 2006: 14).

Hollywood's Alignment

With rival high-definition formats squaring off against each other, the matter of licensed content emerged as a priority for the hardware developers. The alignment of the major Hollywood distributors therefore became crucial to launching the new formats on the market. From the moment the Blu-ray specification was announced, Columbia TriStar Home Entertainment immediately said it would be aligning itself with the parent company Sony. Support for Blu-ray was further strengthened when it was announced on 13 September 2004 that a consortium of investors headed by Sony and cable company Comcast had taken ownership of MGM. As part of the US$5bn deal, Sony gained access to MGM's 4,100-title film library, the largest in Hollywood, which could be combined with the approximately 2,500 titles Sony already owned (Ault, 2004). HD-DVD received encouraging news on 29 November 2004 when Warner, Paramount and Universal simultaneously placed their support behind the format (Sweeting and Hettrick, 2004). Just a week later, however, on 8 December, Disney announced that it would provide titles on Blu-ray (Sweeting, 2004).

All these agreements were made on a non-exclusive basis as the major distributors made cautious commitments while they waited to see which format would prevail. Fox held out, staying on neutral ground by maintaining membership of both the DVD Forum and Blu-ray Disc Association, until on 29 July 2005 the distributor stated that it would be releasing titles for Blu-ray (Sweeting, 2005). This decision split the six major distributors equally between Blu-ray and HD-DVD, with a full-blown format war inevitable. Further support for Blu-ray came in 2005 as Lions Gate (which changed its name to Lionsgate at the end of the year), a major independent distributor, added its support (Netherby, 2005a). In the wake of Fox's decision, Paramount and Warner revised their positions. On 2 October 2005, Paramount made the announcement that it also intended to release titles on Blu-ray together with HD-DVD and, on 21 October, Warner followed suit (Hettrick, 2005a and 2005b).

Warner was now backing both formats. Among the majors, Warner had actively tried to encourage all parties involved to reach a consensus on a unified format, but the decision to offer films to Blu-ray appeared to have a further purpose. When Sony's PlayStation 2 game console came onto the market in 2000, it had the capability to function also as a DVD player. On that occasion, gaming was combined with a video format for which there was an agreed industry standard. But with the launch of PlayStation 3 scheduled for November 2006, it was widely anticipated that Blu-ray would be integrated into the next generation console. If the third generation PlayStation sold in the same volumes as the previous two versions, it would give Blu-ray a strong advantage at an early stage of the new format war. Warner therefore appeared to be covering all bases in anticipation that PlayStation 3 may be the deciding factor in the high-definition battle.

HD-DVD received a small-scale launch in the US on 18 April 2006. Toshiba players and a limited range of titles from Warner and Universal went on sale at selected mass merchants and electronics retailers, including Wal-Mart, Best Buy, Tweeter and Ultimate Electronics. To support the launch, Toshiba paid for a television advertising campaign themed around the slogan 'So Real You Can Feel It'. Warner released *Million Dollar Baby* (Clint Eastwood, 2004, US), *The Last Samurai* (Edward Zwick, 2003, US) and *The Phantom of the Opera* (Joel Schumacher, 2004, US/UK), while Universal put out *Apollo 13* (Ron Howard, 1995, US), *Doom* (Andrzej Bartkowiak, 2005, UK) and *Serenity* (Joss Whedon, 2005, US) (Netherby and Ault, 2006b).

Two months later, on 20 June, Blu-ray players produced by Samsung went on sale at 2,000 stores across the US. Sony Pictures Home Entertainment supported the launch by releasing *The Fifth Element* (Luc Besson, 1997, Fr), *50 First Dates* (Peter Segal, 2004, US), *Hitch* (Jenna Friedenberg and Hannah Fruchtman, 2004, US), *House of Flying Daggers* (Zhang Yimou, 2004, China/Hong Kong), *Underworld: Evolution* (Len Wiseman, 2006, US) and *xXx*

(Rob Cohen, 2002, US) (Netherby and Ault, 2006a). A week later, Lionsgate added *Crash* (Paul Haggis, 2004, US/De), winner of the year's Best Picture Academy Award, to the Blu-ray catalogue, together with *Lord of War* (Andrew Niccol, 2005, US/Fr), *The Punisher* (Jonathan Hensleigh, 2004, US/De) and *Saw* (James Wan, 2004, US). A few MGM titles also appeared as part of the initial run of Blu-ray releases, including *The Terminator* (James Cameron, 1984, US), *RoboCop* (Paul Verhoeven, 1987, US), *The Last Waltz* (Martin Scorsese, 1978, US) and *Species* (Roger Donaldson, 1995, US). Both launches were therefore supported by a range of popular titles from recent years together with selected library titles. Despite Warner placing a foot in both camps, at the time the formats were launched the company's initial run of titles was offered on HD-DVD only.

Retailers set up special high-definition displays in stores, with both HD-DVD and Blu-ray players and discs presented side-by-side. Symptomatic of the industry divisions which had launched two incompatible formats so close together, confusion ensued as a few outlets unwittingly displayed the discs with the wrong players or otherwise included high-definition discs with conventional DVD. To steer customers through the confusion, online retailers created virtual high-definition stores within their sites, offering buying guides to advise customers on the new formats and provide a single point of entry for buying high-definition players, televisions and discs.

With both formats on the market, at the start of July 2006 Amazon.com was offering discs at discounted prices: HD-DVD titles sold for prices between US$19.88 and US$27.99, while Blu-ray discs were priced at US$24.95–35.99. Toshiba's HD-A1 and RCA's HDV5000 HD-DVD players both sold for US$499, which compared to the US$999.99 for either Samsung's BD-P1000 or Sony's BDP-S1 Blu-ray players. By the start of 2007 prices had already dropped: Amazon priced titles for both formats in the range of US$17.45–27.95, while the HD-A1 was available for US$399.99 and Blu-ray players continued to be priced higher, starting at US$589.99 for the BD-P1000. Approximately 200 HD-DVD titles were available in the US, mainly from Warner and Universal but also Paramount and the Weinstein Company. Around 150 Blu-ray titles were available, the majority from Sony, but with others from Disney, Fox, Lionsgate, MGM, Paramount and Warner.

When the PlayStation 3 was launched during November 2006 in Japan, North America, Hong Kong and Taiwan, it confirmed predictions. The machine's optical drive could play Blu-ray discs as well as standard DVDs. Blu-ray drives were also installed in Sony's VAIO range of computers. Sony's move to spread Blu-ray across multiple media platforms may therefore become a deciding factor in this format war.

High-definition promises to further enhance DVD's aura of pristine image quality, advancing the video business into yet another phase of technological change. As a consequence, however, new uncertainties confront the video business as consumer electronics manufacturers divide the market between the two competing and incompatible high-definition formats. When DVD was in development, the Hollywood majors had played a key role in resolving the issue of competing formats, creating the stability necessary for the growth of a mass consumer market. But as the majors have divided their allegiances between the rival high-definition DVD formats, the video business has had to start asking questions again about which format would win out, disrupting the equilibrium which for nearly two decades had prevailed since the ending of the VCR wars.

DIGITAL DELIVERY

Despite their differences, DVD, HD-DVD and Blu-ray all work on the same principle: they offer flexible storage media options for viewing films and other types of audiovisual content in the home or other spaces. Alongside these developments, digitisation has also transformed the technological infrastructures and business models of television delivery systems. From the late 1990s, the pay-TV (PTV) sector has involved an array of subscription television (STV) services, premium channels, pay-per-view (PPV) and video-on-demand (VoD) options delivered by digital cable or satellite systems. Broadband and high-speed connections have also made the internet a more viable network for the streaming or downloading of video content and a further channel for PPV or VoD services.

By 2005, there were 37.3m addressable cable households in the US (i.e. cable-networked homes with a set-top box through which PPV or VoD services could be received) and satellite households had reached 22.3m. Through these platforms, an estimated 24.2m homes or nearly 22 per cent of the total television households in the US could receive VoD services. Internet connectivity had reached higher levels of penetration. An estimated 73.7m or 65.6 per cent of homes in the US owned a PC in 2005, of which 70.7m (63 per cent of US households) had internet access. In 2001, only 10.9m or 10.1 per cent of US homes had access to broadband. Four years later, 36.6m (32.3 per cent of US households) were connected to broadband (based on data cited in MPA, 2006f: 40, 42–4, 46 and 48).

These digital delivery systems presented a direct challenge to the home video business. Not only did the PTV economy offer the same forms of content available on disc or tape, in particular feature films, but also the transactional model of PPV and VoD worked by a similar form of pricing: 'pay-per-view represents an "unbundled" method of pricing, as opposed to the "bundled" pricing of pay-cable. In other words, it allows more direct pricing of a given film or supply of films' (Wasko, 2003: 139). Technologically and commercially, PPV and VoD therefore present direct substitutes for video rental: single items of content can be viewed in the home for single transactions, and with the convenience of never having to leave the home to pick up or return a disc or tape. Additionally, as home viewers have a limited amount of time they can dedicate to watching television or other leisure activities, then the availability of PPV and VoD has the potential to impact on the time available for watching sell-through video purchases. As part of the domestic media ensemble, video must compete for attention with an array of alternative media options, and so time is a very real factor in determining media consumption. According to research by Veronis Suhler Stevenson, a private equity company investing in the media, communications and information industries, the viewing of pre-recorded video software accounted for one of the smallest allocations of time spent on average by media consumers in the US (table 5.7). On average, just under 2 per cent of the time devoted to media consumption was taken up watching video; only attending theatres to see films commanded less time. When at home, US consumers were more likely to spend time listening to the radio and recorded music, or watching broadcast, cable or satellite TV, than watching video.

Home video therefore competes within a very small segment of the attention economy. In this context, it is easy to see how PPV and VoD services present a threat to home video, whether these are delivered by cable, satellite or broadband. Although US consumers spend more time watching cable and satellite television than DVDs or videocassettes, PPV and VoD, however, only account for a small proportion of those hours. In terms of their economic value, PPV and VoD and many other privately consumed entertainment media have struggled to compete against video storage media for a share of the leisure dollar. In 2004, on a per-person average, home video accounted for US$125.31 or over 15 per cent of total spending on media consumption (table 5.8).

Digital delivery systems and home video are most directly thrown into competition through making feature films available for home viewing. Dedicated subscription movie channels appeared on cable in the US from the late 1970s, when Viacom's Showtime (1978–), Warner Amex's The Movie Channel (TMC) (1979–) and Home Box Office's (HBO) Cinemax (1980–) were launched. In 1983, TMC and Showtime merged (with Warner subsequently selling its interest to Viacom in 1986) and that year The Disney Channel also began operations (Hilmes, 1990). Movies from the Hollywood majors were licensed to Cinemax and Showtime/TMC and further such services appeared in the early 1990s with

	Hours
Filmed Entertainment	
Cable and Satellite TV	868
Broadcast TV	678
Consumer Internet	176
Pre-recorded Video and DVD	67
Box Office	12
Wireless Content	11
Subtotal	1,812
Other Entertainment	
Broadcast and Satellite Radio	986
Recorded Music	185
Daily Newspapers	188
Consumer Magazines	124
Consumer Books	108
Video Games	77
Subtotal	1,668
Total	3,480

Sources: adapted from Veronis Suhler Stevenson data in MPA (2006f: 51).

Table 5.7 Per Person Annual Media Consumption Hours in the US (2004)

	US$
Television (broadcast, cable and satellite)	255.36
Home Video	125.31
Consumer Internet	113.48
Consumer Books	89.67
Newspapers	51.62
Recorded Music	49.39
Consumer Magazines	46.88
Other (Box office, video games, interactive TV and wireless content)	85.01
Total	816.72

Sources: adapted from Veronis Suhler Stevenson data in MPA (2006f: 53).

Table 5.8 Per Person Annual Spending on Media Consumption in the US (2004)

the Encore (1991–) and Starz! (1994–) channels from Telecommunications, Inc. (TCI). During the same period, the first PPV services appeared. In 1974, Telecinema operated as an early but short-lived attempt to introduce a PPV offering, but national PPV only emerged when Viewer Choice and Request TV were both launched in November 1985 (Garvey, 2006).

While these services competed against video for the dollars and attention of American consumers, as discussed in the previous chapter, from the early 1980s the value of video for the Hollywood majors increased and considerably surpassed earnings from all television windows. The introduction of subscription film channels and PPV services therefore coincided with, but did not halt, the maturing of the home video market. Annual expenditure on PPV buys in US cable households increased from US$98m in 1990 to US$358m in 1996. In the same period however, consumer spending on video rental alone increased from US$6,629m to US$7,826m (Veronis, Suhler and Associates data cited in Gomery, 2000: 410 and 420).

Internet Distribution

Despite this record of poor performance, new PPV and VoD services continue to be launched across cable, satellite and broadband delivery systems. With the spread of high-speed internet and broadband connectivity, online film distribution in particular has attracted a lot of interest. From the late 1990s, services such as MovieFlix, SightSound and Intertainer appeared at the forefront of internet distribution. While the services made shorts and independent films available, the Hollywood majors offered their films on terms which were not economically viable. The majors also withheld their output from internet distribution over concerns regarding copyright protection.

To guard against the dangers of piracy, the leading Hollywood companies have chosen to set up their own network for legal internet distribution while licensing their films to trusted services offering strong protection systems. Services like MovieFlix and Intertainer were delivering films by video streaming but the Hollywood majors preferred to create a service offering films on a downloadable VoD basis. In August 2001, Sony brought together MGM, Paramount, Universal and Warner to form a joint venture for internet distribution (Hettrick, 2001). Originally called MovieFly but soon renamed Movielink, the VoD service required no subscription. Instead, for a credit card payment, customers could download movies to their computer hard drive for thirty days, during which time the film could be watched once over a 24-hour period. After the thirty days expired or after the film had been watched, the file was automatically deleted. Play, pause, fast-forward and rewind controls provided similar functions to those found on VCRs and DVD players. As Scott Hettrick

(2002b) observed, Movielink set 'itself up as a virtual video rental store, going so far as to use the word "rent" on the clickable icon under the images of the movies being offered'.

Movielink received a soft launch on 11 November 2002 with a catalogue of 170 new and library titles from the partners. Over the next three years, Disney and Fox also licensed films to Movielink. Previously, the two companies had partnered in the VoD joint venture Movies.com before Fox pulled out. While the other majors were backing Movielink, Disney developed its own unique VoD service, Moviebeam, which transmitted films to a television set-top box using existing broadcast signals. When Moviebeam received a trial launch from September 2003 in three US cities, DreamWorks, Fox, MGM, Sony and Universal all licensed films to Disney's service (Sweeting, 2003a).

Although the availability of popular Hollywood features gave internet distribution greater visibility, download rates remained relatively low: in 2003, Movielink was attracting around 6,000 downloads per month, which by 2005 had increased to 100,000 per month (Netherby, 2005b). However, after antitrust concerns were expressed over the collective might of the Hollywood majors and the integration of distribution and exhibition they represented, by June 2006 Movielink was up for sale to a third party.

While setting up Movielink, the Hollywood majors had also begun to license films to other services. CinemaNow was established as a video streaming service in 1999 by the distributor Trimark before it was bought by Lions Gate and attracted investment from Microsoft and Blockbuster. CinemaNow offered both a subscription service, costing US$9.95 per month, and PPV options. Using a territorial rights management system, CinemaNow could geographically limit distribution while also targeting programmes and advertising to customers in particular regions (Rivero, 2001). From 2002, the major distributors began to sign VoD deals with CinemaNow. In February that year, MGM signed a deal for a trial with CinemaNow, offering films for downloading rather than streaming. New releases were priced at US$3.99–4.99, while catalogue titles cost US$2.99 (Hettrick, 2002a). Over the next eighteen months, similar deals were struck with Warner, Universal, Fox and Disney.

Download-to-Own

After entering internet distribution through the VoD model, from April 2006 the majors also began to make their films available for permanent downloads. CinemaNow had been offering independent titles for download-to-own since January 2004, and from April 2006 Fox, MGM, Paramount, Sony, Universal and Warner made their films available for permanent download through either CinemaNow or Movielink. Downloads were offered at prices comparable to

DVD purchases: Movielink offered new titles at prices between US$20 and US$30, while older titles cost US$10–16. Both services imposed limitations on the options for watching these downloads. With CinemaNow, films could only be watched on the computer through which they were downloaded. Movielink allowed copies to be watched on two other computers and for a back-up DVD copy to be taken which would play on a computer but not a free-standing DVD player (Netherby, 2006d). Along with granting permanent downloads, the majors also moved to bring internet distribution in line with the existing home video window. New titles available for permanent download were released on the same day-and-date as DVD. On 4 April 2006, *Brokeback Mountain* (Ang Lee, 2005, US) from Universal became the first film to receive a simultaneous DVD and download-to-own release.

Download-to-Burn

Permanent downloads have not proved to be very popular and the view is widely held that this is due to the limitations of having to watch films on a computer. Internet distributors have therefore looked to move beyond download-to-own and launch download-to-burn services, allowing content to be downloaded then recorded onto disc for playing on standard DVD players. With download-to-burn, broadband services are moving towards a DVD-on-demand model of online distribution. The adult entertainment business pioneered download-to-burn when Download-2-Own.com began offering titles from 900 adult entertainment labels in early 2006. The All Adult Channel, a broadband video-on-demand service owned and operated by CinemaNow, followed a few months later, offering thirty catalogue titles from the major adult entertainment studio Vivid Video (Netherby, 2006a). Movielink announced an agreement on 17 July 2006 with software creator Sonic Solutions through which the service licensed Sonic's technology, enabling downloaded movies to be converted into a format playable on standard DVD players and then burnt to disc. This agreement did not, however, involve the Hollywood majors or other distributors in any commitment to supply content (Sweeting, 2006a). Two days later, CinemaNow launched a working download-to-burn service, offering titles from Disney, Lionsgate, MGM, Sony and Universal. Through the service, customers could download the main feature film plus extras material and burn a single copy to disc, together with printable cover art and DVD labels (Netherby, 2006c). Priced at US$9.99–14.99, downloads sold at levels below the price in stores; however, download times are prolonged and the eventual sound and image quality was inferior to pre-recorded DVDs (Clark, 2006).

Copy protection, however, remains a key issue for the future of download-to-burn. CinemaNow uses FluxDVD, a copy protection system developed by

Coming to a desktop near you: CinemaNow's online service

ACE GmbH, a German company founded by CinemaNow's chief technology officer. By exclusively licensing FluxDVD, CinemaNow is able to hold off competition from rival services. Meanwhile, the Hollywood distributors have explored alternative systems. Pre-recorded DVDs use CSS for copy protection, and compatibility with this system is necessary for playing on all DVD players. Before committing their properties to Movielink or other broadband distributors, the majors are holding on as they wait to be satisfied that CSS can be effectively extended to download-to-burn or if other copy protection solutions can be found.

CONCLUSION

Video-on-demand and broadband internet have all expanded the routes through which video enters the home. However, hard storage media still remain at the centre of the video business. DVD, HD-DVD, Blu-ray, VoD, download-to-own and download-to-burn have taken video into a new digital age, yet many of the same conflicts and lines of tension witnessed with earlier home media continue to endure.

Battles over competing formats seem endemic to the video business. After the VCR and videodisc wars, HD-DVD and Blu-ray are just the latest combatants in the continuing rivalry which characterises innovation in the consumer electronics industry. Introduction of innovations in video hardware or delivery systems continue to depend on securing strong relationships with software suppliers, and the Hollywood majors remain key to influencing technological and commercial change in the video industries. Alongside Japanese technological leadership in consumer electronics, Hollywood remains the other core force in the global video business. Whatever the destinies of high-definition DVD or internet distribution turn out to be, they will depend on the involvement of the major Hollywood majors. By shaping the largest video market in the world, Hollywood is not only influencing the domestic context but also the future of digital video media globally. As the leading worldwide supplier of video software, Hollywood is central to the video business and will continue to influence the prospects of that business for decades to come.

Since the arrival of broadcasting, home storage media have needed to compete against delivery channels. Despite talk of convergence in the media industries, digitisation has not pulled the video business towards a single method of storage or delivery but rather multiplied the various platforms through which video can be accessed by consumers. The digital age has therefore not only seen an increase in the volume of rental or retail transactions conducted over video but has also given consumer markets more routes through which to obtain video. Digital video has therefore further segmented the market and multiplied inter-platform competition between storage and delivery media.

In the digital age, the Hollywood majors have aimed to release films through all video channels. This may suggest that the majors are chasing new revenue streams for filmed entertainment. However, at the moment, VoD services and internet distribution attract so little consumer traffic as to be virtually worthless. Rather than expanding the commercial value of filmed entertainment, it may therefore be more appropriate to see Hollywood's connections with multiple video platforms in strategic terms. While internet distribution is still in an exploratory stage, and while the survival of services remains volatile, the majors may simply be securing a foothold as they wait to see when, or if, the online distribution business takes off. By spreading video releasing over multiple platforms, the Hollywood majors will be able to play one form of outlet or channel off against another. As *Variety*'s Meredith Amdur (2004b: 6 and 72) comments in relation to the buying power of Wal-Mart,

> [u]nlike pickles or pantyhose, movies are a constantly changing packaged good with ever-evolving platforms and technology that keep its manufacturers in the driver's seat.

Studios reckon they can eventually dangle VoD over any Wal-Mart pressure to cut prices. Or they can re-embrace rental as a counterbalance to rising retail leverage.

Placing their marker over all outlets for video gives the Hollywood majors a degree of 'technological leverage' by keeping all channels open and thereby preventing the dominant player in any one sector from imposing unprofitable terms.

6

Illicit Business: The Global Economy of Industrialised Video Piracy

---

'All rights reserved. No copying. Subject to Applicable Laws.' 'Licensed for home viewing only. All other use prohibited.' 'WARNING: All rights of the producer and of the owner of the work reproduced reserved. Unauthorised copying, hiring, lending, public performance, radio or TV broadcasting of this DVD is prohibited.' These statements will be familiar to anyone who has taken the time to study the small print that appears on DVDs from UK and US distributors. Elsewhere, on the reverse of the DVD packaging, an icon may appear of two discs touching one another, with an arrow running between them, and framed in a red circle with a red line running through it, accompanied by the warning 'This DVD is copy protected'. The packaging may carry a small triangle with the letters CP in the middle, and the statement 'Copy Protected Macrovision'. Somewhere the packaging is also likely to carry text to the effect that 'Copyright © 2005 *bfi* Video', '© 2003 Columbia Pictures Industries Inc. All rights reserved', or '2005 DreamWorks Animation LCC and DreamWorks LLC'.

Although the phrasing varies and the names of the relevant parties change, all these statements have the same message: they tell the consumer that while he or she owns the disc, they do not own the work reproduced on the disc. Instead, the work remains protected by copyright, which reserves the rights to use, reproduce or present that work. More than the technology which goes into the making of the videocassette or DVD, copyright continually reminds consumers of the status of videocassettes or discs as carrier or storage media: they only carry copyrighted works into the market but do not make those works the property of consumers.

Copyright is fundamental to understanding the video business. Statements on the protection of rights may be hidden in the minutest print found on videocassettes or discs, but the legal frameworks they point to alert us to the fact that video is not really a business based on the production and exchange of things – films, television programmes, pornography, etc. – but rather a business based on ownership of the rights to copy, distribute or present those things.

Video presents a paradox for property rights. On the one hand, it is only by making videocassettes and DVDs available as packaged public goods that a market can exist for the exploitation of creative works on video. Yet on the other hand, as those works are copied and circulate in the market in hard tangible form, they escape the immediate physical control of those individuals or companies who own the rights to the works. The reproducibility and dispersibility of video has presented a double-edged sword with regard to intellectual property rights. Global markets for video have emerged because low-cost reproduction has enabled copyrighted works to be manufactured in mass volumes on cassette or disc and then transported for sale across vast geographically extended markets. Yet it is the reproducibility and dispersibility of video media, and the global extension of markets, which has resulted in widespread infringement of copyright through the operations of industrialised piracy.

Majid Yar (2005: 679) defines piracy as the term commonly 'refer[ring] to the unauthorized copy and distribution (often, though not necessarily, for commercial gain) of copyright content'. Piracy is a legal concept, concerned with the infringement of copyright, and for the audiovisual industries it is a concept related to technology and commerce. Media and communication technologies provide the tools for copying and distributing pirated materials. As Yar suggests, piracy does not necessarily involve commerce and can be practised by private individuals, but when piracy is organised across large-scale structures for the reproduction of illegal copies and distribution or dissemination of these for sale, it achieves industrial proportions.

Industrialised piracy represents the shadow economy of the video business. Like the legitimate video business, industrialised piracy operates through highly organised facilities for illegal production and extensive, transnational networks of distribution. Certain national territories have become major hubs of pirate production, but the market for illegal recordings does not observe national boundaries. The ease with which industrialised video piracy is able to transnationalise operations exemplifies the 'porous' character of video which Tom O'Regan describes (1991): illegal master recordings cross borders to provide the sources for high-volume replication, while flows of finished pre-recorded cassette and disc units evade customs controls.

To combat video piracy, a range of legislative, enforcement and technological measures have been implemented. Through authorising legislative frameworks to protect intellectual property, governments play a role in the fight against piracy, while police and other local or national enforcement bodies apply these regimes. Through the efforts to combat piracy, the video business is therefore brought into a close working relationship with the state. As Shujen Wang (2003:

16) observes, with video piracy 'multiple networks such as the state, trans-national corporations, criminal organizations, trade associations, hardware and software manufacturers and distributors, transnational trade regimes, and consumers are all inextricably linked and interconnected'.

Initially, this chapter examines the concept of intellectual property and how this applies to video recordings. It then outlines how economic losses and links to organised crime mean that video piracy has become a threat addressed by both industry and law enforcement agencies. The measures taken to combat this threat at national and international levels are discussed. Finally, the chapter looks at the practices of piracy, outlining the various ways in which technology is used to create an industry out of the infringement of copyright.

INTELLECTUAL PROPERTY AND THE VIDEO BUSINESS

Copyright is just one aspect of that branch of the law known as intellectual property. Various categories of intellectual property exist but the main ones are copyright, trademarks and patents (Vaidhyanathan, 2003: 18–20). Intellectual property law is founded on the economics of property rights. At its most basic level, classical economics is based on the supply and demand of scarce resources. Intellectual property law creates property rights by granting 'legally enforceable power to exclude others from using a resource, without need to contract with them' (William Landes and Richard Posner. [1988] 'The Economics of Trademark Law', extracted in Groves, 1997: 527). Intellectual property law deals in intangibles: it turns creations of the mind – inventions, designs, creative works – into property by protecting exclusivity over the rights to legally use or have access to those works. Such works may necessarily circulate in public culture and so appear to be available to everyone, yet property rights create a monopoly for the work, granting ownership over the rights to use, access and present works.

The main economic justification for intellectual property law is that it is only by protecting the rights of the owner that creators will see the remuneration from their works that will provide the motivation for them to refine existing works or create new ones. Peter J. Groves (1997) explains the economic logic of intellectual property when he says that

> Without copyright, there would be no incentive for creative individuals to write novels, paint pictures or compose music. Nor would there be any incentive for publishers, broadcasters and record companies to invest in the exploitation of those works. Creating a property right in these matters enables them to be traded and permits copyright owners to earn money from their work. (p. 261).

By protecting exclusive ownership of the work, intellectual property rights have commercial value, for they define and control who can legally use and access the work. When a DVD carries the statement 'All rights reserved', it is telling the consumer that the property rights relating to the work recorded on the disc remain with whoever owns the rights to the work. So it is only by excluding others from legally using or accessing the work that the disc becomes a viable commercial artefact. When applied in the context of the video business, property rights are therefore fundamental to commodifying video media.

Intellectual property rights are the very lifeblood of the video business. For the consumer electronics industry, patents are vital because they guard 'a monopoly right to the exclusive use of an invention' (p. 103). A trademark 'is a badge of origin ... a sign which indicates who made the goods or provided the services' (p. 511). Scattered across DVD discs and packaging are these signs of origination. When the logo 'DVD Video' appears followed by ™ or ®, it operates as a registered trademark, a signifier for the DVD Format/Logo Licensing Corporation (the organisation of nine electronics manufacturers together with Time Warner who are responsible for licensing use of the DVD format and logo). Similarly, the 'Dolby Digital' logo is a trademark of Dolby Laboratories Licensing Corporation. Trademarks may not only apply to scientific creations. With the 2004 UK DVD release of *Spartacus* (Stanley Kubrick, 1960, US), the front of the packaging proudly announces 'Winner of 4 Academy Awards ®'. On the reverse of the packaging is a note informing that ' "Academy Awards" and "Oscar" are the registered trademarks and service marks of the Academy of Motion Picture Arts and Sciences'. Copyright exists to protect property rights relating to various categories of cultural works, defining ownership of the work. When the *Spartacus* disc therefore includes the text '© 1960 Universal Pictures Company, Inc. & Bryna Productions, Inc. Renewed 1988 Universal Studios', it is documenting the film's history of ownership, from its production by one of the Hollywood majors and Kirk Douglas's independent company, to the rights now held by the distributor. With a DVD, the film or television programme it carries may not be the only copyrighted work included as part of the product. In the case of *Spartacus*, at the bottom of the back page in the small pamphlet included with the disc is the statement 'Packaging Design: © 2004 Universal Studios. All Rights Reserved'.

A DVD bought off the shelf is not a single copyrighted work but rather a packaged collection of rights, covering the core programme, the extras and the artwork. Any single DVD can therefore be read as a synecdoche of the whole legal framework of intellectual property rights which apply in the video business.

International Intellectual Property Law

National instruments of copyright law define what will count as intellectual property and the rights which can be protected. For example, in Britain, under section 1 of the *Copyright, Designs and Patents Act 1988* (the CDPA), the following categories are considered copyrighted works:

> (1) Copyright is a property right which subsists in accordance with this Part in the following descriptions of work –
> (a) original library, dramatic, musical or artistic works,
> (b) sound recordings, films, broadcasts or cable programmes, and
> (c) the typographical arrangement of published editions.
>
> (*Copyright, Designs and Patents Act 1988*, 1988: 1–2)

Section 16 of the CDPA protects a range of rights: the owner retains the rights to copy the work; to issue copies of the work; to perform, show or play the work in public; to broadcast the work or include it in a cable programme service; or to make an adaptation of the work (p. 8). Similarly, as discussed in Chapter 4, the *1976 Copyright Act* in the US protects the rights to reproduce, prepare derivative works, distribute and publicly perform or display works (US Copyright Office, 2003: 16).

Given the easy flow of pirated recordings across borders, national copyright laws alone have proved ineffective as protection against infringement. In the 1990s, moves towards harmonising national laws constructed an international regime linked to trade for the protection of intellectual property rights. At the conclusion of the Uruguay Round of trade negotiations in 1994, the General Agreement on Tariffs and Trade (GATT) was transformed into the World Trade Organisation (WTO). It has been the objective of the WTO to liberalise and expand trade, and in so doing it has taken the role of establishing rules for global trade and acting to resolve any disputes between member nations. Included among the range of agreements administered by the WTO is the *Agreement on Trade-Related Aspects of Intellectual Property Rights* (TRIPs). With the TRIPs agreement, for the first time intellectual property became a component of the international trading system. TRIPs has set requirements for minimum standards relating to intellectual property regulation. Non-compliance with these standards can result in disciplinary actions against WTO members, including sanctions. Trade has therefore become a weapon in the international regime of protection for intellectual property.

Many of the TRIPs provisions relating to copyright were imported from the *Berne Convention for the Protection of Literary and Artistic Works*. Since 1886, the Berne Convention had provided the backbone of moves to harmonise international copyright law. As part of its 'Criteria of Eligibility for Protection', the Convention includes the basic principle of 'national treatment', according to which the creators of copyrighted works from any country which has signed up to the Convention must be afforded the same protection for their works in any other Convention country as the nationals of that country (Kamina, 2002: 367). This provision sets up a framework for reciprocal copyright protection between nations and was incorporated into Article 1(3) of the TRIPs agreement.

As new media technologies have extended not only the range of copyrighted works but also the means for infringing copyright, so the Convention has undergone periodic revision. For example, films were included for the first time under revisions arising from the Berlin Conference of 1908 (p. 18). Again responding to new technologies, additional protection for intellectual property was provided through two treaties passed in 1996 by the World Intellectual Property Organisation (WIPO), the United Nations agency entrusted with developing a stable international intellectual property system. The *WIPO Copyright Treaty* (WCT) and the *WIPO Performances and Phonograms Treaty* (WPPT) built on the *Berne Convention* but included provisions aimed at guarding against new technological methods for infringing copyright. These provisions required contracting parties to introduce prohibitions against the circumvention of copy protection technology and the removal of rights management information. According to the treaties, effective legislation must be implemented to prevent the unauthorised circumvention of technological measures taken by copyright holders to protect their works. Furthermore, it is also a requirement that measures be taken to prohibit the unauthorised removal or alteration of electronic rights management information, and the distribution, importation or making available to the public of works or copies of works when rights management information has been removed or altered without authorisation (WIPO, 1996a: 4–5 and 1996b: 7–8).

In 1998, the WIPO treaties were implemented in US law when the *Digital Millennium Copyright Act* (DMCA) came into effect. The DMCA is divided into five Titles, the first of which adopts the prohibitions against the unauthor-ised circumvention of copyright protection systems and tampering with rights management information taken from the WIPO treaties. These same prohibitions were also integrated into the *EU Copyright Directive* (EUCD), passed by the European Parliament in 2001.

THE PIRACY THREAT

Audiovisual piracy has raised two principal issues among the copyright industries and enforcement agencies. The film and music industries see piracy as a concern in terms of the economic impact of copyright infringement. For these industries, piracy is regarded as a threat measured in terms of lost revenues and trade. For law enforcement agencies on the other hand, piracy has become an issue due to evidence of links between piracy operations and organised crime syndicates.

The Economic Impact of Piracy on the US Copyright Industries

Video piracy is one of the clearest indicators of a globalised media universe. Examples of industrialised video piracy have been uncovered and reported from across the world. Piracy is therefore an international issue.

With the TRIPs agreement, ownership of rights became a key currency in the global trading system. Today, it is reasonable to see divisions in the global cultural economy between 'copyright rich' nations and 'copyright poor' nations. Principal among the copyright rich is the US. Copyright industries in the US can be divided between the 'core' industries of cinema, music, broadcasting, publishing, the press, advertising, theatre and computer software. Total copyright industries encompass these sectors but also other areas of business involved with making and distributing copyrighted works, including retailing, toys and computer hardware. According to the 2004 report *Copyright Industries in the US Economy*, in 2002 the total copyright industries in the US accounted for US$1,254bn or 11.97 per cent of gross domestic product, which totalled US$10,480.8bn (Siwek, 2004: iii). Of this, the core industries contributed US$626.6bn or 5.98 per cent of GDP. The total copyright industries employed 11.476m workers or 8.41 per cent of the national workforce of 136.485m, 5.484m (or 4 per cent of the national total) in the core industries (p. v). Foreign sales and exports for the copyright industries were estimated to have reached US$89.26bn, more than chemicals and related products (US$83.59bn), food and live animals (US$40.3bn), motor vehicles, parts and accessories (US$50.36bn), and aircraft and associated equipment (US$43.88m) (p. vi).

The importance of the contribution made by copyright to the US economy is not matched by any other country in the world. Consequently, the US copyright industries have been at the forefront of legislative and enforcement measures aimed at curbing international industrialised piracy. The impact of international piracy on the copyright industries in the US is monitored by the International Intellectual Property Alliance (IIPA). The IIPA was formed in 1984 as a coalition of seven trade associations representing the core copyright industries: the Association of American Publishers (AAP), Business Software Alliance (BSA), Entertainment Software Association (ESA), Independent Film and Television Alliance (IFTA), Motion Picture Association of America (MPAA), National Music Publishers' Association (NMPA) and the Recording Industry Association of America (RIAA). Through its membership, the IIPA represents 1,900 US companies involved with the production or distribution of copyrighted works (IIPA, 2006a: 1). These can be broken down into the following categories: computer software (for business and consumer use); entertainment software (i.e. interactive video games); motion pictures (films, television programmes, home videos); recorded music; and published works (textbooks, tradebooks, reference and professional publications or journals, in either print or electronic media).

The main goal of the IIPA is to create a safe international market for the US copyright industries: its aim is to establish 'a legal and enforcement regime for copyright that not only deters piracy, but that also fosters technological and cultural development [in foreign countries] and encourages local investment and employment' (p. 1). To pursue this goal, the IIPA works with the US Trade Representative (USTR) to review whether the legal instruments, policies and enforcement practices of foreign countries provide adequate frameworks for the protection of works from the US copyright industries in foreign markets.

Each year, the IIPA files its *Special 301 Report* with the USTR, reviewing the operations and costs of piracy across international territories, and evaluates the current state of copyright protection and enforcement in those territories. Based on this information, the IIPA draws up a 'watch list' of offending nations where copyright legislation and enforcement is regarded as inadequate and makes recommendations to the USTR over trade actions to be taken against those countries. In the *2006 Special 301 Report*, forty-six countries were included on the 301 watch list, most of which were located in Asia, Eastern Europe or Latin America. A further twenty-two nations were classified as deserving of 'special mention'. According to the report's estimates for 2005, piracy across these territories was responsible for US$15,826.8m in trade losses for the US copyright industries. Of this, losses to motion pictures totalled US$1,976m, increasing from US$1,966.5m in 2004 (IIPA, 2006c: 2). For the IIPA's purposes, the category of 'motion picture' piracy covers not only illegal video recordings (cassettes and discs) but also television and cable services that transmit films and television programmes without authorisation, and unauthorised public exhibition using video. Estimates for motion picture piracy in many territories were missing from the *2006 Special 301 Report*, but based on data filed for the 2005 301, estimated losses from piracy were highest in China, Russia, Italy, Mexico and Brazil. Countries with the highest levels of motion picture piracy included China, Kuwait, Paraguay and Indonesia, where piracy was estimated to account for over 90 per cent of the motion picture market (table 6.1).

By Trade Losses				By Piracy Levels				
Losses		Video Piracy Level			Losses		Video Piracy Level	
(US$m)		(%)			(US$m)		(%)	
2004	2003	2004	2003		2004	2003	2004	2003
China	280	178	95	95	China	95	95	280	178
Russia	275	275	80	75	Kuwait	95	95	12	12
Italy	160	140	15	20	Paraguay	95	80	2	2
Mexico	140	50	70	45	Indonesia	92	92	32	29
Brazil	120	120	30	30	Ukraine	90	90	45	45
India	80	77	60	60	Bosnia and Herzegovina	90	90	4	4
Turkey	50	50	45	45	Philippines	85	89	33	33
Ukraine	45	45	90	90	Serbia and Montenegro	85	90	n/a	n/a
Columbia	40	40	75	75	Russia	80	75	275	275
Taiwan	40	42	40	44	Lebanon	80	80	10	10

Source: compiled from IIPA (2005).

Table 6.1 Major Territories for Motion Picture Piracy (2003–4)

Links to Organised Crime

Over an eleven-day period in June 2005, officers from the Hong Kong police were involved in Operation Glaring Sun, raiding over 1,900 locations, including sixty-one pirate optical disc factories, thirty-one brothels, thirty gambling dens and nine drug dens. The raids were directed against the operations run by the Wo Shing Wo and 14K triad gangs. Among the items seized in the raids were 159,000 obscene or pirated optical discs, together with HK$11m in illegal betting slips, 3,000 litres of illicit fuel, 4.51m contraband cigarettes and stashes of various controlled drugs. The total goods were valued at HK$91m (Sinn, 2005). Later the same month and again in Hong Kong, Operation Windpipe was mounted as a joint initiative between the Kowloon West Crime Headquarters and various government offices, including the departments responsible for immigration, labour, customs and excise, and television and entertainment licensing. The operation was conducted as part of measures taken to freeze the assets generated by triad gangs from piracy, drugs, vice, gambling and contraband goods. Police seized goods to the value of HK$4.99m, including 158,200 pornographic and pirated discs, together with drugs, red oil (fuel where duty has not been paid) and contraband cigarettes.

These are just a couple of the operations undertaken in recent years by international law enforcement agencies which have revealed evidence of links between video piracy and organised crime. In their definition of the characteristics of organised crime, the UK's National Criminal Intelligence Service (NCIS) include the 'use of commercial or business like structures', and the organisation of 'operations [which] are international, national or regional' (cited in AACP, n.d.: 6). Organised crime syndicates will frequently engage in multiple lines of illegal activity. In their fight against piracy, the copyright industries have therefore promoted their cause not only in terms of stemming economic losses but also as a moral crusade against criminals who also deal in drug smuggling, trade in illegal munitions and money laundering (IIPA, 2006b: 11). In some cases, the pirates are reported to use the proceeds from piracy to fund terrorism. In Northern Ireland, the Organised Crime Task Force reported in 2002 that 34 per cent of organised crime syndicates in the territory were engaged in producing counterfeit goods (including CDs, clothing and power tools), and that an estimated half of crime groups had either links to, or were controlled by, Loyalist and Republican paramilitary organisations (AACP, n.d.: 14). A report from Interpol in April 2004 included reference to a 2000 case where an illegal CD plant in Russia had been used as a source of funding for Chechen rebels (IIPA, 2006b: 13).

Organised crime is drawn to the huge profits which can be obtained from industrialised piracy. According to reports published in October 2005 from the MPAA's international division, the Motion Picture Association (MPA), criminal revenues from intellectual property theft were estimated to have reached US$512bn in 2004, compared to US$322bn from drug trafficking. Piracy attracts organised crime because the profit margins can be higher than those obtained from drugs, while the chances of arrest are lower and the penalties lighter (cited in IIPA, 2006b: 12). In the case of the Chinese triads, the gangs moved into video piracy due to international police efforts to crack down on the heroin trade (Booth, 1999). Video has therefore provided organised crime with a profitable and less risky line of illegal business.

COMBATING PIRACY

Industrialised piracy not only shadows the legitimate video business but also shares and parallels many of its ways of operating. Illegal recordings come onto the market through a highly organised structure of producers and distributors. The market is fed by duplication or replication plants using master recordings to mass reproduce illegal copies. Just as the legitimate video market rapidly extended across borders to occupy globally extended space and time, so industrialised video piracy operates transnational networks of distribution. To take one example. As the video recording of films from theatre screens became a headache for the legitimate film industry, in the mid-1980s Warner Bros. began to code release prints of their films so that pirated cassettes could be traced back to the theatre and the print from which the recording was taken. By tracking the coding on an illegal cassette copy of *Rocky IV* (Sylvester Stallone, 1985, US), the company was able to trace how the recording went from the US to Thailand, where local subtitles were applied and copies shipped to Malaysia and Singapore. Cassettes were then further distributed to Jordan and then on to Turkey, where new subtitles were produced, and finally copies were shipped to migrant Turkish workers in Germany (Harmetz, 1986).

Links to crime: part of the
www.piracyisacrime.com campaign conducted in the UK by
the Industry Trust for IP Awareness Limited

For Wang, digital media have presented fresh challenges to the legitimate
media industries by aiding video pirates in their efforts to compress time and
space:

> Digital technology has disrupted th[e] balance of power in the film industry. If
> power in this mode of late capitalist expansion lies in one's capacity to overcome
> constraints of both time and space ... then digital technologies present a major
> challenge to existing forms of power and control due to their capacity to erase
> space and reward speed. While technological innovation is instrumental in
> furthering capitalist market expansion, when used by pirates it also seriously
> undermines and challenges the copyright industries' critical need to command
> space and control time. (2003: 2)

Reproducibility and dispersibility have enabled industrialised piracy to rapidly
copy DVDs and swiftly transport these across national and transnational space,
while the internet has made physical boundaries practically irrelevant for unauthorised flows of copyright material.

While noting that piracy operates through transnational networks of distribution, the production of illegal works and efforts to combat such activities

remain rooted in national contexts. As Wang points out, '[p]iracy occurs at the point where deterritorialized forces of capitalism intersect with the reterritorialized forces of the nation . . ., where the cross-bordered flows of information and copyright goods require national law and enforcement to contain, if not eliminate, piracy' (p. 16). National instruments of intellectual property law are bounded by territoriality and despite efforts to internationalise and harmonise international standards for copyright protection, considerable variations still exist between national laws. In many territories, frameworks for copyright protection are considered by the audiovisual industries to be either ineffective or nonexistent. It is due to the inconsistencies or unevenness between the legislative frameworks and enforcement measures implemented by nations to combat piracy and protect copyright that certain territories have become hubs for illegal reproduction and distribution in the global business of industrialised piracy. Observing that pirated product can move rapidly across borders should not therefore mean that sight is lost of how piracy happens in particular territorial contexts.

The MPA's Global Anti-Piracy Programme

Just as the axis of Japanese hardware and Hollywood software structures the legitimate video business, industrial piracy is inextricably bound into a relationship with these corporate forces. As noted in Chapter 3, the smuggling of VCRs manufactured by the major consumer electronics manufacturers was common practice from the earliest years of the video business. Using camcorders and DVD recorders, today pirates work with hardware technology produced by the major manufacturers to illegally produce and reproduce recordings. Industrialised video piracy is, however, a software not a hardware business. In the same way as the legitimate global video market provides an arena for the circulation of copyrighted works from many sources, so pirated software has many origins. Yet, just as Hollywood features predominate in the legitimate market, so Hollywood entertainment is the preferred currency of globalised industrial piracy. Consequently, the MPAA, which represents the collective interests of its members, the Hollywood majors, is at the forefront of Hollywood's global struggle against piracy. 'We're fighting our own terrorist war', claimed the late president of the MPAA, Jack Valenti, in his characteristically forceful manner when railing against video piracy (quoted in Harmon, 2002). By establishing overseas offices and creating partnerships with international anti-piracy organisations, the MPAA has assumed the role of global video police to guard Hollywood product against the onslaught of piracy.

Based on a survey of 20,600 film consumers in twenty-two countries, a 2006 report prepared by LEK Consulting for the MPAA concluded that piracy cost the US film industry approximately US$6.1bn in 2005. Around US$3.8bn of losses came from hard goods (videocassettes, VCDs and DVDs), while the remaining US$2.3bn was accounted for by internet piracy (LEK, 2006). In that year, an estimated US$4.8bn (80 per cent) of losses were believed to be as a consequence of piracy in foreign territories, and the MPAA have consistently addressed piracy as a domestic and international problem. In the LEK study, China (90 per cent), Russia (79 per cent) and Thailand (79 per cent) were identified as the territories with the highest piracy rates (p. 6). However, the developing markets of China and Russia return only low levels of income to the Hollywood majors. The greatest losses to the MPAA members were therefore measured as coming from the mature markets of Mexico (US$483m), the UK (US$406m) and France (US$322m) (p. 7).

Later in 2006, a further study was published by the Institute for Policy Innovation (IPI), a not-for-profit public policy 'think tank' established in 1987 by the former House Republican leader, Dick Armey. The LEK report examined the impact of piracy on the film industry but the IPI study aimed to assess the total economic impact of film piracy by taking the film industry as part of an interlocking system, which draws on supplies and services from many other industries. Consequently, the IPI regarded the economic impact of film piracy as extending beyond the film business itself.

> If the revenue generated by making motion pictures increases (in this case, not by higher demand but by a decrease in piracy), movie companies will make more movies, invest in higher quality, broader distribution or more marketing, or some combination of these activities in order to capture more profits.
>
> As more movies are made, or more is invested in making, marketing and distributing movies, the people and companies that supply movies will make more money. These include, for example, ad agencies, who sell more copy to newspapers and television promoting the films, and the newspapers and television stations that attract the increased volume. . . .
>
> In sum, motion picture piracy affects not only the movie studios, but all the various businesses that supply the industry or buy from the industry, and the people who work in those businesses. Thus, the impact of movie piracy extends well beyond movie stars, all the way to the teenager selling popcorn and candy at the theatre, the company that markets the candy, the farmer that grows the corn, and the workers that pick the farmer's crop. (Siwek, 2006: 3–4)

Considering that the MPAA has frequently complained that film is a risky business and so is deserving of special attention because the majority of the films made fail to turn a profit, it is debatable if increased revenues would ever result in the production of more films, and if they were made, would any one go to see them anyway? Leaving these questions aside, the IPI study concluded that the overall economic impact of film piracy on the US economy resulted in US$20.5bn per annum in lost output, US$5.5bn in lost earnings for US workers, the loss of 141,030 jobs in the film business and other industries, and US$837m in lost tax revenues.

Combating piracy has become one of the MPAA's leading priorities. To protect the interests of its members overseas, the MPAA has established international networks. The MPA operates four regional offices: the Canadian Motion Picture Distributors Association (CMPDA), based in Toronto; MPA Asia Pacific, which is headquartered in Singapore; MPA Europe, Middle East and Africa (MPA EMEA), co-ordinated from Brussels; and the Motion Picture Association–América Latina (MPA-AL) in São Paulo. Starting in 1975, the MPA commenced a worldwide anti-piracy programme. The aims of the programme have been 'to strengthen industry security measures, to strengthen existing copyright protection through legislative activity, to assist local governments in the investigation and prosecution of piracy cases, and to provide technical support in the criminal and civil litigation generated by such investigations' (MPA, n.d.). As part of these initiatives, over several years the MPA has also formed partnerships with, or sponsored the establishment of, international anti-piracy organisations. In 2006, twenty-three of these partnerships were in place, nearly all concentrated in Western Europe (table 6.2). These include organisations with a specific brief to combat audiovisual piracy, such as the German Federation Against Copyright Theft (Gesellschaft zur Verfolgung von Urheberrechtsverletzungen e.V.) (GVU), Federación para la Protección de la Propiedad Intelectual (FAP) in Spain and the UK-based Federation Against Copyright Theft (FACT). However, in Norway the MPAA has linked up with the business law firm SIMONSEN Advokatfirma DA. Many of these anti-piracy organisations were set up in the early 1980s: FACT was founded in 1983, and the GVU and FAP the year after, while in Italy the Federazione Anti-Pirateria Audiovisiva (FAPAV) was established in 1988. These organisations were therefore formed as part of a co-ordinated effort to combat piracy during the first wave of growth in the global video business.

Working in conjunction with local authorities, the MPA are directly involved with piracy measures across international territories. Countries in the Asia-Pacific region have come in for particular attention by the MPA. Operations are directed from the Singapore office, supported by a further twelve anti-piracy offices across the region. In 2005, piracy in the region was believed to account for US$1.2bn of estimated worldwide losses. During that year, the MPA worked with local law enforcement officers to investigate over 34,000 cases of piracy in the Asia-Pacific. More than 10,500 raids were conducted in the region, which netted 34m pirated discs and uncovered fifty-five factory production lines and 3,362 disc burners. As a result of these actions, over 8,000 legal actions were brought (MPA, n.d.).

In August 2006 alone, the MPA was involved with raids in Malaysia, Indonesia and Taiwan. For one such action, representatives from the MPA joined officers from the Malaysian Ministry of Domestic Trade & Consumer Affairs (MDTCA) in a raid on an authorised optical disc factory in Kuala Lumpur which was suspected of manufacturing pirate VCDs or DVDs. According to records found at the premises, over the previous six years the plant had produced 90m pirated discs, creating profits of US$118m (MPA, 2006e). At the end of July 2006, the Special Economic Crimes Division (Krimsus) of the Jakarta Metropolitan Police twice raided Ratu Plaza, a large shopping mall well known as a centre for pirated goods. Although 575,000 pirated DVDs were seized on that occasion, by the start of August the pirates had restocked and when the Krimsus and the MPA returned for a third raid, 801,900 pirated discs were found (MPA, 2006c). Over the following two weeks, further raids conducted by the same authorities uncovered two pirate DVD production plants in the Tangerang area of Jakarta, with over 787,000 pirated VCDs and DVDs seized (MPA, 2006a and 2006b). In Taipei, MPA representatives accompanied police officers to the Venice Theatre in the suburb of Taoyuan on separate occasions to apprehend two men caught attempting to camcord *The Fast and the Furious: Tokyo Drift* (Justin Lin, 2006, US) using mobile phones (MPA, 2006d).

	Organization	www
Austria	Verein für Anti-Piraterie der Film und Videobranche (VAP)	www.vap.cc
Belgium	Belgian Anti-Piracy Federation (BaF)	www.anti-piracy.be
Czech Republic	Česká Protipirátská Unie (CPU)	www.cpufilm.cz
Denmark	AntiPiratGruppen (APG)	www.antipirat.dk
Estonia	Eesti Autoriõiguste Kaitse Organisatsioon (EAKO)	www.eako.ee
Finland	Tekijänoikeuden Tiedotus-Ja Valvontakeskus (TTVK)	www.antipiracy.fi
France	Association de Lutte Contre la Piraterie Audiovisuelle (ALPA)	www.alpa.asso.fr
Germany	Gesellschaft zur Verfolgung von Urheberrechtsverletzungen e.V. (GVU)	www.gvu.de
Greece	Εταιρία Προστασίας Οπτικοακουστικών Έργων (ΕΠΟΕ)	Epoe.hr1.gr
Hungary	Audiovizuális Művek Szerzői Jogait Védő Közcélú Alapítvány (ASVA)	www.asva.hu
Iceland	Samtök Myndrétthafa á Íslandi (SMÁIS)	www.smais.is
Italy	Federazione Anti-Pirateria Audiovisiva (FAPAV)	www.fapav.it
Netherlands	Bescherming Rechten Entertainment Industrie Nederland (BREIN)	www.anti-piracy.nl
Norway	SIMONSEN Advokatfirma DA	www.simonsenlaw.no
Portugal	Federação de Editores de Videogramas (FEVIP)	www.fevip.org
Romania	RO-ACT	www.roact.ro
Serbia and Montenegro	Anti Piratska Asocijacija	www.antipiratskaasocijacija.org.yu
Slovakia	Slovenská Audiovizuálna Protipirátska Únia (SAPU)	www.sapu.sk
South Africa	Southern African Federation Against Copyright Theft (SAFACT)	www.safact.co.za
Spain	Federación para la Protección de la Propiedad Intelectual (FAP)	www.fap.org.es
Sweden	Svenska Antipiratbyrån (APB)	www.antipiratbyran.com
Switzerland	Schweizerische Vereinigung zur Bekämpfung der Piraterie/ Association suisse pour la lutte contre le piratage (SAFE)	www.safe.ch
UK	Federation Against Copyright Theft (FACT)	www.fact-uk.org.uk

Source: compiled from MPAA (2006a).

Table 6.2 MPA International Anti-Piracy Partners (2006)

These raids are illustrative of the MPA's involvement in enforcement operations not only in the Asia-Pacific but worldwide. Current efforts are directed at the manufacturing of pirated recordings with the intention of cutting off supply to the market. However, as the raids at Ratu Plaza demonstrated, industrialised piracy is remarkably adept at recovering from police actions.

Fighting Piracy in Europe – The Federation Against Copyright Theft

Britain is a prime market for pirated recordings of Hollywood movies. Between 1998 and 2003, piracy in Britain was estimated to have cost the US film industry US$393m in lost revenues (MPA, 2004a: 16). According to the study by LEK Consulting, in 2005 the pirate market in the UK was second only to Mexico for losses to the MPA members (LEK, 2006: 7). Malaysia, together with China and Pakistan, are believed to be the main sources of pirate imports into the UK. To confuse UK customs controls, discs are frequently transported to ports elsewhere in Europe and then dispatched to Britain. Pirate DVDs enter the country through the mail, courier deliveries, cargo shipments and passenger luggage. Discs have been discovered hidden in toys, water dispensers, stuffed animals and computer equipment, or disguised as blank CD-Rs. The pirate business in Britain has become so advanced that it now has its own wholesale/retail structures. Rather than importing discs themselves, vendors at street markets and car boot sales will buy discs in bulk from UK-based wholesalers (MPA, 2004a: 14).

As the UK's national anti-piracy organisation, FACT is representative of the MPA's international partners. Headquartered at Isleworth just outside London, FACT is positioned close to the major agglomeration of the film and broadcasting industries based in and around the capital. FACT's thirty-three members bring together various components of the UK video business: the UK subsidiaries of all the major Hollywood distributors; large UK video distributors (e.g. Momentum Pictures, Prism and Video Collection International); leading UK broadcasters (e.g. the BBC and BSkyB); the largest video rentailer (Blockbuster); film laboratories and video replication companies (e.g. Deluxe Laboratories and Technicolor); and the courier firm DHL. In its fight against video piracy, FACT works in conjunction with local police forces, Trading Standards offices, HM Revenue and Customs, and the Department for Work and Pensions. FACT is not a statutory body but it does have the power to prosecute and aids police forces in their investigation and prosecution of piracy activities (FACT, 2006a).

To formalise its relationship with the Metropolitan Police in London, in February 2006 FACT formed a partnership with the Met's Economic and Specialist Crime Command to launch the Film Piracy Unit. Prosecuting under the Proceeds of Crime Act 2002, the unit has worked to seize the proceeds earned by organised crime from piracy (FACT, 2006d). Since its formation, the unit, together with FACT and local Trading Standards authorities, have conducted a number of joint investigations in the south-east of England which have uncovered major piracy production facilities. For example, in April 2006 a joint operation between FACT, the Film Piracy Unit and Waltham Forest Trading Standards led to a raid on a large DVD manufacturing and distribution facility in Leyton, east London. At the premises, police found more than 500 DVD burners capable of producing over 60,000 DVDs each day, with an estimated street value exceeding £250,000 (the average price of pirated DVDs in the UK is £5) (FACT, 2006b: 1).

In recent years, seizures of illegal recordings in the UK have increased dramatically: in 2000, the volume of illegal units seized in raids stood at 154,274 for all formats (VHS, DVD and VCD); five years later, the figure had reached over 2m (table 6.3). As pirate DVDs and more recently DVD-Rs now represent the overwhelming majority of these units, the black market has enjoyed its very own DVD boom. Countries in South and Eastern Asia have been identified as the major sources of imported pirate discs, yet in May 2005 FACT reported large increases in the overall number of pirated discs seized but a substantial reduction in the volume of imported recordings, suggesting a significant rise in home-grown piracy (FACT, 2005a).

FACT is a member of the Alliance Against IP Theft, previously known as the Alliance Against Counterfeiting and Piracy (AACP). Rather like the role which the IIPA performs in the US, AACP was launched in July 1999 as a cross-industry coalition of UK trade organisations representing the copyright industries. The Alliance's other members include the British Association of Record Dealers (BARD), British Phonographic Industry (BPI), the Business Software Alliance (BSA), the British Video Association (BVA), the Cinema Exhibitors Association (CEA), the Copyright Licensing Agency (CLA), the Entertainment & Leisure Software Publishers Association (ELSPA), the Film Distributors Association (FDA) and the Video Standards Council (VSC). In order to promote the interests of the copyright industries to government, the

	2000	2001	2002	2003	2004	2005
VHS	98,371	13,6871	83,387	87,462	11,067	2,520
DVD	9,245	89723	337,617	1,618,203	2,391,398	804,162
DVD-R			93,995	195,256	5,389,943	1,273,120
VCD	46,658	87,337	164,499	126,810	43,874	743
Total	154,274	313,931	679,498	2,027,731	2,985,282	2,080,545

Source: FACT (2006c).

Table 6.3 Seizures of Pirated Video Recordings in the UK (2000–5)

Industrialized production: site of the Leyton raid (photo: FACT)

Alliance supports the All-Party Parliamentary Intellectual Property Group by providing information to Members of Parliament about the value of intellectual property for the UK economy and the efforts to combat piracy. To strengthen the hand of enforcement organisations, the Alliance is also campaigning to see a series of legislative changes in areas including revising the existing framework relating to the burden of proof, and preventative measures to stop the manufacture or adaptation of devices for the purpose of circumventing copyright protection technology (Alliance Against IP Theft, 2006).

MEDIA TECHNOLOGIES AND PIRACY PRACTICES

Historically, the methods and practices of audiovisual piracy have been tied to developments in media technology as piracy has continually proved responsive to technological change. When motion pictures arrived in the last years of the nineteenth century, and before film distribution developed the exchange system of leasing prints to exhibitors, prints were sold outright to exhibitors. Unauthorised duplication of prints was therefore widespread. Producers also frequently copied the narrative subjects of films made by their rivals (Gaudreault, 1985; Segrave, 2003). Audiovisual piracy did not therefore start with video, but when the VCR arrived it provided a low-cost means for illegal reproduction and a new exhibition technology carrying audiovisual works to new spaces of consumption.

In the VCR era, by using compact consumer-level video cameras or camcorders, pirates were able to create a master tape by recording a film off-screen in a theatre. Video therefore became the catalyst for a boom in copyright infringement. Faced with the introduction of new technologies, intellectual property law was required to modernise. According to the CDPA, ' "film" means a recording on any medium from which a moving image may by any means be produced' (*Copyright, Designs and Patents Act 1988*, 1988). Inclusion of the phrase 'on any medium' indicates how the CDPA was the product of the media age in which it came into effect: films were no longer just exhibited in theatres but had become a category of creative work shown across the platforms of television and the VCR as well.

Digitisation subsequently introduced new possibilities and challenges for copy protection. Enthused by the promise of digital fidelity, the legitimate video business embraced DVD, and industrialised piracy followed accordingly. Strong copy protection systems have been built into DVDs but these have proved fallible and can be bypassed by pirates. Broadband internet also provides a new virtual route through which to illegally distribute copyrighted works. Before the legitimate video market worked out business models and technological systems to deliver viable video-on-demand, download-to-own or download-to-burn services, films, pornography, television programmes and music videos were illegally downloadable. Digitisation has not contained but rather multiplied channels for the infringement of copyright.

Today, several procedures are involved with the illegal acquisition, reproduction and distribution of films and other forms of audiovisual copyrighted works. The main types of piracy with direct relevance to the video business are workprint or theatrical release print theft, camcording, optical disc piracy and internet piracy (Media Wildlife, 2006; MPAA, 2006e). It is through these methods that the business of video piracy is now practised.

Workprint and Theatrical Release Print Theft

Theft of film prints is a practice which has existed since the earliest years of cinema. Today, working cuts of a film are sometimes stolen or 'borrowed' from post-production facilities or effects houses. Release prints are also taken from theatres, film depots and courier services. In such cases, suspicion naturally falls on insiders who work as part of the audiovisual industries (Donahue, 2003). For illegal producers, stolen prints are rare but prized sources with clear advantages, for they provide high-quality sources from which a master video recording can be made for the duplication of illegal cassettes or discs. However, the usefulness of stolen prints is limited to only the most streamlined of piracy operations: prints can be difficult to obtain and the telecine transfer process requires specialised technology. Although not strictly print theft, another pre-release 'insider' source of films is provided by so-called 'screener' cassettes and discs used for marketing purposes.

Camcorder Piracy

One of the most prevalent piracy practices, and currently a major concern for rights holders, is the recording of films in theatres using compact video camcorders. Films can be recorded using standard consumer camcorders or cameras with minute pin-hole lenses, and mobile phones with cameras have provided a new addition to the tools for illegal recording. Camcording has caused widespread anxiety among the legitimate film industry because it is relatively easy. Compared to the difficulties entailed with telecine transfer of stolen prints, theatrical camcorder piracy provides a simple and low-cost method of obtaining films. Moreover, pirates can immediately gain access to newly released titles or even films which have yet to receive a release in many territories.

Camcorder piracy aids the temporal and spatial dynamics of illegal production by assisting the speed with which pirated recordings can reach international markets.

> Once a camcorded copy is made, illegal movies often appear online within hours or days of a movie premiere. Pirates sell these 'master recordings' to illicit 'source labs' where they are illegally duplicated, packaged and prepared for sale on the black market, then distributed to bootleg 'dealers' across the country and overseas. Consequently, the film appears in street markets around the world just days after the US theatrical release and well before its international debut. (MPAA, 2006c)

Camcording threatens the organised pattern of sequenced windows employed by distributors to control the release of film to different media in their fact sheets the MPAA now even portray (e.g. MPAA, 2005b: 1) an alternative sequence of pirate release windows which follow on from the official release pattern: camcording piracy coincides with the theatrical release, providing the source for illegal internet distribution and, following the official home video release of the film, pre-recorded discs can be used as masters for pirated DVDs.

However, in cases where theatrical release dates are staggered across international territories, camcordings from one of the earliest release territories can become the source for rapidly produced and distributed discs which arrive in other territories before the official theatrical release. For example, on 22 July 2006, a joint operation involving FACT and the Metropolitan Police raided an

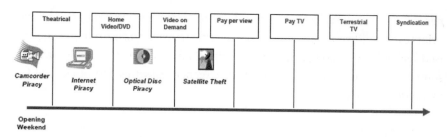

The MPAA's 'piracy timeline' (image: MPAA)

address at the Leyton Mills Retail Park in London. Among the illegal titles seized were *The Devil Wears Prada* (David Frankel, 2006, US) and *Cars* (John Lasseter and Joe Ranft, 2006, US), both of which had not received their theatrical release in the UK (FACT, 2006e). In the case of *The Devil Wears Prada*, the film had opened in theatres across the US on 30 June 2006 but was not scheduled to hit UK screens until 5 October that year. Pirate copies of the film were therefore available more than three months before the theatrical release. In another instance, on Sunday 15 May 2005, *Star Wars: Episode III – Revenge of the Sith* premiered at the annual film festival in Cannes. That same day, FACT and Tower Hamlets Market Services in London seized copies of the film at Brick Lane market, and elsewhere in the city printed counterfeit inlay cards for the film were found after a raid in Woolwich.

In their reporting of the latter incident, FACT referred to the new instalment of the *Star Wars* franchise as a 'pirate blockbuster' (FACT, 2005b). This is an interesting turn of phrase, for it suggests that certain films may achieve exactly the same form of high-profile global saturation release in the pirate market as major event movies gain in the legitimate market. If so, then it is possible to speculate that 'event pirate releases' must impose the same system of seasons on the annual release calendar of the black market as popular Hollywood films do for the legitimate market. As pirate recordings of popular films gain an international release in a matter of days or weeks, then the pirate market will follow the same seasonal highpoints of summer and Christmas as the legitimate release calendar.

To address the issue of pirate copies arriving in international territories before the official theatrical release, starting in 2003 the major Hollywood distributors began to organise for near simultaneous international day-and-date releasing. Before *X2* (Bryan Singer, 2003, US) – the second instalment in the X-Men franchise – hit theatres, 20th Century-Fox were identifying the film as a potential pirate blockbuster. Speaking a couple weeks prior to the film's release, Scott Neeson, Fox's President of Theatrical Releasing, was anticipating '[w]e think this will be one of the most sought after titles for the pirates' (quoted in Kay, 2003c). Fox therefore scheduled the film to open across eighty countries with 7,585 prints over three days starting on 30 April. These efforts practically prevented any piracy of the film prior to it reaching theatres, although a single copy was reported as circulating in China before the release (Kay, 2003b).

Combating piracy is only part of the reasoning behind international day-and-date releasing. Getting a film into theatres across the world takes event marketing onto a global scale, and Fox were conscious that by releasing *X2* internationally they were putting out the first event movie of the year ahead of Warner's much hyped *The Matrix Reloaded* (Andy and Larry Wachowski, 2003, US), due for its own international day-and-date release two weeks later. This strategy reached its apotheosis when on 5 November 2003, *The Matrix Revolutions* (Andy and Larry Wachowski US) was released across fifty countries on 10,103 prints, with the start times scheduled to coincide at the same hour worldwide: the film started simultaneously at 6 a.m. in Los Angeles, 9 a.m. in New York, 5 p.m. in Moscow and 11 p.m. in Tokyo (Holson, 2003). Rolling out across international territories simultaneously also guards against 'spoiler' reviews which may give away plot details or prevent an interval for negative word-of-mouth to be generated around a film. International day-and-date releasing therefore serves not only the purpose of combating piracy but also fuels the hype and sense of event around a film.

Whatever the reasons for using such a strategy, day-and-date releasing has in recent years increasingly brought international distribution into line with the seasonal structure of domestic distribution in North America. Whereas previously, the theatrical release of a film across international territories may have been staggered over a period of months, the simultaneous release of the year's major event movies (which are the films with the greatest potential to become pirate blockbusters) created an international summer season (Kay, 2003a). However, as pirate copies of films have become available across international territories in only a matter of days, frequently appearing in many countries before the scheduled theatrical release, then the piracy market can be said to have operated its own form of near day-and-date releasing for several years.

While conscious of the problems faced by camcording in foreign countries, the MPAA has largely focused its efforts on preventing illegal recordings in the US and Canada. As Hollywood films generally debut in North America, preventing camcording in the domestic territory has been tackled as a matter of urgency to cut off the early supply to overseas territories. At preview screenings, security companies are sometimes employed in theatres to conduct bag searches and inspections using metal detectors. At preview screenings of *X2*, Fox placed security guards wearing night-vision goggles in theatres to scan auditoria for illegal recording (p. 22). Another measure has been the opening of national telephone hotlines, which have been established in the US, Canada and other countries for theatre workers and moviegoers to report criminal activity. Since 2004, anti-piracy trailers have also appeared before the start of film programmes as a method of public education. In March 2006, the MPAA joined with the CMPDA, National Association of Theatre Owners (NATO) and The Motion Picture Theatre Associations of Canada (MPTAC) to launch FightFilmTheft.org, a programme for training theatre workers in Canada and the US. This programme aims to train employees to identify and prevent illegal recording in theatres, with rewards of US$500 offered to employees who take action to stop camcorder piracy (MPAA, 2006b).

Laws prohibiting camcording are in place in several countries. For example, in the US, thirty-nine states and the District of Columbia have passed laws providing state and local authorities with the powers to arrest and prosecute camcorder pirates. On 27 April 2005, the *Family Entertainment and Copyright Act* came into effect, and as part of this legislation, the *Artists' Rights and Theft Prevention Act* or 'ART Act' is aimed at targeting two activities: 'unauthorized recording of motion pictures in a motion picture exhibition facility' and 'infringement of a work being prepared for commercial distribution' (*Family Entertainment and Copyright Act of 2005*, 2005). The latter aims to prevent the release of films before they become publicly available. According to the Act, both offences can be met with threat of imprisonment.

Finally, the MPAA's Office of Technology is supporting the development of various technologies aimed at preventing camcording. Camcorder jamming technologies are in development for installation in theatres to block the operation of cameras or disrupt the recording (Jardin, 2004). Digital Forensic Watermarks are another option: electronic tags included on prints mean that illegal off-screen recordings can be traced back to the original source. For example, the TVS forensic audio-watermarking technology from Florida technology company Trakstar uses a device to emit an inaudible sonic tag from the projection booth to give the information necessary for identifying the theatre and screen where a print was shown, and the time and date when it was shown. Trakstar have also worked on developing PirateEye, a camcorder detection system based on military technology used to locate snipers. A box mounted near the screen facing the audience scans groups of moviegoers with a light-emitting diode and the reflections are read by a camera/sensor. Special software designed by defence contractor Apogen Technologies then processes the images to detect covert camcorders (Healey, 2004; Trakstar, 2006).

Camcorder piracy can bring a timely supply of recent releases and speed the process of illegal production and distribution. Various legal and technical initiatives are in place to prevent camcording, but probably the most significant obstacle to the trade in copies taken from camcorded masters is the question of quality. Recording films off-screen in theatres produces variable results. Recordings can be poorly framed, out of focus, with the heads or bodies of other members of the audience appearing in-frame, and with unclear sound. In their public campaigns, the MPAA and other anti-piracy organisations have therefore focused on the inferior quality of camcorder masters as a way of undermining consumer demand for recordings taken from such sources.

Optical Disc Piracy

Illegal copying of DVD or VCD recordings constitutes optical disc piracy. In some cases, pirated discs are produced at licensed commercial copying facilities and today a great deal of illegal copying around the world is conducted in large factory-scale production operations. Yet, as the cost of the technology necessary for mass reproduction has fallen, then many unlicensed optical disc plants are now in operation. Cheaper technology has also led to the establishment of numerous small-scale pirate 'laboratories' operating out of shops or apartments. In early August 2006, officers from FACT and Trading Standards in the London borough of Hackney raided the house of a woman, where they found 3,500

The 'home entrepreneur' pirate: evidence found in the Hackney raid (photo: FACT)

	Estimated Capacity (m)	Production Lines	Plants
Asia[1]	11,224.5	3,207	540
Europe			
Eastern Europe/CIS[2]	1,427.1	307	92
Western Europe	3,629.5	1,037	189
Americas			
North America	3,052.0	872	198
Central and South America	1,218.0	348	43
Middle East	280.0	80	34
Africa	213.5	61	21
Total	21,044.6	5,912	1,117

Source: compiled and adapted from IIPA (2006b: 8–10)

Notes:
1. Includes Taiwan, where blank recordable discs are produced in huge volumes. Figures here are for production lines and capacity relating to finished pre-recorded discs only.
2. Includes Bulgaria, Kazakhstan and Poland, where capacity is not calculated according to the standard IIPA methodology (3.5m discs, per production line, per annum) but is based instead on plant visits or different capacity estimates per line.

Table 6.4 Global Pirated Optical Disc Production by Region (2005)

pirated DVDs together with thirteen DVD burners in tower units, 1,000 blank DVDs, two colour printers and a PC. Commending the raid, FACT's Director-General described the case as another example of the 'home entrepreneur' pirate (FACT, 2006f). Pirate factories and laboratories are raided frequently, but just as soon as these facilities are closed down, new plants open. Once pirated discs have been produced, they are sold through various channels, including street vendors, open-air markets and online auction sites such as eBay. Most pirated copies are sold in blank packaging without any attempt to mask the illegal status of the product, but in some cases pirates also print full-colour packaging to produce counterfeit copies which are intended to be passed off as the genuine product.

According to IIPA estimates of illegal optical disc production in seventy-nine countries, in 2005 1,117 plants were operating 5,912 production lines, with an annual capacity of 21,044.6m units (table 6.4). Capacity was highest in the Asia-Pacific region, with China, Hong Kong and Taiwan among the largest producers (table 6.5). To estimate production capacity, the IIPA employ a methodology of calculating any single production line to have a

	Estimated Capacity (m)	Production Lines	Plants
China	4,809.0	1,374	86
Hong Kong	2,859.5	817	106
United States	2,590.0	740	181
Taiwan[1]	1,193.5	341	89
Poland	775.0	122	9
Mexico	717.5	205	9
France	714.0	204	18
India	581.0	166	20
Germany	504.0	144	42
Canada	462.0	132	17

Source: compiled and adapted from IIPA (2006b: 8–10)

Notes:
1. Production of finished pre-recorded discs only.

Table 6.5 Pirated Optical Disc Production – Major Territories (2005)

capacity for producing 3.5m discs each year and multiply this by the number of known production lines. The IIPA emphasise that this gives a very conservative estimate, for the volume of 3.5m units per year is based on a production line operating for only eight-hours per day, while many run two eight-hour shifts and, at times of high demand, may operate for twenty-four hours a day. This methodology is based on the time taken to produce DVD units, although a large part of the output from these plants will also comprise production of audio CDs and CD-ROMS, which can often produce copies more quickly (IIPA, 2006d: 6). In recent years, Bulgaria, China, Hong Kong, Indonesia, Macau, Malaysia, the Philippines, Poland, Singapore, Taiwan, Thailand and Turkey have all tightened their regulatory frameworks relating to optical disc piracy. Consequently, production has begun to migrate towards India, Pakistan, Russia and Vietnam due to the looser regulatory regimes in these territories (IIPA, 2006b: 10).

Video copying became widespread in the earliest years of the videocassette business because initially cassettes presented no technical obstacle to illegal reproduction. By the mid-1980s, the MPAA were estimating cassette piracy was losing the film industry between US$500m and US$1bn per annum. As a solution to the problem, copy protection systems were integrated into cassettes. At the start of the 1980s, the CopyGuard system was introduced in the US but proved unsuccessful as it also disrupted playback. In 1985, the Californian company Macrovision introduced a new copy protection system for use in pre-recorded cassettes and to prevent recording from pay-cable services. By using electronic pulses to confuse the automatic gain control on a VCR, which is the system used to regulate the input signal level, Macrovision disrupted and degraded the video image during unauthorised copying. The result was variations in brightness, random line patterns and fluctuating colour (Fantel, 1987). Macrovision was included on cassettes for the first time in April 1985 when the video distributor Embassy released rental-priced copies of the *The Cotton Club* (Francis Ford Coppola, 1984, US) (Harmetz, 1985). After the Hollywood video distributors MCA, CBS-Fox, MGM/UA and Disney adopted the system, Macrovision became the standard-level copy protection technology for the video business, although at best the system only presented an obstacle to consumers and small independent rentailers. By using an image stabiliser device, which could be obtained for as little as US$300, the process could be easily circumvented (Fantel, 1987). Macrovision therefore provided no protection against sophisticated professional pirates.

With the analogue medium of videotape, copying from sources which were already copies resulted in a loss of information, so at each successive stage the next copy lost a 'generation' as image and sound quality was reduced. When transferring films to VCD or DVD, data is lost from the source print through MPEG compression; however, once replicated, commercial copies of discs provide high-quality sources from which illegal copies can be reproduced. VCD and DVD intensified fears among rights holders over the threat of piracy, as these digital disc media effectively made available perfect master recordings to the public, from which exact copies could be made. As DVD re-energised the consumer video market, it therefore also caused a sea-change in the black market as illegal production and distribution moved towards optical disc piracy.

Aware of the potential dangers of digital reproduction, and to avoid the situation witnessed in the early years of videocassettes when no copy protection system was installed, the supporters from consumer electronics, computing and the Hollywood film companies who were behind the development of DVD formed the Copy Protection Technical Working Group (CPTWG) in April 1996 as they worked on the format. Copy protection became one of the key issues around the development of DVD and protracted deliberations over how to make the format safe for rights holders delayed the launch of DVD. Finally, on 29 October, the CPTWG did reach tentative agreement to adopt a copy protection system developed by Matsushita and Toshiba, but were reluctant to stall the launch of the format any further: just a few days later, on 1 November, hardware manufacturers placed DVD players on the market in Japan (Stern and

Stalter, 1996). However, the US launch was held over until March the follow-ing year, by which time full copy protection was installed.

With DVD, the preferred method of protection became the Content Scram-ble System. CSS is an encryption system: using a system of 'keys', DVD discs are encrypted and decrypted by the DVD player. Licensing of CSS to hardware and software manufacturers is co-ordinated through the DVD Copy Control Associ-ation (DVD CCA). Like Macrovision, CSS has not proved to be an entirely robust form of protection. Its weaknesses were most publicly exposed when in October 1999, the teenage Norwegian amateur software engineer Jon Johansen and two others released their programme DeCSS over the internet. By reverse engineering, Johansen and his colleagues were able to identify the decryption source code used in CSS and posted this on the mailing list LiViD (Linux Video and DVD). By using DeCSS, the data on DVDs could be 'ripped' and trans-ferred to a computer hard drive, where that content could be either burnt-to-disc on a recordable DVD format or illegally distributed over the internet.

DeCSS directly challenged the anti-circumvention provision of the WIPO treaties. Consequently, DeCSS was rapidly met with a number of legal actions. When the US magazine *2600: The Hacker Quarterly* posted the programme on its own website <www.2600.com>, the MPAA took out an injunction against the magazine's publisher Eric Corley (aka Emmanuel Goldstein), his company, 2600 Enterprises, and the website (MPAA, 2000). Following the injunction, 2600.com removed DeCCS from its own site but continued to post hyperlinks to other sites from where DeCSS could be downloaded. The matter went to trial in August 2000, when it became the first test case of the DMCA, which had implemented the WIPO provisions two years previously.

Beyond the immediate matter of the case in hand, the incident brought into public focus broader questions over the DMCA, as restrictive copyright protec-tion was pitched against matters of fair use and free speech. Supporters of the defendants took the view that the new copyright law was too restrictive, argu-ing that DeCSS could be employed under fair use by scholars and researchers for non-infringing purposes to legitimately prepare extracts from DVDs, and also that computer code is a kind of speech and so cannot be restricted accord-ing to the First Amendment. But both arguments were rejected by Judge Lewis A. Kaplan, who ruled in favour of Hollywood (Sullivan, 2000). This decision was upheld the following year by the appeals court.

Internet Piracy

After optical disc piracy, the other major challenge which digitisation has pre-sented to the audiovisual industries in their attempts to protect copyrighted works is the enormous potential for using the internet as a decentralised net-

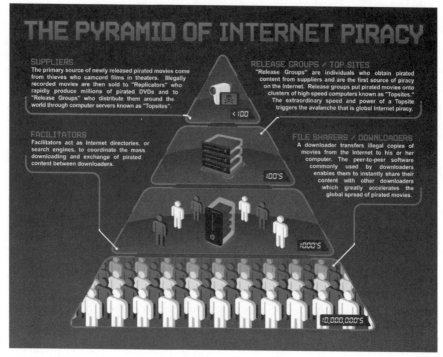

The structure of online piracy (Image: MPAA)

work for the illegal distribution of films and television programmes. Optical disc pirates often sell copies through websites and online auction houses but the greatest threat to copyright presented by the internet is the use of computer networking as a delivery system for unauthorised distribution or webcasting of copyrighted works.

With the internet, industrialised piracy takes on a virtual existence, expanding its geographic reach and speeding up the passage of illegally acquired content across territories. Video content, supplied by camcordings or ripped from commercial DVDs, can be held on computer hard drives, but when that computer is networked, the content can theoretically reach millions of end users across globally extended space. For the pirate business as for the legitimate video business, internet distribution removes the need for duplication, warehousing and transportation to sales outlets. Once a copyrighted work is transferred to a networked server, internet distribution collapses physical distribution and user acquisition into the single act of downloading.

Given the sprawling range of computer networks, it would be easy to lose sight of how internet piracy operates through its own form of structure. The MPAA (2006d) conceptualise this structure as what they call the 'pyramid of

internet piracy', formed from 'suppliers', 'release groups' and 'topsites', 'facilitators', and 'file sharers' or 'downloaders'. Using camcorders, suppliers illegally
record films and sell these for optical disc piracy or to release groups, who place
the recordings on high-speed computers referred to as topsites, from where
files can be distributed. Facilitators function as directories and search engines
by co-ordinating the downloading and exchange of files between downloaders.
After downloading, the files can be watched by users or shared through peer-
to-peer (P2P) networks. In their video presentation *The Global Avalanche of
Piracy*, the MPAA portray the speed and extensity of internet piracy. From the
first topsite, files are shown traversing the world as they pass to facilitators,
which act as hubs for downloaders. Only seven hours after the camcorder copy
was placed on the initial topsite, the number of downloads by facilitators is
shown as totalling 20,503. Through the multiplier effect of networking, after
twenty-four hours, downloads total 62,736 and two days later that figure has
reached 3,922,019.

In this system, a single computer may be used as the wholesale server for
pirated materials. For example, in September 2003, police in Germany, acting
on information from the GVU, raided the Frankfurt-based IT company GATEL,
where they closed down a server with the name Unreality or UNR. The server
was being used to distribute pirated films and video games. With 11 terabytes
of memory, UNR had enough capacity to store 20,000 feature films or 2m music
files and by illegally tapping into the German scientific telecommunications network DFN, UNR could transmit pirated material at the rate of 1Gb per second.
UNR was not open to ordinary internet users but only served selected paying
clients with allocated passwords who paid a fee to the operators of the server to
obtain films and games (Roxborough, 2003).

An alternative method of internet distribution has come through P2P file-
sharing. Since the end of the 1990s, when the illegal music download service
Napstar gained widespread public attention and notoriety, file-sharing has introduced an innovative model of online networked distribution. P2P networks
operate by distributing files between the many members of the network rather
through a few servers. Files of any description, including audio and video files,
can be moved across such networks. Members of the network can make available the files held on their computer to any other members of the network. P2P
networking therefore facilitates file-sharing. Without any centralised servers or
routers, no hierarchy exists in the running or management of the network and
so members become 'peers'. Members of a P2P network also act as both client
and server, downloading from and distributing to other members.

Napster was launched in 1999 as a network to share music files for free. Members registered as part of the network and shared files between their machines,

although central servers were used to keep lists of connected systems and files. By providing the network which enabled peers to distribute copyrighted musical works for free, the major record companies claimed that Napstar facilitated copyright infringement and so they brought legal action against the company. After an injunction was issued ordering the cessation of music sharing, the system was closed down in 2001 and the company's assets were eventually acquired by Roxio, which relaunched Napster as a pay service (Menn, 2003). Napster was a music P2P network, but others like BitTorrent, eDonkey and Grokster have freely distributed both music and video files.

Legal action has been brought against P2P networks by the Recording Industry Association of American (RIAA) or the MPAA alleging that file-sharing infringes copyright. Faced with such action, providers of the software which facilitates file-sharing have frequently agreed to discontinue distribution of the software and also to aid in stopping previously downloaded software from being used for file-sharing. In a particularly high-profile case, the Hollywood film company MGM sued the P2P network Grokster, arguing that by making file-sharing software available, Grokster were knowingly inducing users to commit acts of copyright infringement and were therefore liable. MGM assembled a large coalition of parties from the Hollywood majors, leading recorded music labels and music publishers, professional associations from across the entertainment industries, artists unions and guilds, family groups, academics and online distributors. It was claimed that Grokster encouraged users to illegally share files in order to build a large audience and to attract advertising revenues.

Grokster won when the case was heard by the US District Court for the Central District of California, and the decision was upheld when it went to appeal, before it eventually ended up in front of the Supreme Court. As the case of MGM Studios, Inc. vs. Grokster, Ltd saw a Hollywood film company claiming that a new technology infringed copyright, the case returned to ground covered by the 1984 outcome of the battles between Universal and Sony over Betamax (see Chapter 4). On that occasion, the ruling was made that as the VCR could be used mainly for non-infringing purposes, Sony could not be held liable if recorders were used to infringe copyright. In the Grokster case, the two lower courts took this as a precedent but the Supreme Court reached a unanimous decision and ruled on 27 June 2005 that Grokster's file-sharing software had no substantial non-infringing uses and so by distributing that software the company was liable for infringement committed by users (Triplett, 2005). Grokster agreed to pay US$50m in settlements and on 7 November shut down the file-sharing service.

The decision sent out a warning and, to avoid similar action, on 22 November BitTorrent announced that it would be removing all links to unlicensed content from its site and in future would be working in partnership with the MPAA to combat piracy (Fritz, 2005; MPAA, 2005a). As plans were made to launch a commercial version of BitTorrent to offer movies for sale or rent by downloading, the network agreed a download deal in May 2006 with Warner and by the end of November that year further deals were made with two other Hollywood distributors, 20th Century-Fox and Paramount, together with the independent Lionsgate (Netherby, 2006b and 2006g).

CONCLUSION

For the copyright industries, file-sharing is a major headache, as the number of illegal distributors proliferates exponentially. As with optical disc piracy, a new media technology – in this case the internet – provides benefits to both the legitimate and pirate video industries. Just as rights holders, particularly the major Hollywood film distributors, have moved towards internet distribution through services like CinemaNow, so networked computing is providing a new infrastructure for the illegal exchange of video content. History has therefore shown that the technological forms and systems used by the legitimate film and video industries – from the film print to the videocassette, DVD and the internet – have always found their parallel use in the black market.

As suggested at the opening, the availability of video has created a paradox for the audiovisual industries: videocassettes or discs have opened new markets for copyrighted works but have also exposed those works to increased possibilities of copyright infringement. The emergence of a pirate market paralleling and mirroring the legitimate market is therefore probably an inevitable consequence of the reproducibility, dispersibility and porosity of video media. This could be described as the access paradox: making legitimate recordings more available to consumers always means they become more accessible for illegal reproduction and sale. A further issue raised in particular by optical disc formats such as DVD is, however, the quality paradox. As Chapter 2 discussed, part of the commercial appeal of DVD for consumers has been realised through the 'aura of quality' produced by the format. DVD offers the benefits of high-quality audio and visual presentation, combined with low-cost production, but those benefits are equally available for legal and illegal manufacturers. More than the VCR before it, DVD has therefore provided industrialised piracy with an ideal tool for copyright infringement.

For the copyright industries, the easy flow of illegal video recordings across territories is considered a threat and is described as 'theft'. However, as O'Regan (1991: 122) argues, the black market in video hardware and software proved vital to the formation of video markets in some territories of the developing world. Illegal importation of video hardware provides a route for bypassing tariffs and sales taxes, thereby reducing costs and so extending the availability and adoption of video technology in lower-income economies. In such contexts, the cost of hardware may still remain relatively high. Low-cost reproduction of video software, however, can have a more significant effect on making video recordings affordable. O'Regan argues that '[i]n poorer countries piracy not only allows the development of a [video] system but sustains it' (pp. 122–3). Piracy may therefore not only be an inevitable but also an essential part of the global video business.

The circumvention of copy protection systems, wholesale pirate servers, P2P file-sharing, the statistical weight of reported trade losses and news stories of police raids or units seized all create a picture of video piracy progressively spiralling out of control. As Yar (2005) contends, trade and industry discourse presents piracy as an ever growing epidemic. Piracy does indeed happen and is a corollary of the legitimate video business. But Yar questions the view that the productivity and cost of piracy is forever increasing as the consequence of new technologies for media reproduction and distribution, or the global integration of cultural markets. With the strengthening of copyright law, activities which previously were not prohibited under such legislation suddenly become instances of infringement. Equally, internationalising copyright law immediately extends the problem of piracy by simply including more territories where incidents of infringement will be counted: 'the supposed global growth of "piracy" can be attributed in part to a shifting of the legal "goal posts", rather than simply to any dramatic increase in practices of copying' (p. 686). Copyright infringement is also increasingly subject to criminal prosecution and has become discussed in terms of a criminalising rhetoric which talks of copyright 'theft' and 'links to organised crime'. Furthermore, increases in enforcement activities are producing more raids and netting more seizures, but whether this means more crime is actually happening, or just that more crime is being uncovered, is open to debate. Finally, the statistical reporting of piracy remains questionable. Describing pirate sales as losses to the legitimate copyright industries rests on the fragile presumption that any pirate purchase substitutes for, or displaces, a legitimate purchase. But are 'losses' from piracy actually lost? Would – could? – the buyer of a cheap pirate DVD purchase the full-priced genuine article if the illicit product were not available?

Statistical reporting of piracy therefore rests not only on some questionable methodological procedures but also some doubtful conceptual foundations as well. It is in the interests of the copyright industries to maximise and talk up the figures which support the view that piracy has spun out of control:

From the industry's viewpoint, the inflation of the figures is the starting point for a 'virtuous circle' – high figures put pressure on legislators to criminalize, and on enforcement agencies to police more rigorously; the tightening of copyright laws *produces* more 'copyright theft' as previously legal or tolerated uses are prohibited and the more intensive policing of 'piracy' results in more seizures; these in turn produce new estimates suggesting that the 'epidemic' continues to grow unabated; which then legitimates industry calls for even more vigorous action. What the 'true' underlying levels and trends in 'piracy' might be, however, remain inevitably obscured behind this process of socio-statistical construction. (emphasis in the original, p. 690)

Noting the discursive construction of the piracy 'epidemic' does not mean that piracy is simply an invention of the legitimate copyright industries. Piracy is a very real issue for those industries, but to understand how it is happening and the extent to which it is happening, there is a need to critically interrogate and assess the apparent evidence of its activities and effects. Industry reporting of piracy creates knowledge of the piracy problem. Critically interrogating the piracy issue requires examination of the substance of that knowledge but also the purpose of that knowledge. Yet the very production of that knowledge alone offers just one indication of the ever greater value placed on intellectual property rights by the media industries.

Conclusion: Video Futures

Video media – the VCR, videocassettes, videodisc, VCD and DVD – have transformed the time and the spaces of media consumption. The recordability and reproducibility of videocassettes and DVDs have separated audiovisual media content from institutionally organised timeframes of consumption, liberating the time of consumption from the regimented performance times of film programming in theatres or the fixity of television schedules. Cassettes and discs have also proved endlessly dispersible, as video media have found a place in multiple spaces of consumption. With video, bars, restaurants, schools, shops and buses have all become exhibition venues for audiovisual entertainment. Above all, video media have placed the home within new conditions of mediated existence, further connecting domestic space to the outside world while carrying the outside inside. The dispersal of video media is not confined to a range of locations or places. The porosity of video, its capacity for traversing borders, extends across national and regional territories. For over three decades now, these dynamics of temporal and spatial flexibility have individualised media consumption. At the junction of the temporal and spatial dynamics of video is the individual user, shopper or consumer. This set of forces was established by the VCR during the analogue era of the video business and they have remained as VCD and DVD have taken the video business into the digital age.

This book has explored aspects of the history and operations of video as a global business. In the Introduction, it was suggested that three areas of tension have driven the video business: battles over incompatible formats, competition between hard carrier media and various forms of delivery media, and the perennial fight of copyright holders to protect their works against the effects of industrialised piracy. These conflicts have appeared in various ways throughout this book. As these tensions have defined the history of the video business, then they will continue to play their part in the future shaping of that business.

HIGH-DEFINITION DVD – A DIVIDED FUTURE?

Betamax vs. VHS; DiscoVision vs. CED; MMCD vs. SD; HD-DVD vs. Blu-ray. Through the analogue and digital eras, the video business has been formed and then advanced via a succession of intra-industry conflicts resulting from format battles. As each of these examples has shown, format wars are never just a battle over technological innovation alone. Rivalry between formats draws a range of interests into the fray, from the consumer electronics industry to software suppliers, rentailers and retailers, and now the IT industry. The VCR wars demonstrated that format battles are rarely decided by technology alone: matters of production and marketing affect how formats get into the market and so attract consumers. Format wars are therefore always commercial battles and invariably the destinies of rival video formats have been decided not by technological properties but the marketability of innovations.

High-definition DVD has brought new promises of even greater image quality in video media. Although the current format conflict between HD-DVD and Blu-ray has still to be worked through, what has become immediately clear is that high-definition DVD is creating new uncertainties for the video business. With standard-definition DVD, the video market was able to see a clear sense of direction: the VHS market had peaked and change came in the form of a single DVD format. High-definition DVD has disrupted this stability and certainty, leaving the future state of the market open to speculation: are consumers prepared to replace the still relatively new technology of standard-definition DVD; when will the format war be resolved; will the format war be resolved or will high-definition DVD develop around co-existing incompatible formats; or will the technology fail to take off under the weight of consumer confusion or nervous reluctance to buy players or discs for what could eventually emerge as redundant formats?

Following the lesson of the VCR wars, the format backed by the largest number of hardware manufacturers is likely to be in the best position to create high-volume production and dominate the market. Blu-ray has the strongest backing among electronics manufacturers. Sony is also effectively integrating the format into multiple media platforms. Furthermore, Blu-vay has won the widest support in Hollywood. By the start of 2007, Disney, Fox, MGM and Sony were continuing to exclusively release titles for Blu-ray, while only Universal released exclusively on HD-DVD. As Warner and Paramount were offering their titles on both formats, Blu-ray had attracted the support of nearly all the Hollywood majors.

However, as the example of the games industry has shown, a single common format is not necessary to the growth of a mass market consumer technology in the entertainment business, and a huge global market in entertainment hardware and software can grow and survive through the co-existence of incompatible formats. While the history of the games industry has seen certain platforms gain a dominant market share over others, this has not prevented rival platforms from gaining large consumer bases. In this context, developers in the games business have accepted the need to produce alternative versions of the same content for different platforms. If no single format wins the high-definition

DVD battle, then video may follow the way of the games industry with co-existing and incompatible platforms, and with video distributors conceivably following the line of Warner and Paramount and producing HD-DVD and Blu-ray editions of the same titles.

Warner offered the industry a further option when the company announced at the very beginning of 2007 that it had developed 'Total HD' as a dual-format carrying both Blu-ray and HD-DVD versions of a film on opposite sides of the same disc (Siklos, 2007). When the system was unveiled at a press event on 9 January 2007 during the Consumer Electronics Show in Las Vegas, the Warner stand carried a banner proclaiming 'One World. One Format' (Fritz and Kirsner, 2007). It remains to be seen therefore if high-definition DVD will become a short- or long-term format war, with one side eventually triumphing, or if opposing sides will otherwise reach a state of détente, allowing both formats to co-exist and develop. History suggests that the video business prefers the former.

ANY DEMAND FOR ON-DEMAND?

Networked computing has provided new channels for the delivery of audiovisual content. With video-on-demand, download-to-own and download-to-burn services, consumers are greeted with a panoply of options for accessing and watching the same forms of content available on hard video formats. But will internet distribution provide any serious alternative to the business of hard formats? Certainly at this point in time the technology does not support the commercial aspirations of internet distributors. Downloading may have the immediacy for an on-demand economy, offering more spontaneity and convenience than visiting a video rental or retail outlet, but even with the best performance of high-speed and broadband connections, download times remain slow: 'Until … technical and economic wrinkles are ironed out, video-on-demand may continue to be … video on delay (Wasko, 2003: 152). When compared to DVD playback, the picture quality of downloaded films in full-screen presentation is also noticeably inferior. Finally, while the PC remains the main gateway for accessing the online services, internet film distribution will have to try and impose a 'sit-up' or 'sit-forward' mode of viewing for a type of media consumption for which a relaxed 'sit-back' attitude is more familiar. Internet distribution is unlikely to win over customers until these technological problems are resolved and until downloaded content can be watched in the same social conditions as television.

If taking a technologically centred, teleological perspective, then of course remedies to these problems will be found and inevitably the internet will become a popular platform for video. Download times will get quicker, picture quality will improve and the television, if that it what it is still called, will become an accepted window onto the web. In such a scenario, the ease and convenience of video distribution over the internet will inevitably result in the migration of the video business to the web. Hard video media will disappear as all forms of entertainment will be piped into the home. But are such inevitabilities certain? Talk of convergence, now fuelled by belief in the effects of digitisation, always presumes an ineluctable pull towards the de-differentiation of media platforms and content. Yet history shows that separate media forms have continued to co-exist and multiply. Television broadcasting did not wipe out the film industry and neither did the VCR. Thus although DVD has already signalled the death of the videocassette, there is every reason to presume that hard carrier media in some form or other will still exist for video entertainment.

Not least among the reasons for the survival of hard video media are copy-right holders' concerns regarding the use of the internet as a platform for their works. While Hollywood has made its first steps towards accepting the internet, currently the major companies still appear hesitant in their commitments to online distribution. For as long as the internet provides an active channel for large-scale piracy, concerns will remain over copyright protection. While the majors are keen to protect against what they see as the revenues lost to online piracy, at the same time legal downloading is not providing any significant new business. As profits from videocassettes and DVDs have outstripped all other revenue streams for filmed entertainment for over two decades, the Hollywood majors are keenly aware of how valuable the home video market remains. More-over, in the digital age the video market finally appears to have taken the form which the Hollywood majors have most wanted since the introduction of the VCR. Sales always provided the most direct return to distributors and since the introduction of DVD the market has been solidly built on retail over rental. Fur-thermore, revenue-sharing arrangements now ensure that the major distributors see returns from each rental transaction.

Developments in internet distribution have now moved closer to replicating the options of the video market: VoD provides a form of virtual video rental, while download-to-own and download-to-burn provide substitutes for video sales. Internet distribution does remove replication and distribution costs but when licensing films on the VoD or download-to-own model, inevitably the Hol-lywood majors see a share of revenues going to the third parties who provide these services. DVD or other hard formats may therefore remain more attrac-tive to the majors if the profit margins are higher.

While these issues remain active, a question must linger over whether con-sumers or the Hollywood majors actually want video over the internet. It is certainly debatable whether there is any demand for on-demand among con-sumers or the video business. Rather than VoD or download-to-burn, presently the most significant contribution which the internet is making to the video business is to open up channels for online rental and retail of DVDs. For the short-term future at least, in the video business the instantaneity of on-demand will struggle commercially when balanced against the on-the-shelf immediacy and lucrative margins offered by DVD or other storage media.

PIRACY – VIDEO ARMAGEDDON?

Ironically, it is industrialised piracy which so far has proved most adept at exploiting internet distribution to create a viable business for the delivery of video entertainment. Piracy stands in opposition to the legitimate video business but borrows its ways and means. Audiovisual piracy preceded video but has found in video a tool that suits its needs. The reproducibility, dispersibility and porosity of video have proved ideal qualities for the commercial goals of the pirate industry. Just as the VCR opened a new channel for the distribution of films and other copyrighted content, so industrialised media piracy has used video to further diversify its operations and outlets. As the global dispersal of video media spread to new territories, so piracy not only entered the same territories but also established markets for video where legitimate product was either in scarce supply or non-existent. Piracy may antagonise the legitimate video business, and for that reason appear to somehow resist the economic and cultural power of the overground media industries, but at the most basic level industrialised piracy mimics the legitimate video business because it was precisely that, a business. Piracy continues to represent the revenge of capitalism on capitalism.

Piracy alerts us to the foundations on which the video business is based: intellectual property rights. National and international items of legislation have strengthened the importance and value of intellectual property for the media and cultural industries. As trade has been used as a weapon to impose a rigid international regime for the protection of intellectual property, so more nations have become assimilated into the global economy of intellectual property. Despite stronger legislation and intensified enforcement, industry reporting paints a picture of piracy as an eternal and escalating problem. Yet as Yar's (2005) deconstruction of the piracy 'epidemic' discourse suggests, it is difficult to know or assess the extent of video piracy. Is piracy increasing? How reliable are the figures? Does infringement result in actual economic losses for the copyright industries? Does the strengthening of copyright legislation result in the prevention of infringement or just expand the range of uses which can be counted as incidents of 'theft'?

What does seem certain is that piracy will not go away. Piracy is endemic to video culture, continually co-opting new technologies and colonising new markets.

Videocassettes and now DVDs have created a media market based on the principles of domesticated and individualised consumption. As the old home media of recorded music, radio and broadcast television have now been supplemented by options for video-on-demand and broadband, video media are now firmly embedded among the plethora of consumption options which are available in the domestic media ensemble. After ten years on the market, DVD has now nearly killed off the videocassette, while high-definition formats are already signalling a new wave of technological innovation. Forms of video media will therefore come and go, yet behind those changes tensions over format incompatibility, competition between video and rival media options, and the fight to combat piracy will persist and continue to operate as the underlying dynamics which shape the future of the video business.

Bibliography

AACP. (n.d.) *Proving the Connection: Links Between Intellectual Property Theft and Organised Crime*. London: Alliance Against Counterfeiting and Piracy.

Abel, Richard. (1998) *The Ciné Goes to Town: French Cinema 1896–1914*. Rev. and exp. edn. Berkeley: University of California Press.

Abramson, Albert. (1955) 'A Short History of Television Recording'. *Journal of the Society of Motion Picture and Television Engineers* 64, no. 2: 72–6.

Abramson, Albert. (1973) 'A Short History of Television Recording: Part II'. *Journal of the Society of Motion Picture and Television Engineers* 82, no. 3: 188–98.

Abramson, Albert. (2003) *The History of Television, 1942 to 2000*. Jefferson, NC: McFarland and Co.

'AEG'. (1988) *International Directory of Company Histories*, vol. 1. Ed. Thomas Derdak. Chicago: St James Press. 409–11.

Agrawal, Binod C. (1985) 'Video – A New Diversion for India's Rich'. *Media Development* 32, no. 1: 14–15.

Agrawal, Binod C. (1988) 'India'. *Video World-wide*. Ed. Manuel Alvarado. London: UNESCO/John Libbey. 83–101.

Aho, Jukka. (2001) 'Super Video CD Overview'. <www.uwasa.fi/~f76998/video/svcd/overview /#history> (downloaded 3 November 2005).

Allen, Robert C. (1999) 'Home Alone Together: Hollywood and the "Family" Film'. *Identifying Hollywood's Audiences*. Eds Melvyn Stokes and Richard Maltby. London: British Film Institute. 109–31.

Alliance Against IP Theft. (2006) 'Alliance Campaigns'. <www.allianceagainstiptheft.co.uk/ action/campaigns.html> (downloaded 17 August 2006).

Amdur, Meredith. (2004a) 'Studios Take Walk Around the Block'. *Variety*, 15 March: 4 and 58.

Amdur, Meredith. (2004b) 'Wal-Mart DVDs: The Price is Might'. *Variety*, 19 July: 6 and 72.

American Cinematographer. (1973) 'MCA Demonstrates New Disco-Vision for Use on Standard Home TV Sets' 54, no. 2: 152–3 and 212–17.

Amin, Hussein Y. and Douglas A. Boyd. (1993) 'The Impact of the Home Video Cassette Recorder in Egyptian Film and Television Consumption Patterns'. *Communications* 18, no. 1: 77–88.

Anderson, Chris. (2006) *The Long Tail: How Endless Choice is Creating Unlimited Demand*. London: Random House Business Books.

Armes, Roy. (1988) *On Video*. London: Routledge.

Arthur, Paul. (2004) '(In)Dispensible Cinema: Confessions of a "Making-of" Addict'. *Film Comment* 40, no. 4: 38–42.

Astruc, Alexandre. (1948) 'The Birth of a New Avant-garde: La Caméra-stylo'. (1968) *The New Wave*. Ed. Peter Graham. London: Secker and Warburg/British Film Institute. 17–23.

Ault, Susanne. (2004) 'Sony Finally Snags MGM'. *Video Business*, 13 September. <www.videobusiness.com/index.asp?layout= articlePrint&articleID=CA613459> (downloaded 7 July 2006).

Austin, Bruce A. (1990) 'Home Video: The Second-Run "Theater" of the 1990s'. *Hollywood in the Age of Television*. Ed. Tino Balio. Boston: Unwin Hyman. 319–49.

Barakat, Sohair A. (1983) 'Video Land'. *InterMedia* 11, no. 4/5: 61.

Bausinger, Hermann. (1984) 'Media, Technology and Daily Life'. *Media, Culture and Society* 6, no. 4: 343–51.

BBFC (2006a) 'The History of the Category System'. <www.sbbfc.co.uk/ student_guide_ historycats.asp> (downloaded 2 February 2006).

BBFC (2006b) 'The Video Recordings Act (VRA) 1984'. <www.sbbfc.co.uk/ student_guide_legislation3.asp> (downloaded 2 February 2006).

Benjamin, Walter. (1977) 'The Work of Art in the Age of Mechanical Reproduction'. *Mass Communication and Society*. Eds James Curran, Michael Gurevitch and Janet Woollacott. London: Edward Arnold. 384–408.

Bennett, Hugh. (2004) *Understanding Recordable & Rewritable DVD*. Cupertino, CA: Optical Storage Technology Association.

Bettig, Ronald. (1996) *Copyrighting Culture: The Political Economy of Intellectual Property*. Boulder, CO: Westview Press.

BiB. (2004a) *BiB Television Programming Source Books 2005: Films A–M, Indexes*. Philadelphia, PA: North American Publishing Co.

BiB. (2004b) *BiB Television Programming Source Books 2005: Films N–Z, Indexes*. Philadelphia, PA: North American Publishing Co.

Blockbuster. (2000) *2000 Annual Report*. Dallas: Blockbuster Inc.

Blowen, Michael. (1988) 'E.T. May Be Late Getting Home'. *The Boston Globe*, 28 October: 55.

Blume, Stephen E. (2006) 'The Revenue Streams: An Overview'. *The Movie Business Book*. International 2nd edn. Ed. Jason E. Squire. Maidenhead: Open University Press. 333–59.

Booth, Martin. (1999) *The Dragon Syndicates: The Global Phenomenon of the Triads*. London: Doubleday.

Bowman, Jim and Jonathan Martin. (1993) 'Matsushita Electric Works, Ltd'. *International Directory of Company Histories*, vol. 7. Ed. Paula Kepos. Detroit: St James Press. 302–3.

Boyd, Douglas A. (1987) 'Home Video Diffusion and Utilization in Arabian Gulf States'. *American Behavioral Scientist* 30, no. 5: 544–55.

Boyd, Douglas A. (1989) 'The Videocassette Recorder in the USSR and Soviet-Bloc Countries'. *The VCR Age: Home Video and Mass Communication*. Ed. Mark R. Levy. Sage: Newbury Park. 252–70.

Boyd, Douglas A. and Nawaf Adwan. (1988) 'The Gulf States, Jordan and Egypt'. *Video World-wide*. Ed. Manuel Alvarado. London: UNESCO/John Libbey. 159–79.

Boyd, Douglas A. and Joseph D. Straubhaar. (1985) 'Developmental Impact of the Home Video Cassette Recorder on Third World Countries'. *Journal of Broadcasting and Electronic Media* 29, no. 1: 5–21.

Brent, Willie. (1998) 'Chinese Gov't Ends Vid Format Battle'. *Variety*, 21 December: 22.

Briggs, Asa. (1995) *The History of Broadcasting in the United Kingdom vol. 5: Competition 1955–1974*. Oxford: Oxford University Press.

Brinkley, Joel. (1998) 'New Recorded Format Draws Criticisms from Rivals'. *The New York Times* sec. C, 12 October: 5.

Brodie, John and J. Max Robins. (1994) 'Synergy, Schmynergy!'. *Variety*, 21 March: 1 and 70–1.

Bruck, Connie. (1994) *Master of the Game: Steve Ross and the Creation of Time Warner*. New York: Penguin.

Business Week. (1984) 'VCRs That Spout the Party Line'. 3 September: 40.

Cadavid, Amparo. (1983) 'Before Television'. *InterMedia* 11, no. 4/5: 45.

Cellitti, David Robert. (1998) 'World on a Silver Platter: A Brief History of Optical Disc'. <www.oz.net/blam/DiscoVision/LaserMagic 1998.htm> (downloaded 18 October 2005).

Chandler, Alfred J. (2001) *Inventing the Electronic Century: The Epic Story of the Consumer Electronics and Computer Industries*. New York: Free Press.

Clark, Mike. (1993) 'VHS and Laser Discs Still Have Their Charms'. *USA Today*, 11 November: 12D.

Clark, Samantha. (2006) 'Smooth Burning'. *Video Business*, 20 July. <www.videobusiness.com/index.asp?layout= articlePrint&articleID=CA6355518> (downloaded 22 August 2006).

Cohen, Kerstan. (1996) 'Philips Electronics N.V.'. *International Directory of Company Histories*, vol. 13. Ed. Tina Grant. Detroit: St James Press: 400–3.

Coleman, W. F. Kobena. (1983) 'A Vivid Choice'. *InterMedia* 11, no. 4/5: 49.

Conservative Party. (1983) *1983 Conservative Party General Election Manifesto*. <www.conservative-party.net/manifestos/1983/1983–conservative-manifesto.shtml> (accessed 2 February 2006).

Copyright, Designs and Patents Act 1988. (1998) London: HMSO.

Crowdus, Gary. (1999) 'A Film Archive for the Home Viewer: Interview with Peter Becker of the Criterion Collection'. *Cineaste* 25, no. 1: 47–50.

Cubitt, Sean. (1993) *Videography: Video Media as Art and Culture*. Houndmills: MacMillan.

Cumberbatch, Guy. (1994) 'Legislating Mythology: Video Violence and Children'. *Journal of Mental Health* 3, no. 4: 485–94.

Cusumano, Michael A., Yiorgos Mylonadis and Richard S. Rosenbloom. (1992) 'Strategic Maneuvering and Mass-market Dynamics: The Triumph of VHS Over Beta'. *Business History Review* 66, no. 1: 51–94.

D'Alessandro, Anthony. (2001) 'Top Grossing Pics of 2001'. *Variety*, 7 January: 38–9.

D'Alessandro, Anthony. (2004) 'The Top 250 of 2003'. *Variety*, 12 January: 14–15.

D'Alessandro, Anthony. (2005) 'Domestic Top 250 of 2004'. *Variety*, 10 January: 14–15.

Davis, Darrell William. (2003) 'Compact Generation: VCD Markets in Asia'. *Historical Journal of Film, Radio and Television* 23, no. 2: 165–76.

Dean, Peter, Dominic Pride and Steve McClure. (1993) 'Nimbus Claims Video Compression on CD'. *Billboard*, 20 February: 8.

DeGeorge, Gail. (1996) *The Making of a Blockbuster: How Wayne Huizenga Built a Sports and Entertainment Empire for Trash, Grit and Videotape*. New York: John Wiley and Sons.

Doherty, Thomas. (2001) 'DVD Commentary Tracks: Listening to the Auteurs'. *Cineaste* 26, no. 4: 78–80.

Donahue, Ann. (2003) 'Piracy: An Inside Job'. *Variety: VLife Supplement*, 8 December: 66–8 and 89.

Epstein, Edward Jay. (2006) *The Big Picture: Money and Power in Hollywood*. New York: Random House.

FACT. (2005a) 'New Figures Reveal US as Emerging Producer of Pirate DVDs'. Press Release, 19 May. <www.fact-uk.org.uk/site/downloads/press_releases/review%20APP.doc> (downloaded 17 August 2006).

FACT. (2005b) 'Star Wars Finale Set to be Pirate Blockbuster'. Press Release, 20 May. <www.fact-uk.org.uk/site/downloads/press_releases/lease%20final.doc> (downloaded 17 August 2006).

FACT. (2006a) 'FACT: Who We Are'. <www.fact-uk.org.uk/site/about/index.htm> (downloaded 17 August 2006).

FACT. (2006b) 'Largest Ever Pirate DVD Manufacturing and Distribution Facility Raided'. Press Release, 7 April. <www.fact-uk.org.uk/site/media_centre/pressreleases/documents/LEYTONWEBRELEASE.pdf> (downloaded 17 August 2006).

FACT. (2006c) 'Media Centre/Statistics'. <www.fact-uk.org.uk/site/media_centre/dvd_seiz_0405.html> (downloaded 17 August 2006).

FACT. (2006d) 'Metropolitan Police Film Piracy Unit'. 23 February. <www.fact-uk.org.uk/site/about/metpolice.html> (downloaded 17 August 2006).

FACT. (2006e) 'Multi Agency Operation Targets Prolific DVD Sellers in Leyton'. Press Release, 25 July. <www.fact-uk.org.uk/site/media_centre/documents/LeytonMillsweb.pdf> (downloaded 17 August 2006).

FACT. (2006f) 'Online Pirate DVD Seller Raided in London: Equipment and Thousands of Counterfeit Films Seized'. Press Release, 8 August. <www.fact-uk.org.uk/site/media_centre/documents/HackneyAugweb.pdf> (downloaded 17 August 2006).

Family Entertainment and Copyright Act of 2005. (2005) <www.copyright.gov/legislation/pl109-9.html> (downloaded 11 August 2006).

Fantel, Hans. (1987) 'Video: Tangles in the Anti-copying Thicket'. *The New York Times* sec. 2, 30 August: 22.

Farhi, Paul. (1989) 'Columbia Acceptance of Bid Puts Sony into the Big Time'. *The Washington Post*, 28 September: E1.

Feingold, Benjamin S. (2006) 'Home Video Business'. *The Movie Business Book*. International 2nd edn. Ed. Jason E. Squire. Maidenhead: Open University Press: 409–17.

Ferguson, John. (1999) 'In the Premiere League'. *Video Home Entertainment (Kids' Kollection Supplement)*, 25 September: 4–5.

Fisher, Bob. (2000) 'Indelible Compressions'. *American Cinematographer* 81, no. 5: 96–101.

Forsythe, Victor L. C. (1983) 'Video Parties – And Fewer Cars Stolen'. *InterMedia* 11, no. 4/5: 52–3.

Fritz, Ben. (2005) 'MPAA Buddies Up to Bit Player'. *Daily Variety*, 23 November: 1.

Fritz, Ben and Scott Kirsner. (2007) 'High (Def) Anxieties'. *Variety*, 15 January: 3.

Ganley, Gladys and Oswald Ganley. (1987) *Global Political Fallout: The VCR's First Decade, 1976–1985*. Norwood, NJ: Ablex.

Garvey, Ronald. (2006) 'Pay-per-view'. The Museum of Broadcast Communications. <www.museum.tv/archives/etv/P/htmlP/payperview/payperview.htm> (downloaded 10 July 2006).

Gaudreault, André. (1985) 'The Infringement of Copyright Laws and its Effects (1900–1906)'. *Framework* no. 29: 2–14.

Gelatt, Roland. (1977) *The Fabulous Phonograph 1877–1977*. 2nd rev. edn. London: Cassell.

Gilligan, Gregory J. (1998) 'A View of the Future?: Circuit City's Divx Could Change the Way We Watch Movies'. *Richmond Times Dispatch* (Virginia), 8 June: D14.

Ginsberg, Charles P. (1956) 'A New Magnetic Video Recording System'. *Journal of the SMPTE* 65, no. 5: 302–4.

Ginsberg, Charles P. (1981) 'The Horse of the Cowboy: Getting Television on Tape'. *Television* 18, no. 12: 11–17.

Goldstein, Seth. (1998a) 'Indie Video Retailers Plan Suit Against Studios, Blockbuster'. *Billboard*, 18 July. <www.lexisnexis.com/uk/business/results/docview/docview.do?risb= 521_T1033904642&format=GNBFI&sort= BOOLEAN&startDocNo=1&resultsUrlKey =29_T1033904644&cisb=22_T1033904643 &treeMax=true&treeWidth=0&csi=5545& docNo=5> (downloaded 7 April 2006).

Goldstein, Seth. (1998b) 'MGM Licenses Titles for the Divx System'. *Billboard*, 11 April. <www.lexisnexis.com/uk/business/results/docview/docview.do?risb=21_T1033904664 &format=GNBFI&sort=BOOLEAN&start DocNo=1&resultsUrlKey=29_T1033904666 &cisb=22_T1033904665&treeMax=true&tree Width=0&csi=5545&docNo=3> (downloaded 7 April 2006).

Gomery, Douglas. (2000) 'The Hollywood Film Industry: Theatrical Exhibition, Pay TV, and Home Video'. *Who Owns the Media: Competition and Concentration in the Mass Media Industry*. 3rd edn. Eds Benjamin M. Compaine and Douglas Gomery. Mahwah, NJ: Lawrence Erlbaum Associates. 359–435.

Graham, Margaret. (1986) *RCA and the VideoDisc: The Business of Research*. Cambridge: Cambridge University Press.

Graser, Marc. (1999) 'Divx Takes Digital Dive'. *Variety*, 21 June: 9.

Greene, Jay. (1994) 'Sumner's Star Rises'. *Variety*, 21 February: 1 and 184.

Gregory, Gene. (1981) *The Japanese Electronics Industry*. Tokyo: Sophia University.

Griffin, Nancy and Kim Masters. (1997) *Hit and Run: How Jon Peters and Peter Guber Took Sony for a Ride in Hollywood*. New York: Touchstone.

Gronow, Pekka and Ilpo Saunio. (1998) *An International History of the Recording Industry*. London: Cassell.

Groves, Peter J. (1997) *Sourcebook on Intellectual Property Law*. London: Cavendish.

Hain, Andy and David Browne. (2003a) 'Philips N1500'. *Total Rewind*. <www.totalrewind.org/philips/P_1500.htm> (downloaded 14 October 2005).

Hain, Andy and David Browne. (2003b) 'Philips N1502'. *Total Rewind*. <www.totalrewind.org/philips/P_1502.htm> (downloaded 14 October 2005).

Hain, Andy and David Browne. (2003c) 'Philips N1700'. *Total Rewind*. <www.totalrewind.org/philips/P_1700.htm> (downloaded 14 October 2005).

Hain, Andy and David Browne. (2003d) 'Telcan and Wesgrove'. *Total Rewind*. <www.totalrewind.org/revolution/R_telwes.htm> (downloaded 14 October 2005).

Harding, Thomas. (1997) *The Video Activist Handbook*. London: Pluto.

Harmetz, Aljean. (1985) '*Cotton Club* Cassettes Coded to Foil Pirates'. *The New York Times* sec. C, 24 April: 15.

Harmetz, Aljean. (1986) 'Film Industry Escalates War Against Pirates'. *The New York Times* sec. C, 23 June: 14.

Harmetz, Aljean. (1988a) '*E.T.*, Box Office Champ, Sets Video Records'. *The New York Times* sec. C, 27 October: 21.

Harmetz, Aljean. (1988b) 'Wearing Spielberg Down to Put *E.T.* on Cassette'. *The New York Times* sec. C, 17 May: 18.

Harmon, Amy. (2002) 'Black Hawk Download; Moving Beyond Music, Pirates Use New Tools to Turn the Net into an Illicit Video Club'. *The New York Times* sec. G, 17 January: 1.

Harper, Graeme. (1999) 'Dooming the Video'. *Sight and Sound* 9, no. 6: 18–20.

Harper, Graeme. (2001) 'DVD: The Shift to Film's New Modernity'. *CineAction* no. 56: 20–5.

Hazelton, John. (2004a) 'The Beauty of "The Beast"'. *Screen International*, 16 April: 12–14.

Hazelton, John. (2004b) ' "Virtual" DVD Rentals Wake up to Reality'. *Screen International*, 16 April: 13.

Hazelton, John. (2006) 'Rivals Line Up for Battle'. *Screen International*, 17 March: 14–15.

Healey, Jon. (2004) 'Turning the Camera on Movie Pirates'. *Los Angeles Times*, 19 September: C1 and 12.

Hendley, Tony. (1985) *Videodiscs, Compact Discs and Digital Optical Discs*. Hatfield: Cimtech.

Herskovitz, Jon. (1997) 'Firms Boost Japan's DVD Rentals'. *Daily Variety*, 16 December: 39.

Hettrick, Scott. (1997) 'Uni Makes it a Gang of Four Majors Set for DVD'. *The Hollywood Reporter*, 11 July: 4 and 46.

Hettrick, Scott. (1998a) 'Betamax Redux'. *The Hollywood Reporter*, 24 February: 12.

Hettrick, Scott. (1998b) 'Boxoffice Titans Could Float a New DVD Format'. *The Hollywood Reporter*, 20 February: 1 and 85.

Hettrick, Scott. (1998c) 'Fox to Play for Pay with Divx'. *The Hollywood Reporter*, 19 February: 1 and 8.

Hettrick, Scott. (1998d) 'Netflix Puts DVD Rentals on Web'. *The Hollywood Reporter*, 16 April: 6–23.

Hettrick, Scott. (1998e) 'Par Jumps on DVD Wagon; Fox, DreamWorks Still Out'. *The Hollywood Reporter*, 28 April: 13 and 71.

Hettrick, Scott. (2001) 'Five Align for Internet Movie Service'. *Video Business*, 16 August. <www.videobusiness.com/index.asp?layout=articlePrint&articleID=CA619308> (downloaded 12 July 2006).

Hettrick, Scott. (2002a) 'CinemaNow Downloads MGM'. *Video Business*, 19 February. <www.videobusiness.com/index.asp?layout=articlePrint&articleID=CA618867> (downloaded 9 July 2006).

Hettrick, Scott. (2002b) 'Movielink Video on Demand Open for Business'. *Video Business*, 11 November. <www.videobusiness.com/index.asp?layout=articlePrint&articleID=CA617793> (downloaded 9 July 2006).

Hettrick, Scott. (2005a) 'Paramount Embraces Blu-ray'. *Video Business*, 2 October. <www.videobusiness.com/index.asp?layout=articlePrint&articleID=CA6262261> (downloaded 6 July 2006).

Hettrick, Scott. (2005b) 'Warner Joins Blu-ray Camp'. *Video Business*, 21 October. <www.videobusiness.com/index.asp?layout=articlePrint&articleID=CA6276046> (downloaded 6 July 2006).

Hight, Craig. (2005) 'Making-of Documentaries on DVD: *The Lord of the Rings* Trilogy and Special Editions'. *The Velvet Light Trap* no. 56: 4–17.

Hilmes, Michelle. (1990) 'Pay Television: Breaking the Broadcast Bottleneck'. *Hollywood in the Age of Television*. Ed. Tino Balio. Boston: Unwin Hyman. 297–318.

Hindes, Andrew. (1998) 'Majors Sharing, Indies Paring'. *Variety*, 14 September: 9 and 14.

HMSO. (1984) *Video Recordings Act 1984*. London: HMSO.

Holson, Laura M. (2003) 'Wrapping Up a Trilogy with a Global Assault'. *The New York Times* sec. E, 5 November: 1.

Howe, Tom. (2005a) '1970: Telefunken Teldec VideoDisc Player Prototype'. *CED Magic*. <www.cedmagic.com/history/teldec-1970.html> (downloaded 18 October 2005).

Howe, Tom. (2005b) '1975: Telefunken Teldec Production VideoDisc Player'. *CED Magic*. <www.cedmagic.com/history/teldec-1975.html> (downloaded 18 October 2005).

IFPI. (2001) *The Recording Industry in Numbers 2001*. London: International Federation of the Phonographic Industry.

IIPA. (2005) 'Appendix A: IIPA 2005 "Special 301" Recommendations'. Washington, DC: International Intellectual Property Alliance.

IIPA. (2006a) 'Factsheet'. <www.iipa.com/pdf/IIPA%20Fact%20Sheet%2009212006.pdf> (downloaded 15 August 2006).

IIPA. (2006b) 'IIPA Special 301 Letter to USTR'. Washington, DC: International Intellectual Property Alliance.

IIPA. (2006c) '2006 Special 301 Report – Appendix A: IIPA 2006 "Special 301" Recommendations'. Washington, DC: International Intellectual Property Alliance.

IIPA. (2006d) '2006 Special 301 Report – Appendix B: Methodology'. Washington, DC: International Intellectual Property Alliance.

ISO. (2001) 'MPEG: Achievements and Current Work'.<www.chiariglione.org/mpeg/mpeg_general.htm> (downloaded 1 November 2005).

Jamgocyan, Nik. (1998) 'Share Issue'. *Screen International*, 1 May: 13.

Jardin, Xeni. (2004) 'An Eye on Movie Theater Pirates'. *Wired*, 12 November.

<www.wired.com/news/digiwood/0,1412,65683,00.html> (downloaded 11 August 2006).

Kabira, Chosei. (1983) 'A Japanese Without a VCR'. *InterMedia* 11, no. 4/5: 59.

Kamina, Pascal (2002) *Film Copyright in the European Union*. Cambridge: Cambridge University Press.

Karon, Paul and Adam Sandler. (1997) 'Disney Dives into DVD'. *Variety*, 8 September: 33.

Katz, Elihu. (1983) 'A Second TV Channel?'. *InterMedia* 11, no. 4/5: 55–6.

Kay, Jeremy. (2003a) 'Global Warming'. *Screen International*, 12 September: 22–3.

Kay, Jeremy. (2003b) 'X2 Global Rampage Keeps Pirates at Bay'. *Screen Daily*, 6 May. <www.screendaily.com/print.asp?storyid=12195> (downloaded 4 July 2006).

Kay, Jeremy. (2003c) 'X-Men Tackle Mutant Pirate'. *Screen International*, 18 April: 1–2.

Kendrick, James. (2001) 'What is the Criterion? The Criterion Collection as an Archive of Film as Culture'. *Journal of Film and Video* 53, no. 2/3: 124–39.

Kipps, Charles. (1989a) 'Col's Future is Sony-Side-Up'. *Variety*, 27 September: 1 and 5.

Kipps, Charles. (1989b) 'Sony and Columbia: A Tidy Case of Hardware Meeting Software'. *Variety*, 27 September: 5.

Kittler, Friedrich A. (1999) *Gramophone, Film, Typewriter*. Stanford, CA: Stanford University Press.

Klain, Stephen. (1977) 'H'wood Pix on Home Tape at $50 Per'. *Variety*, 7 December: 1 and 90.

Klinger, Barbara. (2006) *Beyond the Multiplex: Cinema, New Technologies, and the Home*. Berkeley: University of California Press.

Klopfenstein, Bruce C. (1989) 'The Diffusion of the VCR in the United States'. *The VCR Age: Home Video and Mass Communication*. Ed. Mark R. Levy. Sage: Newbury Park. 21–39.

Koenigsberg, Allen. (1990) 'One Hundred and One Significant Patents: Illustration and Commentary'. *The Patent History of the Phonograph 1877–1912*. Ed. Allen Koenigsberg. New York: APM Press. xxii–lxxii.

Krämer, Peter. (1996) 'The Lure of the Big Picture: Film, Television and Hollywood'. *Big Picture, Small Screen: The Relations between Film and Television*. Eds J. Hill and M. McLoone. Luton: John Libbey Media/University of Luton Press. 9–46.

Kristof, Nicholas D. (1986) 'X-rated Industry in a Slump'. *The New York Times* sec. 3, 5 October: 1.

Kumar, Keval J. (1985) 'India's Video Boom: Threat or Alternative?'. *InterMedia* 32, no. 1: 18–20.

Landis, David. (1993a) 'Pop in a CD – and Watch a Movie'. *USA Today*, 27 October: 1D.

Landis, David. (1993b) 'Video CDs Newest Choice in Home Viewing'. *USA Today*, 11 November: 12D.

Lardner, James. (1987) *Fast Forward: Hollywood, the Japanese, and the Onslaught of the VCR*. New York: W. W. Norton.

Learmonth, Michael. (2005) 'Store Wars!'. *Variety*, 11 November: 1 and 62.

Leeds, Alex. (2003) 'Movies without Borders'. *Film Comment* 39, no. 1: 64 and 67.

LEK. (2006) *The Cost of Movie Piracy*. Los Angeles: LEK Consulting.

Lewis, Jon. (2002) *Hollywood v. Hard Core: How the Struggle over Censorship Saved the Modern Film Industry*. New York: New York University Press.

Luh, James C. (2001) 'Breaking Down DVD Borders'. *The Washington Post*, 1 June: E01.

Lyons, Eugene. (1966) *David Sarnoff*. New York: Harper and Row.

McClure, Steve. (1993) 'Hardware Giants Assess Video CD Future: Even with Standard, Compatibility Questions Remain'. *Billboard*, 11 September: 6.

McDougal, Dennis. (1998) *The Last Mogul: Lew Wasserman, MCA, and the Hidden History of Hollywood*. New York: Crown.

Manovich, Lev. (2001) *The Language of New Media*. Cambridge, MA: MIT Press.

Markoff, John. (1997) 'Companies Roll the Dice on Digital Videodisks'. *The New York Times* sec. D, 9 January: 2.

'Matsushita Electric Industrial Co., Ltd'. (1990) *International Directory of Company Histories*, vol. 2. Ed. Lisa Mirabile. Chicago: St James Press. 55–6.

Mebold, Anke and Charles Tepperman. (2003) 'Resurrecting the Lost History of 28mm Film in North America'. *Film History* 15, no. 2: 137–51.

Media Wildlife. (2006) 'What Are the Different Types of Piracy?'. <dazed.adc.rmit.edu.au/~s3088639/blog/?p=275 (downloaded 11 August 2006).

Menn, Joseph. (2003) *All the Rave: The Rise and Fall of Shawn Fanning's Napster*. New York: Crown Business.

Monush, Barry (ed.). (1991) *1991 36th Edition International Television and Video Almanac*. New York: Quigley.

Monush, Barry (ed.). (1992) *1992 37th Edition International Television and Video Almanac*. New York: Quigley.

Monush, Barry (ed.). (1993) *1993 38th Edition International Television and Video Almanac*. New York: Quigley.

Monush, Barry (ed.). (1994) *1994 39th Edition International Television and Video Almanac*. New York: Quigley.

Monush, Barry (ed.). (1995) *1995 40th Edition International Television and Video Almanac*. New York: Quigley.

Moore, Jerrold Northrop. (1976) *A Voice in Time: The Gramophone of Fred Gaisberg 1873–1851*. London: Hamish Hamilton.

Morita, Akio with Edwin M. Reingold and Mitsuko Shimomura. (1987) *Made in Japan: Akio Morita and Sony*. London: Fontana.

Morley, David. (2000) *Home Territories: Media, Mobility and Identity*. London: Routledge.

Morton, James. (1994) *A Guide to the Criminal Justice and Public Order Act 1994*. London: Butterworths.

MPA. (n.d.) *Anti-Piracy Fact Sheet: Asia-Pacific Region*. <www.mpaa.org/AsiaPacificPiracyFactSheet.pdf> (downloaded 11 August 2006).

MPA. (2002) *2001 U.S. Economic Review*. Los Angeles: MPAA Worldwide Market Research.

MPA. (2003) *U.S. Entertainment Industry: 2002 MPA Market Statistics*. Los Angeles: MPA Worldwide Market Research.

MPA. (2004a) 2004 *European Country Piracy Fact Sheets. November*. <www.mpaa.org/EuropeanPiracyFactSheet.pdf> (downloaded 11 August 2006).

MPA. (2004b) *U.S. Entertainment Industry: 2003 MPA Market Statistics*. Los Angeles: MPA Worldwide Market Research.

MPA. (2005) *U.S. Entertainment Industry: 2004 MPA Market Statistics*. Los Angeles: MPA Market Research.

MPA. (2006a) '135 CD/VCD Burners Seized, Nine Arrested in Pirate Burner Lab Raid by Jakarta Police'. News Release, 11 August. <www.mpaa.org/press_releases/2006_08_11.pdf> (downloaded 20 August 2006).

MPA. (2006b) 'Five DVD/VCD Lines Seized, Five Arrested in Raid on Pirate Disc Factory in Indonesia'. News Release, 15 August. <www.mpaa.org/press_releases/2006_08_15_indo.pdf> (downloaded 20 August 2006).

MPA. (2006c) 'Jakarta Police Seize 801,900 Pirated DVDs in Raid on Notorious Ratu Plaza Shopping Mall'. News Release, 11 August. <www.mpaa.org/press_releases/2006_08_11.pdf> (downloaded 20 August 2006).

MPA. (2006d) 'Taiwan Movie Pirate Arrested Camcording *The Fast and the Furious: Tokyo Drift*'. News Release, 22 August. <www.mpaa.org/press_releases/2006_08_22.pdf> (downloaded 23 August 2006).

MPA. (2006e) 'Three DVD/VCD Lines Seized, Seven Arrested in Raid on Licensed Factory in Malaysia'. New Release, 7 August. <www.mpaa.org/press_releases/2006_08_07.pdf> (downloaded 20 August 2006).

MPA. (2006f) *U.S. Entertainment Industry: 2005 MPA Market Statistics*. Los Angeles: MPA Market Research and Analysis.

MPAA. (1998) 1997 *U.S. Economic Review*. <www.mpaa.org/useconomicreview/1997/vcr97.htm> (downloaded on 11 February 1999).

MPAA. (2000) 'Motion Picture Studios Seek Modification of January 20 Injunction in DeCSS Case'. News Release, 5 April. <www.mpaa.org/dvd_release_4_5.asp> (downloaded 15 August 2006).

MPAA. (2005a) 'BitTorrent and MPAA Join Forces'. News Release, 22 November. <www.mpaa.org/bittorrent_announcement_final.pdf> (downloaded 10 October 2006).

MPAA. (2005b) *2005 US Piracy Fact Sheet*. <www.mpaa.org/USPiracyFactSheet.pdf> (downloaded 11 August 2006).

MPAA. (2006a) 'International Anti-Piracy Organizations'. <www.mpaa.org/inter_organizations.asp> (downloaded 11 August 2006).

MPAA. (2006b) 'MPAA, NATO, CMPDA & MPTAC Launch FightFilmTheft.org to Fight Illegal Camcording in Theaters'. Press Release, 13 March. <www.mpaa.org/press_releases/2006_03_13_web.pdf> (downloaded 20 August 2006).

MPAA. (2006c) 'Theatrical Camcorder Piracy'. <www.mpaa.org/piracy_theatrical_cam.asp> (downloaded 11 August 2006).

MPAA. (2006d) 'The Pyramid of Internet Piracy'. <www.mpaa.org/pyramid_of_piracy.pdf> (downloaded 12 August 2006).

MPAA. (2006e) 'Who Are Movie Thieves?'. <www.mpaa.org/piracy_whoAre.asp> (downloaded 11 August 2006).

Naficy, Hamid. (2004) 'Islamizing Film Culture in Iran: A Post-Khatami Update'. *The New Iranian Cinema: Politics, Representation and Identity*. Ed. Richard Tapper. London: I. B. Tauris. 26–65.

Nakayama, Wataru, William Boulton and Michael Pecht. (1999) *The Japanese Electronics Industry*. Boca Raton: Chapman & Hall/CRC.

Nathan, John. (2001) *Sony: The Private Life*. London: HarperCollinsBusiness.

Neale, Steve. (1998) 'Widescreen Composition in the Age of Television'. *Contemporary Hollywood Cinema*. Eds Steve Neale and Murray Smith. London: Routledge. 130–41.

Negus, Keith. (1997) 'The Production of Culture'. *Production of Culture/Cultures of Production*. Ed. Paul du Gay. London/Milton Keynes: Sage/Open University Press. 67–104.

Neopolitan, Matt. (2003) 'Quality is the Trademark of Criterion Collection DVDs'. *Billboard*, 17 May: 46.

Netflix. (2006) 'Fact Sheet'. <www.netflix.com/MediaCenter?id=1005&hnjr=8> (downloaded 14 July 2006).

Netherby, Jennifer. (2004) 'Revenue Sharing in the DVD Age'. *Video Business,* 24 November. <www.videobusiness.com/index.asp?layout=articlePrint&articleID=CA612556> (downloaded 13 July 2006).

Netherby, Jennifer. (2005a) 'Lions Gate Goes with Blu-ray'. *Video Business*, 17 August. <www.videobusiness.com/index.asp?layout=articlePrint&articleID=CA635586> (downloaded 10 July 2006).

Netherby, Jennifer. (2005b) 'Studios Key to Online Success'. *Video Business*, 31 March. <www.videobusiness.com/index.asp?layout=articlePrint&articleID=CA627187> (downloaded 9 July 2006).

Netherby, Jennifer. (2006a) 'Adult Content Already Hot on Burning'. *Video Business*, 7 April. <www.videobusiness.com/index.asp?layout=articlePrint&articleID=CA6322925> (downloaded 22 August 2006).

Netherby, Jennifer. (2006b) 'BitTorrent Expands Download Service Content'. *Video Business*, 29 November. <www.videobusiness.com/index.asp?layout=articlePrint&articleID=CA6395661> (downloaded 16 January 2007).

Netherby, Jennifer. (2006c) 'CinemaNow Satisfies Burning Desire'. *Video Business*, 19 July. <www.videobusiness.com/index.asp?layout=articlePrint&articleID=CA6354445> (downloaded 22 July 2006).

Netherby, Jennifer. (2006d) 'Download-to-Own Dawns in US'. *Video Business*, 3 April. <www.videobusiness.com/index.asp?layout=articlePrint&articleID=CA6321278> (downloaded 9 July 2006).

Netherby, Jennifer. (2006e) 'Netflix Sues Blockbuster'. *Video Business*, 4 April. <www.videobusiness.com/index.asp?layout=articlePrint&articleID=CA6322053> (downloaded 14 July 2006).

Netherby, Jennifer. (2006f) 'Report Predicts Disc Downturn in '07'. *Video Business*, 27 December. <www.videobusiness.com/index.asp?layout=articlePrint&articleID=CA6402797> (downloaded 5 January 2007).

Netherby, Jennifer. (2006g) 'Warner Partners with BitTorrent'. *Video Business*, 9 May. <www.videobusiness.com/index.asp?layout=articlePrint&articleID=CA6333062> (downloaded 16 January 2007).

Netherby, Jennifer and Susanne Ault. (2006a) 'Blu-ray Bows with Titles, Hardware'. *Video Business*, 21 June. <www.videobusiness.com/index.asp?layout=articlePrint&articleID=CA6346170> (downloaded 4 July 2006).

Netherby, Jennifer and Susanne Ault. (2006b) 'HD DVD Set to Launch Quietly'. *Video Business*, 13 April. <www.videobusiness.com/index.asp?layout=articlePrint&articleID=CA6324750> (downloaded 4 July 2006).

New Media Markets. (1993) 'Philips Puts First Film on CD as Formats Multiply'. 21 October. <www.lexisnexis.com/uk/business/results/docview/docview.do?risb=21_T1033904664&format=GNBFI&sort=BOOLEAN&startDocNo=1&results UrlKey=29_T1033904666&cisb=22_T1033904665&treeMax=true&tree Width=0&csi=5545&docNo=3> (downloaded 7 April 2006).

Newsweek. (1989) 'The Perceived Threat: A *Newsweek* Poll'. 9 October: 64.

New York Times, The. (1982) 'X-Rated Movies Still Major Factor in the Video Market'. sec. D, 21 January: 4.

Nichols, Peter M. (1993) 'Home Video'. *The New York Times* sec. D, 3 December: 19.

Nmungwun, Aaron Foisi. (1989) *Video Recording Technology: Its Impact on Media and Home Entertainment*. Hillsdale, NJ: Lawrence Erlbaum Associates.

Noglow, Paul and J. Max Robins. (1994) 'Sumner Swallows Wayne's World'. *Variety*, 10 January: 1 and 71.

Nulty, Peter. (1979) 'Matsushita Takes the Lead in Video Recorders'. *Fortune*, 16 July: 110–12 and 16.

Ochiva, Dan. (2006) 'Entertainment Technologies: Past, Present and Future'. *The Movie Business Book*. International 2nd edn. Ed. Jason E. Squire. Maidenhead: Open University Press: 499–529.

Ogan, Christine. (1985) 'Cultural Imperialism by Invitation'. *Media Development* 32, no. 1: 2–4.

O'Regan, Tom. (1991) 'From Piracy to Sovereignty: International Video Cassette Recorder Trends'. *Continuum: An Australian Journal of the Media* 4, no. 2: 112–35.

Owen, Richard. (1983) 'An Elite Revolution'. *InterMedia* 11, no. 4/5: 75.

Parisi, Paula. (1988a) 'Consumers Queue Up for E.T. Vids'. *The Hollywood Reporter*, 28 October: 3 and 49.

Parisi, Paula. (1988b) 'E.T. Goes Home Vid with Record 10 Million Preorders'. *The Hollywood Reporter*, 16 September: 1 and 38.

Parisi, Paula. (1988c) 'E.T. Goes Home with Sell-through $19.95 Video Tag'. *The Hollywood Reporter*, 6 May: 3 and 8.

Parisi, Paula. (1988d) 'Sell-through Propels Home Video to New Heights in 1988'. *The Hollywood Reporter*, 29 December: 1, 4 and 19.

Parisi, Paula. (1993) 'Par Films to Philips CD-I'. *The Hollywood Reporter*, 3 June: 1 and 17.

Petley, Julian. (1984) 'A Nasty Story'. *Screen* 25, no. 2: 68–74.

Petley, Julian. (1994) 'In Defence of "Video Nasties"'. (2001) *The Media Studies Reader*. Eds Tim O'Sullivan and Yvonne Jenkins. London: Arnold. 188–95.

Philipscdi.com. (2006) 'History of the Philips CD-I'. <www.philipscdi.com/history.htm> (downloaded 21 July 2006).

Prince, Stephen. (2000) *A New Pot of Gold: Hollywood under the Electronic Rainbow, 1980–1989*. Berkeley: University of California Press.

Rawsthorn, Alice. (1995) 'Sony and Philips Take Multimedia Disc War to Hollywood'. *Financial Times*, 15 August: 4.

Rayns, Tony. (2000) 'No Zone Layer'. *Sight and Sound* 10, no. 9: 5.

Reesman, Bryan. (2001) 'Building a Better DVD: Special Features and Surprise Extras Add Excitement to the Format'. *Billboard*, 18 August: 56 and 78.

Rentrak. (2006) 'Rentrak: Supplier Terms'. <www.rentrakonline.com/pdfs/SupplierTerms.pdf> (downloaded 28 June 2006).

Rivero, Enrique. (2001) 'CinemaNow Restricts Regional Streams'. *Video Business*, 27 February. <www.videobusiness.com/index.asp?layout=articlePrint&articleID=CA6201121> (downloaded 9 July 2006).

Rollins, Nita. (1991) 'Something Borrowed, Something Taped: Video Nuptials'. *Wide Angle* 13, no. 2: 32–8.

Rosenbloom, Richard S. and Karen J. Freeze. (1985) 'Ampex Corporation and Video Innovation'. *Research on Technological Innovation, Management and Policy*, vol. 2. Ed. Richard S. Rosenbloom. Greenwich, CT: JAI Press. 113–85.

Rothman, Wilson. (2004) 'I Don't Rent. I Own'. *The New York Times* sec. G, 26 February: 1.

Rourke, Elizabeth with Carrie Rothburd. (2000) 'Blockbuster Inc.'. *International Directory of Company Histories*, vol. 31. Ed. Tina Grant. Farmington Hills, MI: St James Press. 56–60.

Rybczynski, Witold. (2001) *Home: A Short History of an Idea*. London: Pocket Books.

Salamie, David E. (1999) 'Victor Company of Japan, Limited'. *International Directory of Company Histories*, vol. 26. Ed. Jay P. Pederson. Farmington Hills, MI: St James Press. 511–13.

Salamie, David E. (2001) 'SANYO Electric Co., Ltd'. *International Directory of Company Histories*, vol. 36. Ed. Jay P. Pederson. Farmington Hills: St James Press. 399–403.

Sanger, David E. (1991) 'Toshiba Rewrites a Hollywood Script'. *The New York Times* sec. D, 9 October: 1.

Sarathy, M. A. Partha. (1983) 'Video on the Bus'. *InterMedia* 11, no. 4/5: 53.

Schauer, Bradley. (2005) 'The Criterion Collection in the New Home Video Market: An Interview with Susan Arosteguy'. *The Velvet Light Trap* no. 56: 32–5.

Schmemann, Serge. (1983) 'Video's Forbidden Offerings Alarm Moscow'. *The New York Times* sec. 1, 22 October: 1.

Schiesel, Seth. (2002) 'Viacom's Chief Defends Deals by Blockbuster with Studios'. *The New York Times* sec. C, 14 June: 1.

Schubin, Mark. (1980) 'An Overview and History of Video Disc Technologies'. *Video Discs: The Technology, the Applications and the Future*. Eds Efrem Sigel, Mark Schubin and Paul F. Merrill. White Plains, NY: Knowledge Industry Publications. 7–51.

Schwartz, Tony. (1981) 'The TV Pornography Boom'. *The New York Times* sec. 6, 13 September: 44.

Screen Digest. (1978a) 'JVC VHD/AHS Video Disc'. November: 206–10.

Screen Digest. (1978b) 'Video Disc Survey'. November: 211–14.

Screen Digest. (1979a) 'Huge Magnavision Player Mark-up'. August: 143.

Screen Digest. (1979b) 'IBM Joins MCA for Video Discs'. October: 181.

Screen Digest. (1979c) 'Magnavision and DiscoVision on the Market'. February: 27–34.

Screen Digest. (1979d) 'Massive Premium on Magnavision Prices'. July: 104.

Screen Digest. (1979e) 'Philips/Sony Pact on Video Discs'. November: 204.

Screen Digest. (1979f) 'Price Rise Already for Magnavision'. August: 144.

Screen Digest. (1980a) 'Pioneer Reveals Its Video Disc Player'. April: 82.

Screen Digest. (1980b) 'Sluggish Growth of US Video Disc Sales'. December: 224.

Screen Digest. (1981a) 'Video Disc Players: Ten Models on the Market'. July: 134.

Screen Digest. (1981b) 'World Video Status Report'. November: 213–18.

Screen Digest. (1981c) 'World Video Statistics Report: 2'. December: 234–6.

Screen Digest. (1982a) 'MCA and IBM Sever Video Disc Links'. March: 41.

Screen Digest. (1982b) 'Sadistic Video Ads Rebuked'. June: 104.

Screen Digest. (1983a) 'World Video Population at 30 Million'. May: 89–94.

Screen Digest. (1983b) 'World Video Population Reaches 40m'. November: 207–14.

Screen Digest. (1984a) 'RCA's Decision and Video Disc's Outlook'. May: 87–9.

Screen Digest. (1984b) 'Video Disc Players'. December: 227–8.

Screen Digest. (1984c) 'Video Manufacturing and Market Reports'. June: 110–14.

Screen Digest. (1986a) 'National Video Market Reports'. December: 249–51.

Screen Digest. (1986b) 'World VCR Manufacturing Capacity'. July: 129–31.

Screen Digest. (1986c) 'World Video Statistics Review'. November: 225–9.

Screen Digest. (1990a) 'Testing Time for Video Software'. December: 273–80.

Screen Digest. (1990b) 'World Video Homes Reach 200m Level'. November: 249–52.

Screen Digest. (1991a) 'High Definition Television: Preparing to Happen'. January: 9–16.

Screen Digest. (1991b) 'World VCR Survey: One in Three TV Homes'. June: 129–36.

Screen Digest. (1992) 'World Video Recorder Market Research Maturity'. June: 129–33.

Screen Digest. (1993) 'World VCR Markets: Back to Growth'. June: 129–33.

Screen Digest. (1995) 'World VCR Population Set for Steady Growth'. August: 177–80.

Screen Digest. (1996) 'DVD Video and DVD-ROM: A Global Status Report'. December: 273–80.

Screen Digest. (1997a) 'DVD Software Choice Expanding in Japan'. November: 258.

Screen Digest. (1997b) 'Video Hardware Markets: VCRs Stable as DVD Starts to Move'. July: 158–60.

Screen Digest. (1997c) 'World-wide Video Markets: No Longer VHS Dominated'. November: 249–56.

Screen Digest. (1998a) 'Sony Japan Follows Warner into DVD Rental'. August: 186.

Screen Digest. (1998b) 'Worldwide Video Markets: The End of the Beginning?'. November: 249–56.

Screen Digest. (1999) 'Worldwide Video Software Markets'. November: 293–300.

Screen Digest. (2000a) 'DVD Video Recorders Hit Market'. October: 317.

Screen Digest. (2000b) 'DVD Video Recorders Poised for Market Launch'. February: 62.

Screen Digest. (2000c) 'Worldwide Video Software Markets'. November: 341–8.

Screen Digest. (2001) 'Asia-Pacific Video Market'. December: 373–6.

Screen Digest. (2004) 'World DVD Markets in Position'. November: 333–40.

Screen Digest. (2005a) 'DVD Retail Rules Film Spending'. August: 230.

Screen Digest. (2005b) 'DVD Take-up Equals VCRs in 1990'. January: 11.

Screen Digest. (2005c) 'High Definition Television'. October: 306–8.

Screen Digest. (2005d) 'World DVD Growth Slows to Crawl'. November: 333–40.

Screen Digest. (2006) 'World DVD Turns Corner'. November: 365–72.

Segrave, Kerry. (2003) *Piracy in the Motion Picture Industry*. Jefferson, NC: McFarland & Co.

Seguin, Denis. (2000) 'MPAA Takes Issue with Scour.com'. *Screen International*, 4 August: 1 and 4.

Seguin, Denis. (2003a) 'A Little Extra Something'. *Screen International*, 10 October: 22.

Seguin, Denis. (2003b) 'The Rest is History'. *Screen International*, 10 October: 23.

Sendit.com (2005) 'Help On … Digital Versatile Disc Regions'. <www.sendit.com/help/ help_dvd_regions> (downloaded on 23 October 2005).

Shales, Tom. (1977) 'All I Want for Christmas Is My Own TV Show … '. *The Washington Post*, 24 November: C1.

'Siemens AG'. (1990) *International Directory of Company Histories*, vol. 2. Ed. Lisa Mirabile. Chicago: St James Press. 97–100.

Sigel, Efrem (1980) 'The Consumer Market for Video Discs'. *Video Discs: The Technology, the Applications and the Future*. Eds Efrem Sigel, Mark Schubin and Paul F. Merrill. White Plains, NY: Knowledge Industry Publications. 53–67.

Siklos, Richard. (2007) 'New Disc May Sway DVD Wars'. *The New York Times* sec. C, 4 January: 1.

Singer, Ben. (1988) 'Early Home Cinema and the Edison Home Projecting Kinetoscope'. *Film History* 2, no. 1: 37–69.

Sinn, Dikky. (2005) 'Police Freeze $90m and Arrest 1,600 over 11 Days; Mainland and Macau Also Make Big Catches in Joint Anti-Triad Operation'. *South China Morning Post*, 20 June: 1.

Sirower, Mark L. (1997) *The Synergy Trap: How Companies Lose the Acquisitions Game*. New York: Free Press.

Siwek, Stephen E. (2004) *Copyright Industries in the US Economy*. Washington, DC: Economists Incorporated/International Intellectual Property Alliance.

Siwek, Stephen E. (2006) *The True Cost of Movie Piracy*. Lewisville, TX: Institute for Policy Innovation.

Smith, Anthony (ed.). (1998) *Television: An International History*. 2nd edn. Oxford: Oxford University Press.

Solman, Gregory. (2001) 'Picture Perfect?'. *Film Comment* 37, no. 3: 52–7.

Sony. (2005a) 'Not Quite Suitable for the Home – the U-matic VTR'. <www.sony.net/Fun/SH/ 1–13/h3.html> (downloaded 14 October 2005).

Sony. (2005b) 'The Video Cassette Tape'. <www.sony.net/Fun/SH/1–13/h1.html> (downloaded 14 October 2005).

Sony. (2005c) 'This is a Revolution!'. <www.sony.net/Fun/SH/1–13/h5.html> (downloaded 14 October 2005).

Sreberny, Annabelle. (2000) 'The Global and the Local in International Communications'. *Mass Media and Society*. 3rd edn. Eds James Curran and Michael Gurevitch. London: Arnold. 93–119.

Sreberny-Mohammadi, Annabelle and Ali Mohammadi. (1994) *Small Media, Big Revolution: Communication, Culture and the Iranian Revolution*. Minneapolis: Minnesota University Press.

Stalter, Katharine. (1997) 'Sony, WB Set DVD Date'. *Variety*, 13 January: 150 and 166.

Stern, Christopher and Katharine Stalter. (1996) 'Taking DVD for a Spin'. *Variety*, 4 November: 41.

Sterngold, James. (1994) 'Sony, Struggling, Takes a Huge Loss on Movie Studios'. *The New York Times* sec. A, 18 November: 1.

Stewart, Al. (1989) 'Sony into Vid Big League via Col Deal; 8m Push on?'. *Variety*, 4 October: 45.

Straubhaar, Joseph D. and Carolyn Lin. (1989) 'A Quantitative Analysis of the Reasons for VCR Penetration Worldwide'. *Media Use in the Information Age: Emerging Patterns of Adoption and Consumer Use*. Eds Jerry L. Salvaggio and Jennings Bryant. Hillsdale, NJ: Lawrence Erlbaum Associates. 125–45.

Stroughton, Stephanie. (1999) 'Circuit City's Slipped Disk: Firm Concedes Defeat, Abandons Divx Technology'. *The Washington Post*, 17 June: E1.

Sullivan, John. (2000) 'Judge Halts Program to Crack DVD Film Codes'. *The New York Times* sec. C, 18 August: 1.

Sweeting, Paul. (1998) 'Indies Aim Slingshots at Goliath Blockbuster'. *Variety*, 20 July: 11 and 59.

Sweeting, Paul. (1999) ' "Something" About Revenue Sharing'. *Variety*, 8 February: 28.

Sweeting, Paul. (2003a) 'Disney's Moviebeam Bows, With Other's Help'. *Video Business*, 29 September. <www.videobusiness.com/index.asp?layout=articlePrint&articleID=CA615833> (downloaded 9 July 2006).

Sweeting, Paul. (2003b) 'Rev-Share Rumble: Disney Sues Blockbuster'. *Video Business*, 3 January. <www.videobusiness.com/index.asp?layout=articlePrint&articleID=CA617187> (downloaded 13 July 2006).

Sweeting, Paul. (2004) 'Disney in Blu-ray Camp'. *Video Business*, 8 December. <www.videobusiness.com/index.asp?layout=articlePrint&articleID=CA612611> (downloaded 6 July 2006).

Sweeting, Paul. (2005) 'Fox Adopts Blu-ray Disc Format'. *Video Business*, 29 July. <www.videobusiness.com/index.asp?layout=articlePrint&articleID=CA631765> (downloaded 6 July 2006).

Sweeting, Paul. (2006a) 'Movielink Signs Download-to-Burn Deal'. *Video Business*, 16 July. <www.videobusiness.com/index.asp?layout=articlePrint&articleID=CA6353674> (downloaded 18 July 2006).

Sweeting, Paul. (2006b) 'The Video Retailer'. *The Movie Business Book*. International 2nd edn. Ed. Jason E. Squire. Maidenhead: Open University Press: 419–36.

Sweeting, Paul and Scott Hettrick. (2004) 'Four Studios Choose HD DVD Format'. *Video Business*, 29 November. <www.videobusiness.com/index.asp?layout=article Print&articleID=CA612564> (downloaded 6 July 2006).

Talty, Stephan (1991) 'Family Record'. *Film Comment* 27, no. 3: 50–3.

Tashiro, Charles. (1996/7) 'The Contradictions of Video Collecting'. *Film Quarterly* 50, no. 2: 11–18.

Taubman, Philip. (1985) 'Oh Comrade, Can I Borrow Your *Rambo* Cassette?'. *The New York Times* sec. A, 9 December: 2.

Taylor, Jim. (1998) *DVD Demystified*. New York: McGraw-Hill.

Taylor, Simon (ed.). (2002) *Home Entertainment: Market Assessment 2000*. London: Key Note Ltd.

Temko, Ned. (1983) 'Kremlin Sees Threat in Uncensored Videocassttes'. *Christian Science Monitor*, 12 May: 2.

Terazono, Emiko. (1991) 'Japan is Top Video Target'. *The Financial Post*, 24 September: 12.

Thompson, John B. (1995) *The Media and Modernity: A Social Theory of the Media*. Cambridge: Polity Press.

Trakstar. (2006) 'PirateEye'. <www.trakstar.net/pirateEye.com> (downloaded 11 August 2006).

Triplett, William. (2005) 'Grokster Tuned Out'. *Daily Variety*, 28 June: 1.

Trumbell, Robert. (1983) 'Videotapes of Slaying Smuggled into Manila'. *The New York Times* sec. A, 13 September: 9.

TV Guide. (1987) 'This Week's Programs'. 14 November: A-31–215.

TV Guide. (1989) 'This Week's Programs'. 6 May: 63–234.

Usami, Shoso. (1988) 'Japan'. *Video World-wide: An International Study*. Ed. Manuel Alvarado. Paris/London: UNESCO/John Libbey. 71–82.

US Copyright Office. (2003) *Copyright Law of the United States of America and Related Laws Contained in Title 17 of the United States Code*. Washington, DC: US Copyright Office.

Vaidhyanathan, Siva. (2003) *©opyrights and ©opyrongs: The Rise of Intellectual Property*. New York: New York University Press.

Variety. (1978) 'Fox Buys Magnetic Video $7.2-M Cash'. 29 November: 5.

Variety. (1983) 'Big Rental Films of 1982'. 12 January: 13, 46 and 52.

Variety. (1986) '50 Top Grossing Films: Based on *Variety*'s Theater Sample (Week Ending May 21)'. 28 May: 9.

Viacom. (2005) *Form 10-K*. New York: Viacom.

Video Week. (1998a) 'Divx is a Little "Title-Challenged" Right Now – Sharp'. 22 June. <www.lexisnexis.com/uk/business/results/docview/docview.do?risb=21_ T1033863871 &format=GNBFI&sort=BOOLEAN&start DocNo=26&resultsUrlKey=29_T103386387 3&cisb=22_T1033863872&treeMax=true&t reeWidth=0&csi=244971&docNo=33> (downloaded 7 April 2006).

Video Week. (1998b) 'Divx's Success Rests on Title Exclusivity – IBM's Bell'. 30 March. <http://www.lexisnexis.com/uk/business/ results/docview/docview.do?risb=21_T10338 34548&format=GNBFI&sort=BOOLEAN &startDocNo=1&resultsUrlKey=29_T10338 34550&cisb=22_T1033834549&treeMax= true&treeWidth=0&csi=244971&docNo52 > (downloaded 7 April 2006).

Video Week. (1998c) 'Europeans Circumventing DVD Regional Coding'. 20 July. <www.lexisnexis.com/uk/business/results /docview/docview.do?risb=21_ T1033834586 &format=GNBFI&sort=BOOLEAN&start DocNo=1&resultsUrlKey=29_T1033834588 &cisb=22_T1033834587&treeMax=true&tr eeWidth=0&csi=244971&docNo=3> (downloaded 7 April 2006).

Video Week. (1998d) 'Few Surprises in Divx Introductory Market Launch'. 15 June. <www.lexisnexis.com/uk/business/results/ docview/docview.do?risb=21_

T1033863844&format=GNBFI&sort= BOOLEAN&startDocNo=26&resultsUrlKey= 29_T1033863846&cisb=22_T1033863845&tr eeMax=true&treeWidth=0&csi=244971&do c No=26> (downloaded 7 April 2006).

Video Week. (1998e) 'More Than 30 Titles Listed for Divx Launch'. 8 June.<www.lexisnexis.com/ uk/business/results/docview/docview.do?risb= 21_T1033887108&format=GNBFI&sort5 BOOLEAN&startDocNo=1&resultsUrlKey =29_T1033887110&cisb=22_T1033887109 &treeMax=true&treeWidth=0&csi=244971 &docNo55> (downloaded 7 April 2006).

Video Week. (1998f) 'Richmond and San Francisco are Divx Introductory Markets'. 23 March. <www.lexisnexis.com/uk/business/ results/docview/docview.do?risb=21_ T1033887151&format=GNBFI&sort= BOOLEAN&startDocNo=1&resultsUrlKey =29_T1033887153&cisb=22_T1033887152 &treeMax=true&treeWidth=0&csi=244971 &docNo=3> (downloaded 7 April 2006).

Video Week. (1998g) 'Warner Bows Lower DVD Price Tiers'. 13 July. <www.lexisnexis.com/ uk/business/results/docview/docview.do?risb= 21_T1033887164&format=GNBFI&sort= BOOLEAN&startDocNo=1&resultsUrlKey =29_T1033887166&cisb=22_T1033887165 &treeMax=true&treeWidth=0&csi=244971 &docNo=2 > (downloaded 7 April 2006).

Video Week. (1998h) 'Warner in 5-Market DVD Rental Test'. 13 April. <www.lexisnexis.com/ uk/business/results/docview/docview.do?risb= 21_T1033887177&format=GNBFI&sort= BOOLEAN&startDocNo=1&resultsUrlKey =29_T1033887179&cisb=22_T1033887178 &treeMax=true&treeWidth=0&csi=244971 &docNo.3> (downloaded 7 April 2006).

Vogel, Harold L. (1990) *Entertainment Industry Economics: A Guide for Financial Analysis*. 2nd edn. Cambridge: Cambridge University Press.

Vogel, Harold L. (1998) *Entertainment Industry Economics: A Guide for Financial Analysis*. 4th edn. Cambridge: Cambridge University Press.

Vogel, Harold L. (2001) *Entertainment Industry Economics: A Guide for Financial Analysis*. 5th edn. Cambridge: Cambridge University Press.

Wagstyl, Stefan. (1989) 'Sony Starts to Peddle Dreams'. *Financial Times*, 28 September: 29.

Wang, Shujen. (2003) *Framing Piracy: Globalization and Film Distribution in Greater China*. Lanham, MD: Rowen and Littlefield.

Wasko, Janet. (1994) *Hollywood in the Information Age*. Cambridge: Polity Press.

Wasko, Janet. (2003) *How Hollywood Works*. London: Sage.

Wasser, Frederick. (2001) *Veni, Vidi, Video: The Hollywood Empire and the VCR*. Austin: University of Texas Press.

Waterman, David. (1985) 'Prerecorded Home Video and the Distribution of Theatrical Feature Films'. *Video Media Competition: Regulation, Economics, and Technology*. Ed. Eli M. Noam. New York: Columbia University Press. 221–43.

Watson, David. (2005) 'Appeals Court Revives Suit Against Blockbuster by Independent Video Rental Companies'. *Metropolitan News Enterprise*, 23 November: 1.

Weiner, Rex and Katharine Stalter. (1997) 'DVD Dividing H'wood'. *Variety*, 17 March: 1, 51 and 71.

Weinstein, Joshua L. (1988) 'E.T. is a Hit – Again'. *St Petersburg Times* (Florida), 28 October: 1B.

Winston, Brian. (1996) *Technologies of Seeing: Photography, Cinematography and Television*. London: British Film Institute.

WIPO. (1996a) *WIPO Copyright Treaty (WCT)*. Geneva: WIPO.

WIPO. (1996b) *WIPO Performances and Phonograms Treaty (WPPT)*. Geneva: WIPO.

Yar, Majid. (2005) 'The Global "Epidemic" of Movie "Piracy": Crime-wave or Social Construction?'. *Media, Culture and Society* 27, no. 5: 677–96.

Zimmermann, Patricia R. (1995) *Reel Families: A Social History of Amateur Film*. Bloomington: Indiana University Press.

Index

Page numbers in **bold** type indicate detailed analyses/case studies; those in *italics* denote illustrations; *t* = table; *f* = figure